Polygonal Modeling: Basic and Advanced Techniques

Mario Russo

Wordware Publishing, Inc.

Library of Congress Cataloging-in-Publication Data

Russo, Mario.
    Polygonal Modeling : basic and advanced techniques / by Mario Russo.
      p. cm.
    Includes bibliographical references and index.
    ISBN-13: 978-1-59822-007-0
    ISBN-10: 1-59822-007-1 (pbk.)
    1. Computer graphics.   2. Geometrical models--Data processing.
    3. Polygons. I. Title.
    T385.R865 2005
    006.6'93--dc22   2005025871
                                      CIP

ISBN-13: 978-1-59822-007-0
ISBN-10: 1-59822-007-1
10 9 8 7 6 5 4 3 2 1
0510

All inquiries for volume purchases of this book should be addressed to Wordware Publishing, Inc., at the above address. Telephone inquiries may be made by calling:

(972) 423-0090

Contents

Contents

Contents

Introduction

Computer graphics are expanding rapidly. New tools to apply to computer-generated imagery are created and improved upon every week. The palette of the digital artist is very broad these days, and it's getting much broader as new features appear that make life easier for the CG artist. Every artistic medium requires mastery of technique, and digital sculpture is no different. Digital sculpture is surely one of the most interesting aspects of computer graphics today and requires study just as any other traditional sculpture technique.

The main focus of this book is polygonal modeling. It provides a thorough discussion on the theory of polygons, how polygons work, how to understand the workflow structure, and how to enjoy the main benefits of a well-planned model. While this book is intended to be non-software specific, the appendices do cover some of the basic functions of polygonal modeling and navigation in 3ds Max and Maya. Many of the major 3D packages available use the same theory and principles on polygons.

If you are already familiar with a 3D package, you may want to skip Chapter 1. If not, you will probably find some useful information there about how 3D space works and the basics of polygonal modeling. Also, be aware that it is impossible to cover every available feature, attribute, and tool for polygonal modeling. New tools are constantly in development, including stand-alone modeling software (commercial and free) and even scripts, plug-ins, extensions, and extra resources for 3D packages like 3ds Max, Maya, Softimage XSI, LightWave, and so on. No application has every tool, but if you understand the basic concept of the modeling topology and how to build it correctly, you can pretty much model just about anything with the standard tools like moving, cutting, extruding, selecting, and so forth.

As an artist myself and an avid reader of CG books, I have noticed that many books on CG have too much text and not enough images to illustrate the process (even the "practical guide" ones). With this book I have included hundreds of images and used a more visual approach to make the process easier to follow, as artists are visually oriented and more inclined to learn from images. This book is intended to be a comprehensive guide to polygonal modeling for artists to use with any application with the most basic set of polygonal creation and polygon editing tools.

Why Polygons?

Polygonal meshes have been present since the early days of computer graphics because of their characteristics of easy computation, rendering, and data storage. But today, when there are other (and newer) modeling surfaces like NURBS, why use polygons? These are some of the advantages of using polygons:

▶ Ease of computation

▶ Reduced amount of time to plan the entire structure cage

▶ Ease of modeling complex organic shapes

▶ High degree of flexibility

▶ Local refinement (not possible with NURBS)

▶ Can be used as multi-resolution meshes

According to the Alias Maya glossary, a polygon is "an n-sided shape defined by a group of ordered vertices and the edges that are defined between pairs of those vertices. Polygons can be either simple shapes, such as polygonal primitives, or complex models built from the various Maya polygonal tools. A polygonal object can be closed, open, or made up of shells, which are disjointed pieces of geometry." Note that other software packages may call polygons meshes.

This means that with polygons you can build any kind of object, digitally sculpture it, and freely manipulate its structure by joining parts, ripping off parts, and merging others, without compromising the overall structure when done well. This way any kind of shape can be achieved with polygons.

What Is in This Book?

Here is a summary of each chapter in this book:

Chapter 1, "Polygonal System Basics," covers the basic concepts of the general polygon structure, including customization, layouts, display features, attributes, and common operations.

Chapter 2, "Polygon Operations," contains more specific descriptions of the most basic and common operations such as extruding, cutting, merging, and duplicating. Additionally, the chapter covers the concept of pivots, holes on the mesh, Soft Selection, and the basics of gizmos and manipulators that work with polygonal sub-elements.

Chapter 3, "Polygon Subdivision," presents an overview of the theory and history of general polygonal systems. Among the techniques discussed are Chaikin's algorithms for curves, Doo-Sabin surfaces, and the Catmull-Clark, Loop, Butterfly, and Kobbelt subdivision methods. With this theoretical base established, we move to more practical matters with examples of how Catmull-Clark subdivision works and the results we can produce with it. Throughout the chapter we discuss how to plan a successful model, both organic and inorganic, as well as advanced techniques for modeling.

Chapter 4, "Visual References," is dedicated to the importance of having references for modeling and explains how to prepare blueprints/model sheets before modeling.

Chapters 5 through 9 are practical chapters that teach step by step how to build a topologically correct human body, both male and female, with polygons using different techniques (single polygon and box modeling). Adding details such as eyeballs, eyelashes, and teeth are also demonstrated.

Chapter 10, "The Ogre Head," provides a lesson on modeling a basic ogre head to use with ZBrush in Chapter 11. This chapter also provides an introduction to displacement.

Chapter 11, "Introduction to ZBrush," discusses the basics of ZBrush sculpting and the tools available.

Chapter 12, "Cartoon Modeling," is dedicated to cartoon character modeling with lessons for two types of cartoon characters including body, head, and hands.

Chapter 13, "Modeling for Games," addresses real-time surfacing and structure regarding OpenGL display and processing.

Additionally, the appendices provide a quick start guide to modeling in 3ds Max and Maya.

What Is Not in This Book?

This book does not discuss the following topics:

▶ NURBS or patch modeling techniques

▶ Blob surfacing techniques

▶ Complete coverage of all the tools, plug-ins, shortcuts, and extensions available for polygonal modeling

▶ Rendering or texturing techniques

Chapter 1

Polygonal System Basics

Customization

Mastering the tools of your 3D application is only a small part of the battle. It is highly recommended that you customize the keys of your application since the default keys often aren't the perfect combination for you. When you customize the keys and shortcuts, you fit the keys to match your needs and the program adapts to you as much as possible in the most ergonomic and efficient way. 3D applications tend to have enormous numbers of commands, tools, editors, and options, and if you don't map shortcuts for your keyboard, it can stress your muscles and slow you down. Think about the modeling process: You pan the camera, rotate the camera, zoom the camera, scale, move, rotate, zoom again, pan — all done using the mouse. Customization also allows you to change colors, the display, and many other preferences. Of course, not everything can be changed or mapped to your keyboard or customized in some way, but the most important things (depending on the software you are using) probably are.

Here are a few suggestions for customization:

▸ Map the viewport controls for your keyboard like this:

    A = Pan

    S = Rotate

    D = Zoom

    F = Zoom to selected object

▸ Map the manipulation controls like this:

    Q = Select

    W = Move

    E = Rotate

    R = Scale

Layouts

The choice of a good layout will vary depending on your project. If you are an animator, it is desirable to have an animation editor (such as a graph editor, dope sheet, etc.) in a viewport to quickly access when needed. There are a number of ways to set up your layout, as shown in Figure 1-1, but for modeling purposes, you will have four standard viewports: Top, Front, Side (right or left), and Perspective.

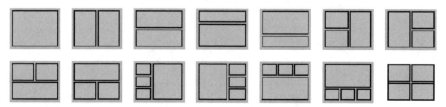

Figure 1-1

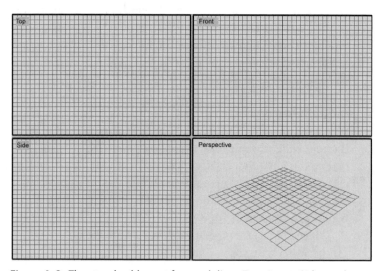

Figure 1-2: The standard layout for modeling: Top, Front, Side, and Perspective views.

3D Polygonal Surface

Before discussing modeling features, attributes, and techniques, you must understand what a 3D surface is. The mesh you will be working on is a group of vertices and edges that form polygons. The 3D surface is generated by advanced mathematic algorithms that put a "skin" over the mesh so you perceive a three-dimensional shape. Note that what you see in the viewport of your software is a "rough draft" compared to a rendered image. When you move your mesh inside the viewport, it is redrawn in real time.

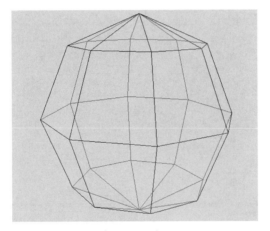

Figure 1-3: A wireframe render.

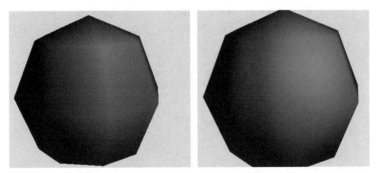

Figure 1-4: Left, real-time surfacing. Right, final rendering of the same sphere with the same number of polygons.

3

Space

All of the 3D elements — polygons (meshes), NURBS surfaces, particles, lights, cameras, and helpers/constraints — exist inside a 3D world based on Cartesian space. When working with 3D modeling in any software, you will be dealing with a three-dimensional world. This seems pretty obvious in theory, but in practice it means a lot of training, thinking in 3D, and in-depth knowledge of using the tools and accessing the viewports of the software that you are using to model your mesh.

Every manipulation inside a 3D world must be planned inside a Cartesian system with three axes: X, Y, and Z.

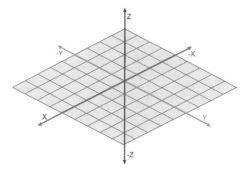

Figure 1-5: 3D space.

In most cases, 2D software uses X and Y coordinates. Figures 1-6 and 1-7 show the difference between an orthogonal view (2D) and a perspective view of the same elements in a space.

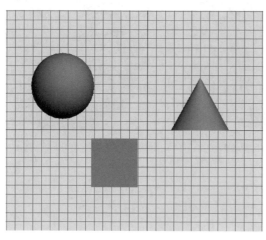

Figure 1-6: Orthogonal view (2D).

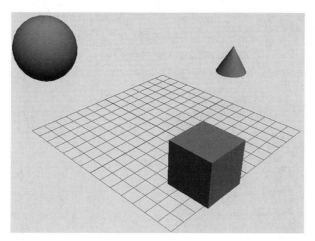

Figure 1-7: Perspective view (3D).

In 3D, all three axes are used to model, light a scene, animate, and more.

Axis

The axis is probably the most used feature when you model and/or manipulate an object. If you want to move a vertex, edge, polygon, or entire object, or maybe scale it down or up, or rotate it, you will be accessing one or more axes. An axis is usually represented by arrows in the color red for X, green for Y, and blue for Z. Some packages like 3ds Max and Maya have a different gizmo for each operation (move, rotate, or scale) so that when you turn on the tool you know how the operation will perform.

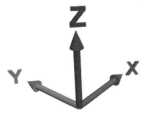

Figure 1-8

Polygonal Structure

The polygonal structure consists of three basic sub-elements: vertexes, edges, and faces or polygons, as shown in Figure 1-9.

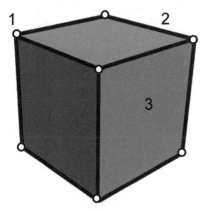

Figure 1-9: 1 indicates a vertex, 2 indicates an edge, and 3 indicates a polygon composed of two faces.

As you can see, the cube in the above figure has eight vertices, 12 edges, and six quad polygons. The edges connect the vertices and form an n-sided polygon. In this case, we have a four-sided polygon, or quad polygon made with two tris.

NOTE:
In 3ds Max you can select the Border sub-object to select all the edges around an open hole of your mesh.

Polygonal Attributes

Polygonal attributes represent the properties of the mesh, how it will look, how you will deal with its elements, and more. Among these attributes are Name and Display.

Name

When modeling complex objects or a scene, it is very useful to name your objects when you create them. If you model a bolt and you are working on an object that uses a lot of bolts, you may want to name them bolt000, bolt001, etc., so you can select all of them from a list and apply one texture to all of them with one command. Naming your objects is also useful when you have to find an object in a complex scene and for general organization.

NOTE:

Name your objects as soon as you create them, and be sure to give them a descriptive name. Finding and renaming objects after the fact can be a cumbersome process.

Display

Display defines the mesh aspect in your viewport. It is common for most 3D applications to have the display options shown in Figure 1-10.

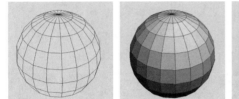  

Figure 1-10: From left, wireframe, edged+facets, edged+smooth, and smooth without wires display options.

Wireframe display disables the 3D surfacing and shows only the wires, or the mesh. Options related to backface wires or backface cullings will display properties of the wires that would not be seen if the viewport display were set to shaded view. The back sides of these faces will receive the same shading as the front sides.

Backfacing culling usually means that the back sides of the faces won't be visible. Figure 1-11 shows a sphere with and without backface culling.

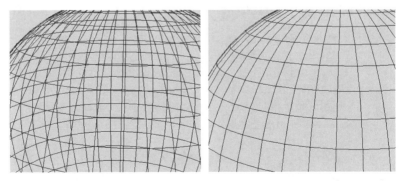

Figure 1-11: Left, wireframe with backface culling off. Right, wireframe with backface culling on.

Selecting

When modeling, you can often select the whole mesh or sub-elements (vertex, edge, face/polygon) of the mesh. Depending on the package you are using, the selection can be made in several ways. Whatever color scheme/user preference you choose for your viewport, keep in mind that the colors for the selected sub-element and the non-selected sub-element must be easily discernible.

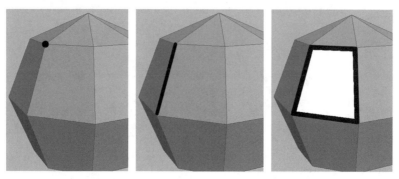

Figure 1-12: From left, vertex selected, edge selected, and polygon selected.

NOTE:

The lessons and examples in this book use the selecting scheme shown in Figure 1-12. Selected vertices are shown as black dots, selected edges are black lines, and selected faces are white with black borders.

Colors and Shading

For modeling purposes it is recommended that you use a neutral color, like gray. However, if you wish, you can paint your mesh any color you like using the material/texture/shade editor. Depending on the model on which you are working, you may want to change the shading for a more appropriate look. It's up to you to choose what best fits your needs.

NOTE:

If you are using Maya, the UV will appear as part of the sub-element of the mesh, along with vertex, edge, polygon, etc. UVs are used for texture mapping, not polygonal modeling, so they are not discussed in this book.

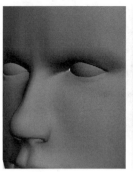

Figure 1-13

Appropriate shading sometimes makes it easier to detect mesh errors like those shown in Figure 1-13. There are a few unnecessary vertices near the left eye that cause a modeling imperfection. Adding a specular value to the shader makes it easier to detect the problem and fix it.

Normals

According to the 3ds Max user reference, a *normal* is a unit vector that defines which way a face or vertex is pointing. The direction in which the normal points represents the front of the outer surface of the face or vertex, which is the side of the surface that is normally displayed and rendered. This means that when you are not using a "force two-sided" option and the normal is flipped to the other side, you will not see the surface. Game programmers use normal manipulations for hardware acceleration and pixel shader effects, but for modeling purposes what really matters is that the normals show us the visible surface. It's where we'll be working. An extruded face or edge follows the polygon's normal.

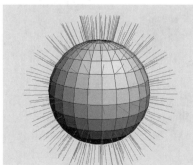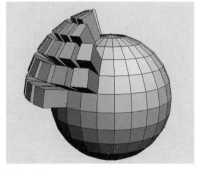

Figure 1-14: Left, normals. Right, extruded polygons.

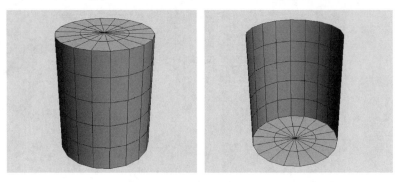

Figure 1-15: Notice the flipped normals on the right. External polygons are invisible and internal polygons become visible.

Polygonal Creation

There are a number of ways to model an object. Most polygonal meshes start from a primitive, a polygon operation with splines, or a single polygon.

Starting from a primitive is the most common way to create polygons. Complex shapes can be made starting with a box (box modeling), but there are other primitives that you can start from, like a sphere, a cylinder, a torus, or a plane.

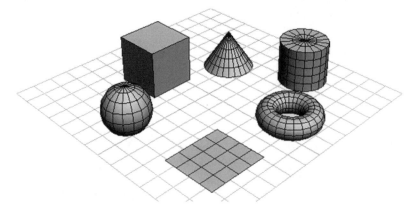

Figure 1-16: Primitives.

You can also start with a spline (or curve) and then apply some modification tool, like rotation, extrusion, or loft, to generate a new mesh.

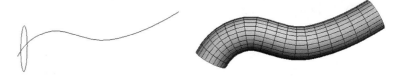

Figure 1-17: Starting from a spline.

By starting from a single polygon you can obtain full control over your mesh if you correctly plan the topology of the object. When you start with a single polygon, it is common to progress the modeling by extruding the edge of the polygon until you get a shell of faces, as shown in Figure 1-18.

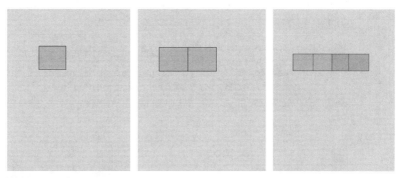

Figure 1-18: Starting from a single polygon and then extruding the lateral edges three times.

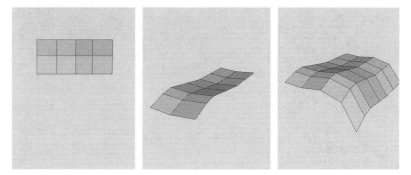

Figure 1-19: Selecting the bottom edges and extruding them a couple of times gives us a quad polygon surface that started from a single polygon. With this method it is possible to create complex inorganic forms, as well as organic ones. With a good blueprint, you can use this method to model cars or any other vehicle.

Operational Tools

Operational tools are commands or modifiers that perform an operation using two meshes, two lines or curves, or a single line and generate a new mesh as a result. Using operational tools can save time in many cases. For example, if you need to model a vase, using a Lathe operational tool is much easier than box modeling. If you need to model a cable, you can certainly make it by extruding a cylinder, but lofting is much quicker and more accurate. Let's take a look at some of the most common operational tools available.

Extrusion

Extrusion is a modifier that picks a shape and raises a mesh from it that adds depth. See Figure 1-20.

> **NOTE:**
>
> The process described as extrusion in this book is referenced as loft in Maya and is mostly for NURBS surfaces that are later converted to polygons.

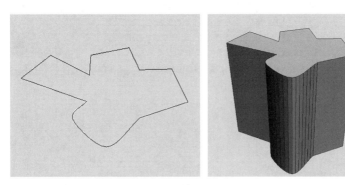

Figure 1-20: Using the Extrusion tool.

Lathe

The Lathe tool creates a 3D object by rotating a curve or line.

When using the Lathe tool, the pivot point of the object must be centered correctly (the + in the following figure). If the pivot is not centered correctly, it may cause undesirable results. The Lathe tool usually allows you to shape the rotation in all three axes (X, Y, and Z).

Figure 1-21: Using the Lathe tool.

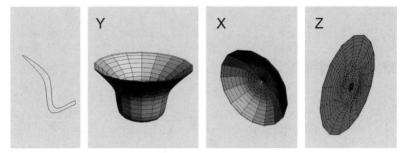

Figure 1-22: Using the Lathe tool in the X, Y, and Z axes.

Loft

Loft creates a 3D object that extrudes one or more shapes along one path. Figures 1-23 and 1-24 show examples of using the Loft tool.

NOTE:
The process described as loft in this book is referenced as extrusion in Maya and is mostly for NURBS surfaces that are later converted to polygons.

Figure 1-23: 3D object generated by lofting with two splines: a shape and a path. The figure on the right shows a slight decrease of the loft scale after the operation.

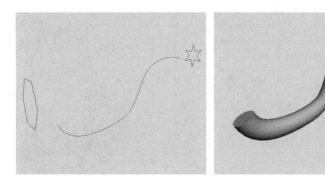

Figure 1-24: 3D object generated by lofting with three splines: two shapes (circle and six-pointed star) and the path. The circle is lofted to one half and the star is lofted to the other half.

Distribution Over a Surface

Automatic placement of an object over other surfaces is the fastest option when you need to model some peculiar objects or scene, such as setting stones in a modeled or fractal-generated terrain in a random way, but you don't want to or can't place them one by one.

NOTE:
Maya has an advanced particle system that allows you to per-form a huge number of scatter effects over an object surface and animate it.

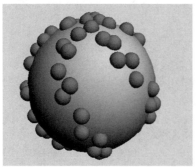

Figure 1-25: Automatically placing objects.

Boolean Operations

Boolean polygonal operations aren't popular among 3D modelers because they reconfigure your mesh and often this configuration isn't topologically correct. This means that when you smooth your Boolean-operated mesh, it will probably have some mesh flaws. Sometimes you don't even have to smooth your mesh to see its flaws. However, in some circumstances, Boolean operations can be useful (otherwise, they probably wouldn't be included in most 3D packages as a tool). The golden rule is: If you can avoid using Boolean operations, avoid them. But if you can't, be sure to do everything you can to check and correct all the flaws in your mesh. See Chapter 3 for more information about Booleans.

A Boolean operation is one that, given an A object and a B object (as shown in Figure 1-26), creates a new shape. Boolean operations include subtraction, union, and intersection.

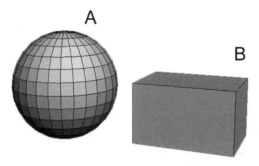

Figure 1-26

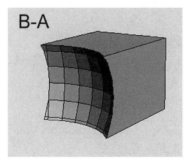

Figure 1-27: Boolean subtraction.

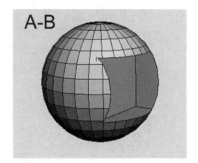

Figure 1-28: Boolean subtraction.

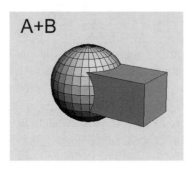

A+B

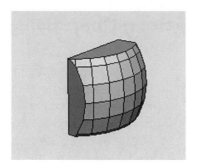

Figure 1-29: Boolean union.

Figure 1-30: Boolean intersection.

Pass-Through Mode

Another useful property you may set for your object is the "pass-through" or "x-ray" mode. Not all 3D applications have it, but in some circumstances it can be very useful, such as when you're modeling a complex robot with a lot of mechanical parts inside it. It is also useful when rigging your character or in a situation where you need to see through a shaded mesh.

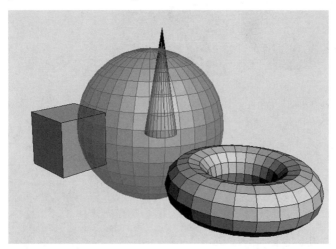

Figure 1-31: Pass-through mode activated for the sphere. You can see the cube and the cone through the sphere.

Global Deformations

In this book, the polygonal tools that affect the mesh globally by a cage, lattice, or similar resource are classified as "global deformations."

Lattice

Lattice is a cage that affects the whole shape by manipulating the cage's vertices. In Figure 1-32, the image on the left shows a base cylinder without any modification, the center image shows the applied lattice, and the right image has some lattice vertex tweaks and scaled down top vertices.

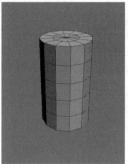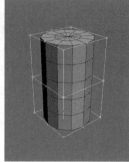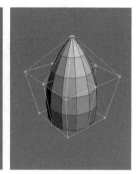

Figure 1-32

Figure 1-33 shows the same cylinder as Figure 1-32 with extra extrusion to get a more interesting shape. The image on the right shows the cylinder with the same lattice operation plus two levels of subdivision.

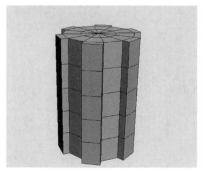

Figure 1-33

Twist

Twist operations are self explanatory. They twist the object, generating very interesting results, but most cases require a good
polygonal resolution to give smooth results. The following image
shows the modified cylinder from the above exercise with different
Twist parameters.

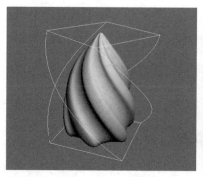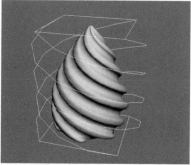

Figure 1-34

Figure 1-35 shows a basic line extrude with a high number of
segments.

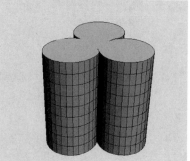

Figure 1-35

Figure 1-36 shows the basic line extrude from Figure 1-35 twisted
to model a rope.

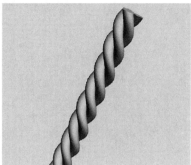

Figure 1-36

Bend

Bend is another self-explanatory tool. It deforms the mesh according to the angle in the parameter. Figures 1-37 to 1-39 show several examples of using the Bend tool.

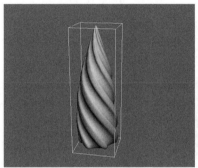
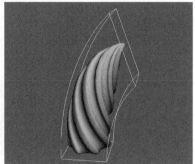

Figure 1-37: Bending in the Z axis.

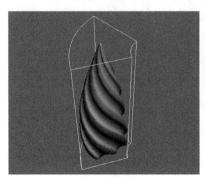
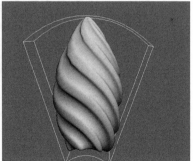

Figure 1-38: Bending in the Y axis and in the X axis.

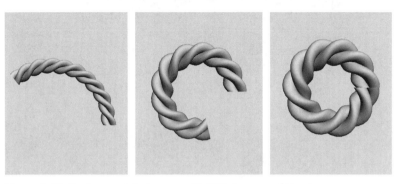

Figure 1-39: Earlier modeled rope, with 360 degrees of Bend.

Polygon Reduction

Every object in your viewport is computed to display in real time, which requires a fast CPU, but even with a fast computer the high number of polygons starts to slow everything down. Sometimes a high-resolution poly for distant objects is not needed; in this case, polygonal reduction tools are the best choice to increase the speed and make the objects in your scene lighter. Figures 1-40 to 1-43 show the results of using polygonal reduction tools.

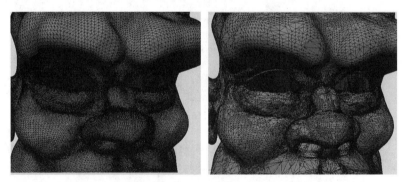

Figure 1-40: Left, original object with 109,170 vertices. Right, after the reduction operation there are 55,385 vertices.

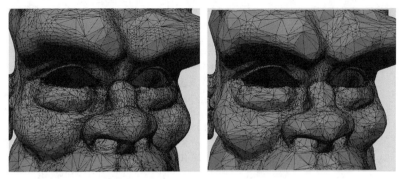

Figure 1-41: Left, 24,232 vertices. Right, 11,981 vertices.

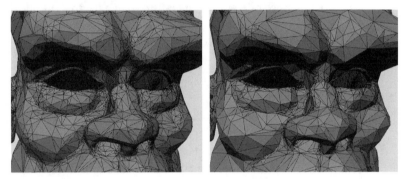

Figure 1-42: Left, 6,837 vertices. Right, 4,333 vertices.

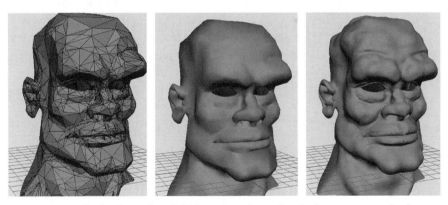

Figure 1-43: Left, the figure has 2,985 vertices shown in wireframe; center, the figure is the same model without the wireframe; and right, the figure is the original mesh with 109,170 vertices.

Organizational Tools

In this book we use the term "organizational tools" for tools or features that allow the user to improve the organization of a complex scene or model in order to avoid losing time looking for specific objects and to optimize speed.

Hide and Freeze

Hide is used to hide objects in your scene. The objects are still there, but you can't see or select them in your viewport; you will need to unhide them from the appropriate editor.

The name for the Freeze feature may vary from application to application. Its main function is to lock the selected object for any viewport selection or transformation, such as translation, rotation, or scaling.

Layers

Layers have became an industry standard for computer graphics and multimedia. However, layers behave a little differently in 3D. In 2D applications like Photoshop or Flash, layers are used to determine the depth of the elements inside the layers. In other words, layers determine what is under what. In 3D applications, layers are used like groups; if you add all the spheres to layer1, all the cubes to layer2, all the tori to layer3, then hide layer2, all the cubes (and any other objects) assigned to layer2 will be hidden (or reflect whatever properties that layer may have). It's a quick way to set properties globally for all objects of a single group without having to select them individually. For character setup, for example, a technical director usually puts the bones of the character and the skin mesh in separate layers to make it easier to lock one and unhide the other.

Conclusion

In this chapter we got a quick overview of the basics of the polygonal world. We covered the importance of customization, aspects of 3D surfacing, Cartesian space, and polygonal structure aspects and properties, along with some of the most common general deformation tools and organizational features inside 3D packages.

Chapter 2

Polygon Operations

Before you start adding polygons to and cutting polygons from your shape, it is crucial that you understand how to manipulate its sub-elements because every modification and tool you apply to your mesh will affect the position and/or the number of vertices, polys, or edges of your mesh.

The Move, Rotate, and Scale tools are self-explanatory; they move, rotate, and scale the selected sub-element. Each tool usually has its own manipulator gizmo. Move is represented by three pointed arrows, Rotate by a spherical gizmo, and Scale by a triangular gizmo, as shown in Figure 2-1.

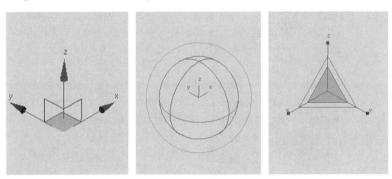

Figure 2-1: From left, the Move, Rotate, and Scale tool gizmos.

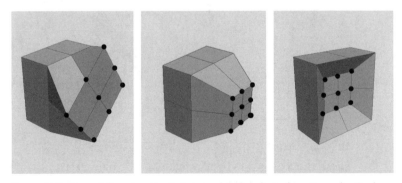

Figure 2-2: From left, using the Rotate tool with selected vertices, the Scale tool with selected vertices, and the Move tool, moving the selected vertices backward after a scaling operation.

These tools can affect sub-elements of an object, as shown in Figure 2-2, or the entire object, as shown in Figure 2-3.

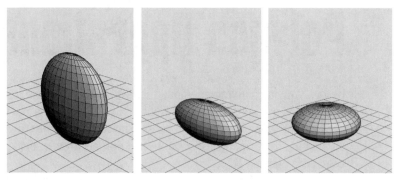

Figure 2-3: From left, scaling in the X axis, scaling in the Y axis, and scaling in the Z axis.

Another interesting point to mention when working with sub-elements, or even an entire object, is the orientation of the gizmo in relation to the object. Most 3D packages will likely have a few options and allow you to choose the one most appropriate to your modeling. By World and By Local are pretty basic and the most common.

When the By World option is selected, it doesn't matter how much you have moved or rotated your object, the gizmo will be related to your viewport, as shown in the following figure.

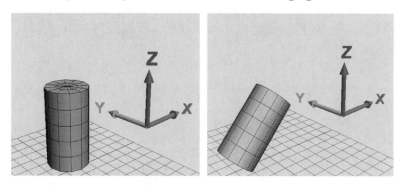

Figure 2-4: Using the By World option.

When the By Local option is selected, rotating your object will cause the axis gizmo to also rotate and remain local to the object's internal axis. This can be very useful in some cases.

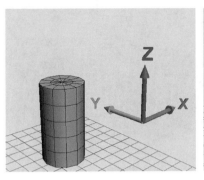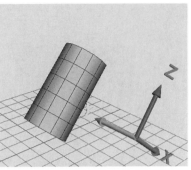

Figure 2-5: Using the By Local option.

Cutting Polygons

The Cut tool is one of the most used tools for polygonal modeling. When you cut or manually divide the polygon, you add an edge. Every edge adds tension to the mesh, as we'll see in the next chapter. The procedure for cutting a polygon is specific to each modeling application. For example, since version 5 of 3ds Max there has been an indicator cursor that shows whether you are over an edge or vertex. In Maya, when you click on the edge and hold, you snap the cut starting point to the clicked edge; when you move the mouse you can reposition the starting point. 3ds Max 5 allows you to cut as many polygons as you wish with one cut. Maya 6.5 lets you cut one polygon at time.

Figures 2-6 and 2-7 show examples of using the Cut tool.

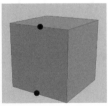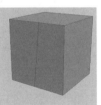

Figure 2-6: Click on the origin point (where you want the cut to start), then click on the destination point to generate a new line.

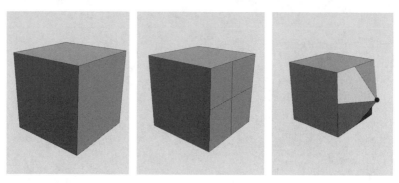

Figure 2-7: Here we have made a "+" cut in the face of a box and pulled the vertex forward.

Extruding

The Extrude tool described here refers to extrusion of the polygon's sub-elements, like a face, edge, or vertex. Face extrusion is oriented by its element normal, generating new faces along the side of the origin extrusion and extruded face. Edge and vertex extrusion are similar to face extrusion. These processes extrude the selected sub-object, obeying the topology and using the object's normal as the direction reference.

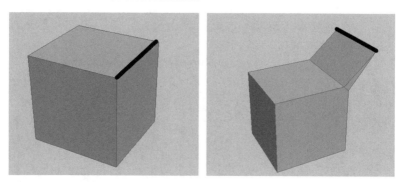

Figure 2-8: Edge extrusion.

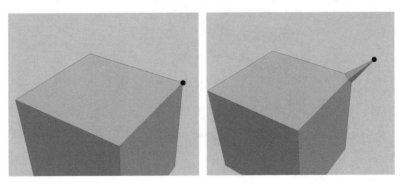

Figure 2-9: Vertex extrusion.

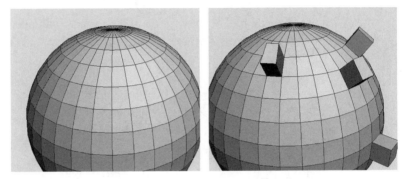

Figure 2-10: Face extrusion.

Figure 2-11 shows extrusion operations combined with rotation operations.

Figure 2-11: Face selected, extruded, rotated a bit, extruded again, rotated, and extruded. Note that you can extrude as many times as you wish, and every time you extrude the face, new edges stay where you stopped the last extrusion.

Most 3D packages give you several options for extrusion, including group extrusion, extruding by polygon, and extruding by local normal.

With the Extrude by Group option, you extrude the selected polygons as a group.

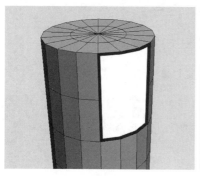
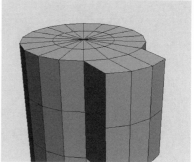

Figure 2-12: Extruding group.

With the Extrude by Polygon option, the polygons will be extruded independently from each other.

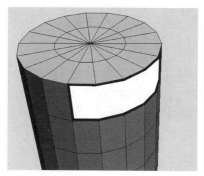
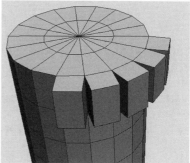

Figure 2-13: Extruding by polygon.

With the Extrude by Local Normal option, the polygons follow the local normal of each polygon, but they stay together as a group.

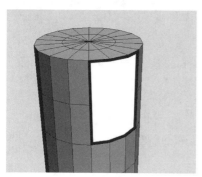
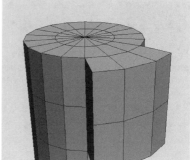

Figure 2-14: Extruding by local normal.

Chamfer/Bevel

Chamfer and Bevel can produce very similar results. In some applications, however, the name related to its function may vary, causing confusion. Let's take a look at the tools.

It is very common to see beveling functions applied over 3D text, giving the result shown in Figure 2-15.

Figure 2-15: Beveling text.

In 3ds Max, beveling applied to a box face will give us the result shown in Figure 2-16.

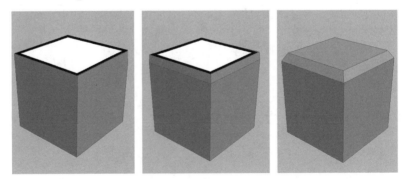

Figure 2-16: Beveled box face in 3ds Max.

Additionally, depending on the parameters that are set for this tool, the shape can vary considerably, as shown in Figure 2-17.

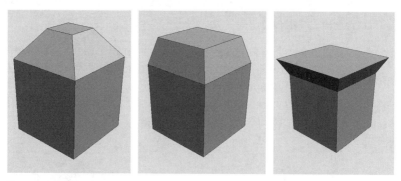

Figure 2-17: Using the Bevel tool.

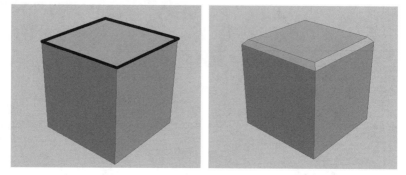

Figure 2-18: Selecting the top edges and applying the Chamfer command.

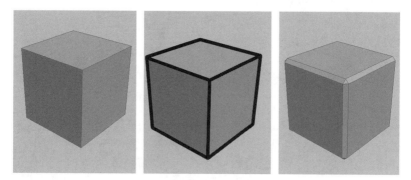

Figure 2-19: Using the Bevel tool in Maya. The same result could be achieved by extruding the face up and then scaling the extruded face down a bit.

Note that the variety of options allows you to reach the same result in different ways; just choose the quickest or easiest method for you.

Attach and Detach

Detach is the operation to use when you have a mesh and want to separate parts of it into two distinct meshes.

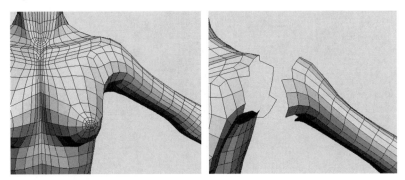

Figure 2-20: Detaching.

Remember, every time you detach a piece of the mesh, each piece will be an independent mesh that can have different properties, textures, and so on.

Attach is a very useful operation that allows you to join two different meshes and merge them as one. If you are modeling a full human body, you may want to model the head, the limbs, and the torso separately and then merge them into one single mesh. After the attach operation, all the parts of the human body you've modeled will be treated as one for any further operations you may apply. However, they do not necessarily have to share the same texture. You can merge two meshes and preserve the texture coordinates, shaders, and textures applied to each one.

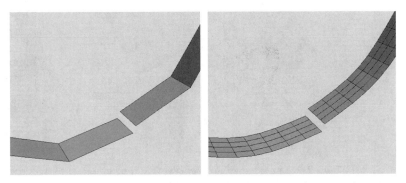

Figure 2-21: An attached mesh without merged vertices. After smoothing is applied, the meshes continue, disconnected from each other.

When you attach two distinct meshes, they will be a single mesh but will not have continuity. The attach operation does not merge the vertices automatically; you'll need to merge the vertices one by one.

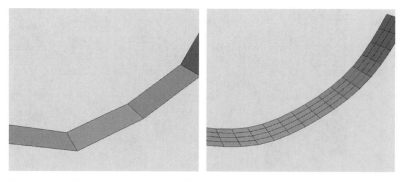

Figure 2-22: The attached mesh with the vertices welded. The smoothing is applied continuously when the vertices are matched and welded.

Welding

Welding is probably the most common tool for fixing a mesh that has errors or matching two meshes after an attach operation.

Welding works differently in different applications. In 3ds Max, you cannot weld a vertex that isn't near a hole or a vertex that does not have an edge connecting through the targeted vertex. You can do this in Maya, but it may have undesirable results on your mesh. This book recommends "safe" techniques that you can apply using just about any 3D modeling program you wish.

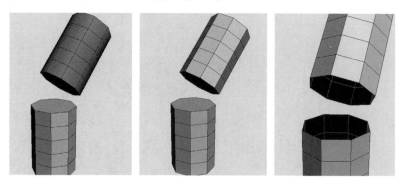

Figure 2-23: In Maya you can easily weld the vertices of the attached cylinders, but in 3ds Max you must delete the cap hole.

To use the Weld command, you select the matching vertices one by one and apply the command. See Chapter 3 for information on welding meshes that do not have the same number of vertices.

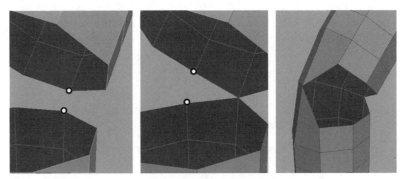

Figure 2-24: Using the Weld command.

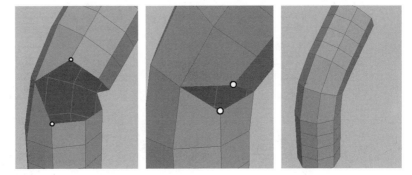

Figure 2-25: Welding two cylinders with the same number of sides.

Duplicate and Mirror

One of the most common tools in computer graphic applications is the Duplicate tool. This tool makes a copy of the selected object (usually with all the properties of the original object).

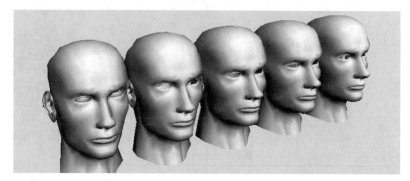

Figure 2-26: Duplicating along the X axis.

The Mirror tool duplicates the object and mirrors it across an axis.

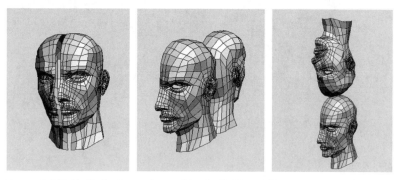

Figure 2-27: Half of a face mirrored in the X, Y, and Z axes.

Pivot Point

The pivot point is an attribute that represents the object's location and governs transformations such as rotation and scale. When the pivot point is centered, the scaling and rotation operations use the center point as their origin. When the pivot point is aligned to a corner, the scaling and rotation operations use that corner as their origin.

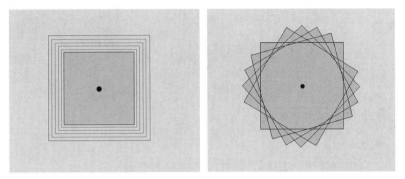

Figure 2-28: Centered pivot point.

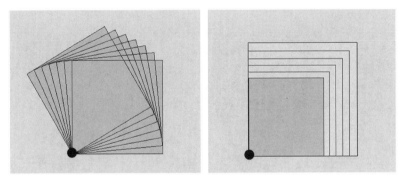

Figure 2-29: Pivot point with the origin in a corner.

Holes

A hole is a missing face in your mesh. It's not desirable in most cases, but if you know how to work with it, it may be useful.

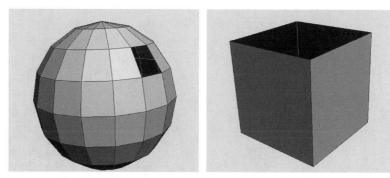

Figure 2-30: A hole in a mesh.

Smoothing a Mesh with a Hole

A mesh that contains a hole can be smoothed. Figures 2-31 to 2-38 show different smoothing operations.

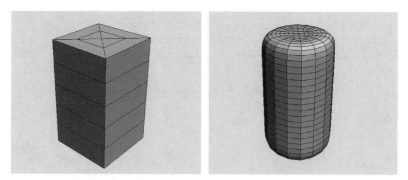

Figure 2-31: The subdivision computes the cap as a tension generator on this four-sided cylinder. Every edge contributes to the new mesh generated by the subdivision process shown on the right.

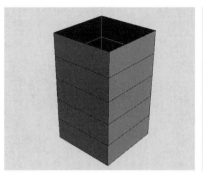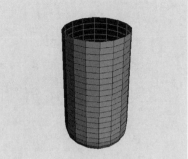

Figure 2-32: Left, a four-sided cylinder without a cap. Right, the same cylinder subdivided. As you can see, Catmull-Clark subdivision does a great job on quad polygon shapes, and the four-sided cylinder becomes a smooth cylinder after a few subdivision steps.

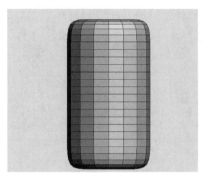

Figure 2-33: Left, the cylinder with a cap, after subdivision. Right, the cylinder with a hole. Notice that the hole does not generate tension on the mesh when subdividing.

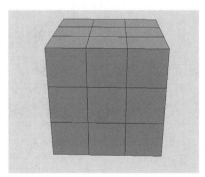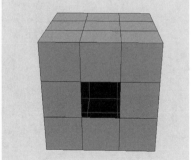

Figure 2-34: To show how subdivision performs on a quad hole, we pick a cube and delete the middle face on one side.

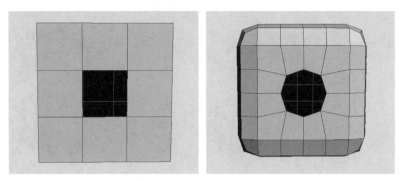

Figure 2-35: Left, the same hole without subdivision. Right, with one level of subdivision.

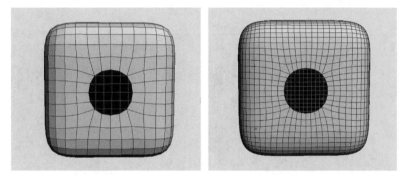

Figure 2-36: Left, two levels of subdivision. Right, three levels of subdivision.

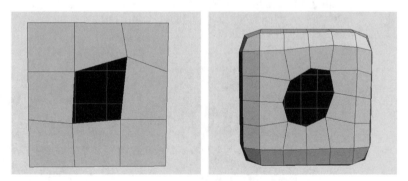

Figure 2-37: The same cube but with the hole distorted a bit.

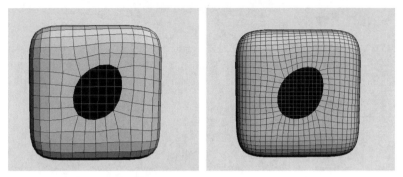

Figure 2-38: More levels of subdivision.

Soft Selection

Soft Selection, SoftModificator, DragNet — the name can vary from application to application but the purpose is similar: to select a sub-element and apply an influence for its neighboring elements. For example, if you move a vertex, the neighboring vertex will also be moved, depending on the Attenuation parameter of this tool. It's like a magnetic tool attracting the nearest sub-elements of the selected sub-element.

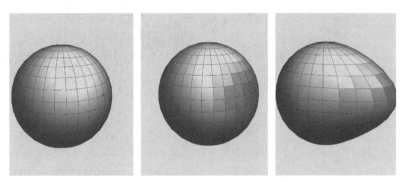

Figure 2-39: Using Soft Selection.

Soft Selection tools are very useful for reshaping your objects and adjusting their proportions and volume.

Mesh Errors

Mesh errors are any undesired artifacts or holes, or continuity errors on the mesh. It's not uncommon to find errors on the mesh.

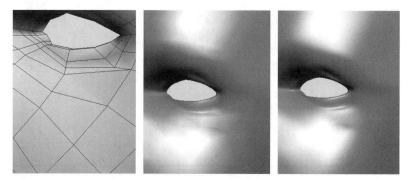

Figure 2-40: Left, an error mesh. Depending on the viewport shading, it may be hard to find out where the error is before subdivision. Middle, shading with a high specular level (subdivision level 1). The error is still not easy to find. Right, the figure has two levels of subdivision and it is more obvious now where the gap is.

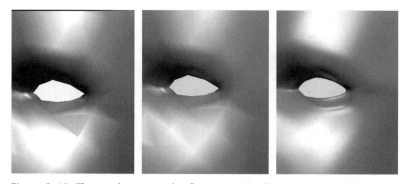

Figure 2-41: The mesh error in this figure is caused by two vertices that are too close. The solution is to merge them together.

Figure 2-42: Note the problem on the chin.

To find and correct mesh errors, smooth the object and carefully watch the geometry while searching for them. Mesh errors can produce undesirable results at render time.

Chapter 3

Polygon Subdivision

Polygon Subdivision Theory

Subdivision (also called smoothing) is a process for generating smooth surfaces by refining a polygonal mesh. The basis for subdivision can be traced back to the 1940s and '50s when G. de Rham used "corner cutting" to describe smooth curves. Since then, many researchers and scientists have worked on this topic, but it was only in the mid-1970s that the practical use of subdivision theory as applied to computer graphics started to take a definitive shape. In this chapter we discuss subdivision algorithm theory and provide a number of examples. All of the subdivision methods described in this chapter are classified by three criteria:

▶ Type of mesh: quadrilateral (quad) or triangular (tri)

▶ Type of refinement: primal (vertex insertion) or dual (cut-corner)

▶ Type of scheme: approximating or interpolating

The mathematical procedures that define the subdivision process are called "masks." In this chapter we show the visual representations of the subdivision schemes for control points with the coefficients of the subdivision mask.

Arbitrary topology means that the edges, vertices, and the whole graph formed by the mesh cage can be arbitrary; that is, the vertices of the mesh may be of arbitrary degrees. In arbitrary topology, we classify the valence of the vertices when 6 degrees as tri and when 4 degrees as quad. Ordinary vertices have a valence of 4, and extraordinary vertices have a valence other than 4.

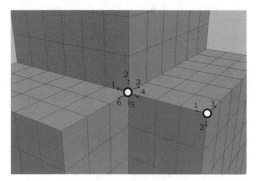

Figure 3-1: Two extraordinary vertices with valences of 6 and 3.

Chaikin's Algorithms for Curves (1974)

In 1974, George Chaikin introduced one of the first algorithms for refinement (cut-corners). In contrast to his predecessors, Chaikin developed an algorithm that worked directly on control polygons. His new algorithm generated a new control polygon by cutting the corner.

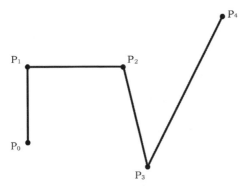

Figure 3-2: The initial, unrefined polygonal line with five P points: P0, P1, P2, P3, and P4.

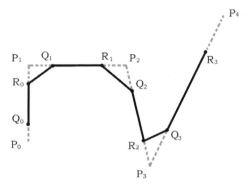

Figure 3-3: Refinement step 1. Chaikin's method generates Q and R points, while cutting the corners add refinement to the line.

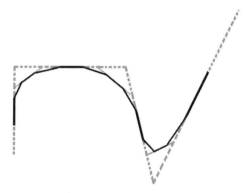

Figure 3-4: Refinement step 2.

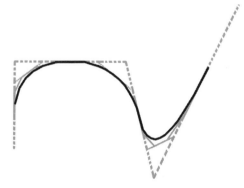

Figure 3-5: Refinement step 3. When increasing the refinements, the curve gets smoother.

Doo-Sabin Surfaces (1978)

Daniel Doo and Malcom Sabin adapted Chaikin's polygon refinement technique for the bi-quadratic uniform B-spline and developed a new procedure for surface generation. Doo-Sabin is a dual approximating scheme for meshes of arbitrary topology. All the vertices have a valence of 4 after the first subdivision refinement.

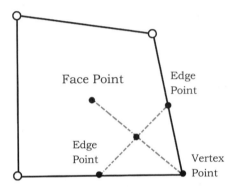

Figure 3-6

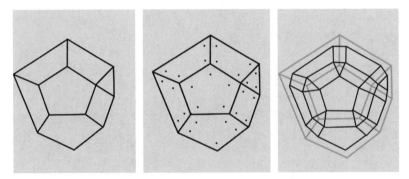

Figure 3-7: Left, an unrefined mesh. Center, vertices placed by the Doo-Sabin method and then connected. Right, the subdivided shape is shown in black and the original, unrefined mesh is shown in gray.

Catmull-Clark Subdivision (1978)

The algorithm proposed by Edward Catmull and Jim Clark is the most widely known and used. When the mesh is subdivided, new vertices (face points) are placed at the center of each unrefined face and in the center of each unrefined edge, and then new edges are created to connect these new vertices. It's an approximating primal scheme.

These are the steps of Catmull-Clark subdivision:

1. The face points are created by averaging positions of the polygon's unrefined vertices.

2. Edge point locations are calculated by averaging the center point of an unrefined edge and the locations of the two new adjacent face points.

3. The positions of the old vertices are reconfigured using the following equation:

$$\frac{Q}{n} + \frac{2R}{n} + \frac{S(n-3)}{n}$$

Figure 3-8: Variable **Q** represents the average of the new vertices (face points) surrounding the unrefined vertex. Variable **R** represents the average of the edge's midpoints that share the unrefined mesh. Variable **S** is the original, unrefined mesh. Variable **n** is the number of edges that share the old unrefined vertex.

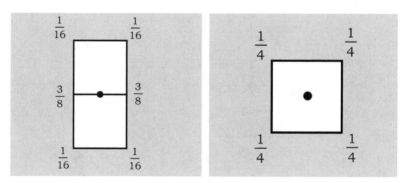

Figure 3-9: Left, a mask scheme for an edge vertex. Right, a mask for a face vertex.

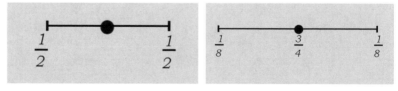

Figure 3-10: Left: a mask for boundary odd vertices. Right, a mask for even vertices.

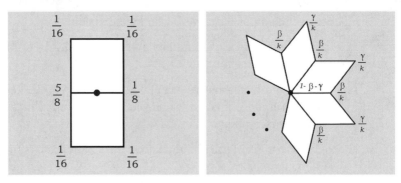

Figure 3-11: Left, a mask for extraordinary vertices. Right, a mask for interior even vertices.

Catmull-Clark is an excellent scheme for ordinary vertices (valence of 4, quads) but also works with valences that are greater than or less than 4.

The following figures demonstrate the Catmull-Clark subdivision scheme.

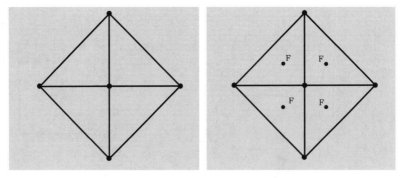

Figure 3-12: An unrefined cube primitive seen from the top view. The face points are generated and placed using the Catmull-Clark subdivision method.

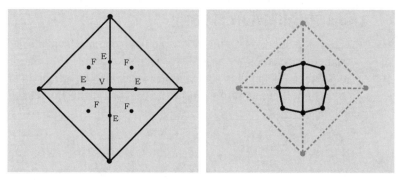

Figure 3-13: New vertex points (F) generated from the (E) points (see Figure 3-11). These new vertices are then connected, forming the subdivided shape.

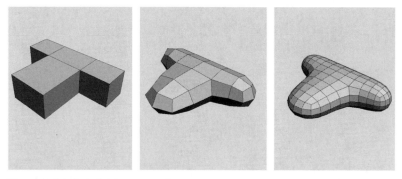

Figure 3-14: Subdivision example.

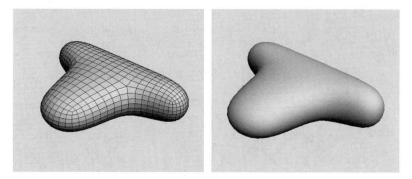

Figure 3-15: Refinement of subdivision example.

Loop Subdivision (1987)

The Loop subdivision method is an approximate primal scheme for triangular meshes proposed by Charles Loop in 1987. The Loop method can be applied to triangular arbitrary polygonal meshes.

The following figures show the masks for the Loop subdivision scheme.

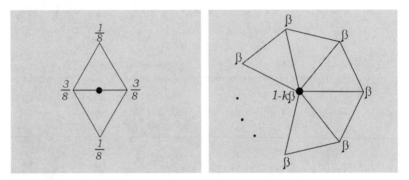

Figure 3-16: Interior rules. Left, rules for odd vertices. Right, rules for even vertices.

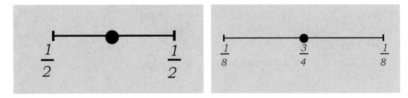

Figure 3-17: Special rules for creases and boundaries. Left, rules for odd vertices. Right, rules for even vertices.

Figures 3-18 to 3-21 show Loop subdivision in action.

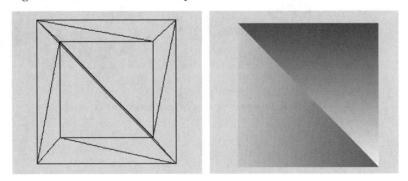

Figure 3-18: Unrefined mesh cube with 12 (tri) polygons.

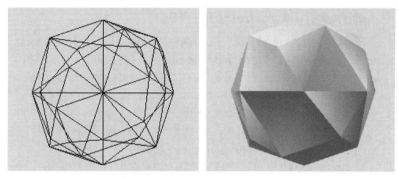

Figure 3-19: First level of subdivision, 48 faces.

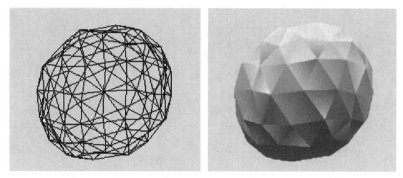

Figure 3-20: Second level of subdivision, 192 faces.

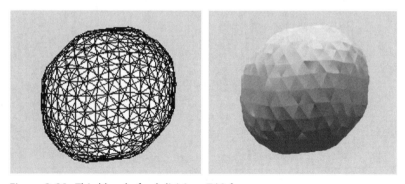

Figure 3-21: Third level of subdivision, 768 faces.

Butterfly Subdivision (1990)

Butterfly subdivision is a method proposed by Dyn, Gregory, and Levin and is primal and interpolating for triangular meshes. In the original subdivision scheme, artifacts often appeared on the mesh after the subdivision interpolation. In 1996, Denis Zorin's Modified Butterfly Subdivision scheme improved on the Butterfly method, solving the problems of the old scheme yet retaining the simplicity of the original scheme and improving the smoothing.

Figures 3-22 to 3-25 show the subdivision steps for the Butterfly scheme using a triangulated cube.

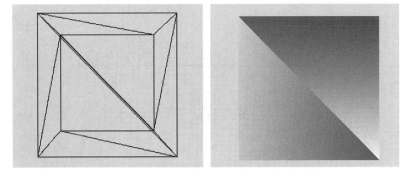

Figure 3-22: Unrefined mesh cube with 12 (tri) polygons.

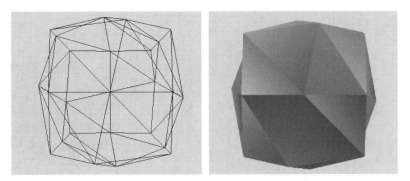

Figure 3-23: First level of subdivision, 48 faces.

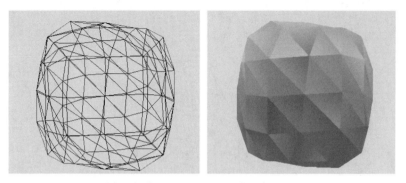

Figure 3-24: Second level of subdivision, 192 faces.

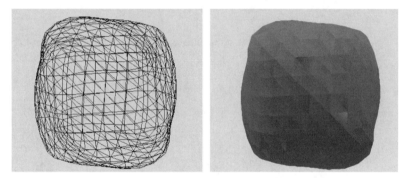

Figure 3-25: Third level of subdivision, 768 faces.

Kobbelt Subdivision (1996)

The Kobbelt subdivision method is interpolating and primal, and works on quadrilateral meshes. The difference is that vertices are fixed during the interpolation process and the rules for edges and faces are referenced to the unrefined mesh.

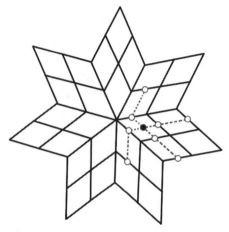

Figure 3-26: Kobbelt's scheme for computing a vertex adjacent to an extraordinary vertex.

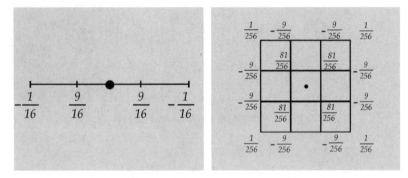

Figure 3-27: Left, a regular mask for edge, crease, and boundary vertices. Right, a regular mask for a face vertex.

Continuity

Continuity can be defined as the smoothness of an object's edge. Computer-generated models should not contain any faceted polygons, gaps, or hard edges in the final result (unless they are deliberate). Some modeling formats, like Maya's subdivision surfaces or NURBS, have implicit continuity, but balancing the weight of the mesh must be carefully planned when using polygons.

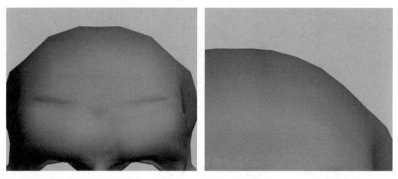

Figure 3-28: Left, bad continuity. Note the facets at the top of the head. Right, after one step of subdivision. There are still some artifacts.

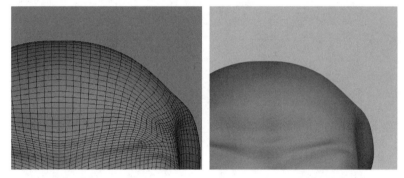

Figure 3-29: The same object with two levels of subdivision. We can almost see the facets in wireframe, but at render time they are nearly imperceptible.

Subdivision and Wire Tension

Most 3D applications use Catmull-Clark subdivision. It is the industry standard for dealing with polygonal geometry. As this subdivision algorithm works best with meshes with ordinary vertices (valence 4, quads), effort has been made to keep the methods and techniques quad as much as possible. When that's not possible, non-quad polygons are used in areas of less deformation.

The difference between a cube polygon with six faces (quad) (see Figure 3-30) and a cube with 12 faces (tri) (see Figure 3-31) is very clear after some Catmull-Clark subdivision: The edges across the tri faces generate unnecessary tension, giving a deformed look to the cube during the subdivision process.

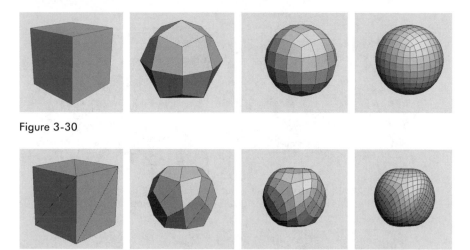

Figure 3-30

Figure 3-31

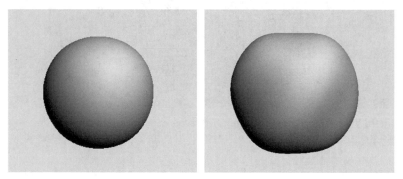

Figure 3-32: Left, final result of cube subdivision of six quad faces. Right, final result of cube subdivision of 12 tri faces.

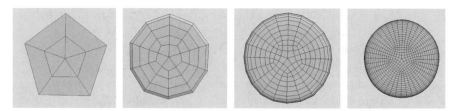

Figure 3-33: Subdivision process of a pentagon cylinder mesh.

Starting from a Primitive

"Imagination is greater than knowledge," Einstein once said. Using this as a golden rule when starting polygonal modeling from a primitive will bring you good results. Knowing your primitives well and planning what they can become is a very good starting point. Don't think about primitives in terms of what they are; think about the possibilities. A box can be a pipe, a cylinder can be a vase, and a cone can be a flower. When starting from a primitive, the sky is the limit.

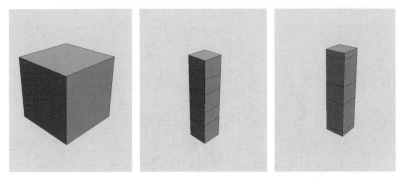

Figure 3-34: We extrude the cube a few times. Each line adds more tension.

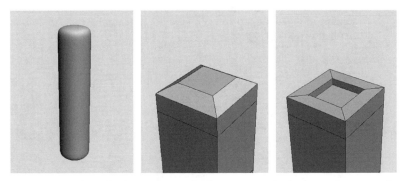

Figure 3-35: The cube becomes a cylinder. We extrude the top polygon, scale it down, and extrude in.

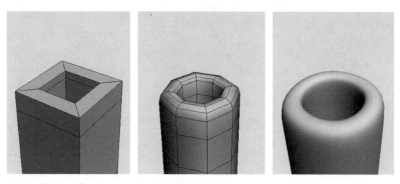

Figure 3-36: After some subdivision we get a tube made from a cube.

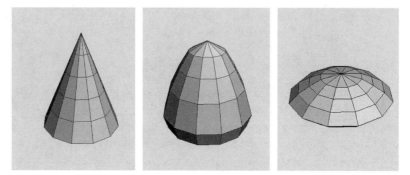

Figure 3-37: With a rigid cone primitive, you can scale up the body vertices and push down the top vertex a little bit, making the cone smoother. Then scale down the whole object.

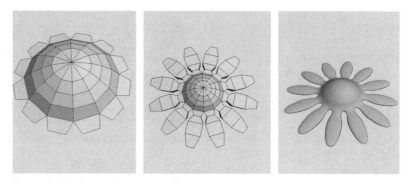

Figure 3-38: A cone becomes a flower.

Giving It the Shape You Want

Creating the desired shape when modeling polygonal objects is all about understanding how subdivision works. The desired shape often depends on careful cuts and dense and structured wires. A well-planned mesh can give desired results without excessive hours of cutting and reshaping. Here we discuss some of the most important aspects of planning complex geometry: edge flow and edge loops.

Edge Flow

The edge flow represents the actual structure of your model and how the topology must be constructed in order to work correctly according to the anatomy of the model or object when animated and to avoid unwanted gaps, hard edges, or subdivision artifacts.

Notice in Figure 3-39 that the lines of the male model (at left) follow the flow of the human anatomy to provide the correct tension and deformation of the muscles after the subdivision. The female model's abdomen (at right) is not correct from the muscle structure standpoint, but the base mesh as shown can provide a good structure for an abdomen without bumpy musculature.

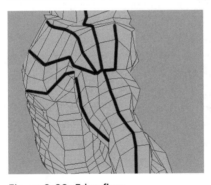 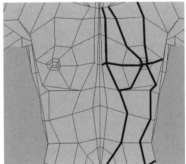

Figure 3-39: Edge flow.

Edge Loop

Edge loops occur when the end of the line encounters the beginning, forming a loop.

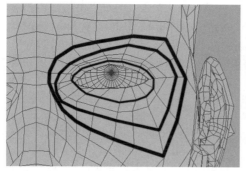 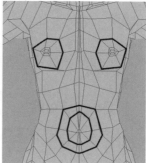

Figure 3-40: Edge loops.

The same thing occurs when a line contours a model and returns to its origin.

Subdivision and Iterations

Polysmooth is a term for smoothing polygonal surfaces, and is also called subdivision, which was discussed earlier in this chapter. The iterations correspond to the number of subdivisions, meaning the higher the iteration value, the higher the number of polygons and the smoother the surface. One secret to working with a 3D scene is to manage the weight of the elements in the scene. This means, in geometry terms, that you need to carefully watch the number of visible objects in your viewport and the density of the mesh (number of polygons). Sometimes a higher number of polygons (high iteration value) is necessary for a good general resolution of the object (better continuity).

The following figures are two examples of smoothing with changing iteration values.

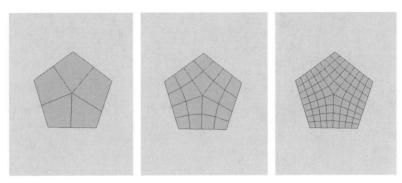

Figure 3-41

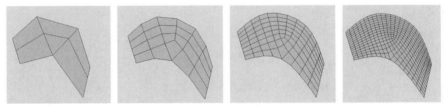

Figure 3-42

Inorganic Modeling

Inorganic modeling is not the easiest approach for polygonal modeling if you need precision. However, polygons can do a great job if you plan the mesh and use it wisely. Here we discuss techniques for successful inorganic modeling.

Soft Edges

The look of edges is very important in the creation of realistic inorganic objects. Cut objects are among the few real-life objects that have sharp edges, similar to those we get when creating box primitives in 3D applications. In 3D, the corners of inorganic objects must have at least a hint of a soft edge to improve the look and realism of the objects (the shading also benefits from edges that are not too sharp). In this section we describe how to control the creation of hard and soft edges, using Figures 3-43 to 3-53 as examples.

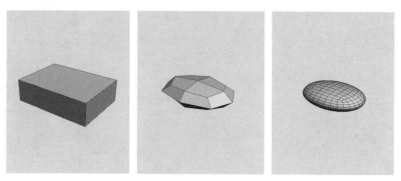

Figure 3-43: There is not enough tension to hold the box's shape after subdivision.

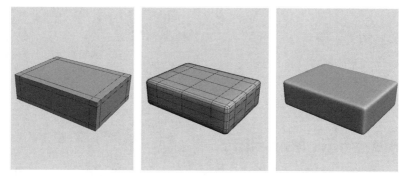

Figure 3-44: Adding edges improves the tension and holds the box shape.

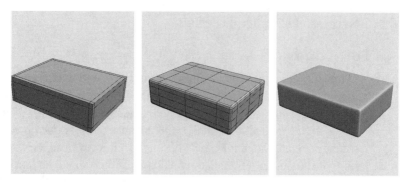

Figure 3-45: When the extra edges are too close to the original box edges, the tension is higher and the border gets sharper; when the extra edges are farther away, the border gets rounder.

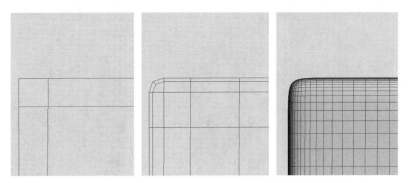

Figure 3-46: In this example we see clearly how the subdivision performs a smoother look to the box.

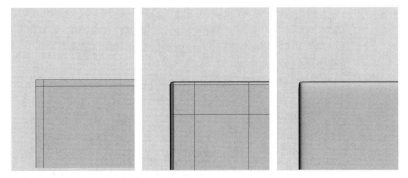

Figure 3-47: The closer the edges, the sharper the border.

When there are extraordinary vertices (valence other than 4, which is the case of the vertices on the top border of the cylinder in Figure 3-48), the subdivision algorithm has to perform operations to compensate for the lack of vertices.

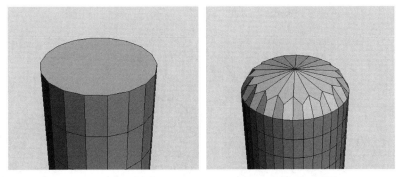

Figure 3-48: In this case, where there is a valence of 3, there is one vertex missing that keeps it from having an ordinary valence of 4.

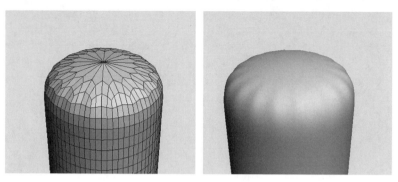

Figure 3-49: When we see the result without the wireframe, some ripples appear on the smoothed border.

To correctly generate the cap polygons in order to avoid unwanted tension during subdivision, select the top polygon, extrude up, scale down, and move down to align with the top edges, as shown in Figure 3-50.

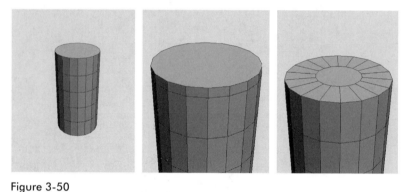

Figure 3-50

Repeat the operation.

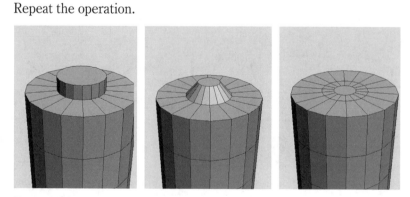

Figure 3-51

Then you can select all the edges and weld them together, as shown in Figure 3-52.

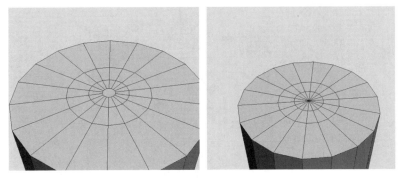

Figure 3-52

Now you have a nice top that you've made manually.

Bump

Modeling circular edge loops by hand is the safest way to carve or bump polygonal objects and reduce mesh errors. When you cut an eight-sided edge, you have the opportunity to plan how the mesh will behave because you can cut, remove edges, and merge vertices as much as you need.

First we cut an "X" in the top of the box, then cut a "+" to give us eight intersecting lines. Then we draw a poly-circle in the middle, as shown in Figure 3-53.

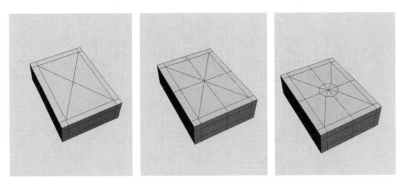

Figure 3-53

Select the polygons inside the circle and extrude it a little bit, then extrude again. This will generate tension in the base. Extrude again, a little higher.

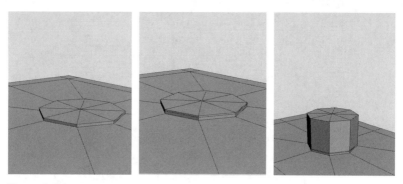

Figure 3-54

After the extrusion, scale down the top polygons. You may want to cut near the top of the extruded object to improve the tension at the top.

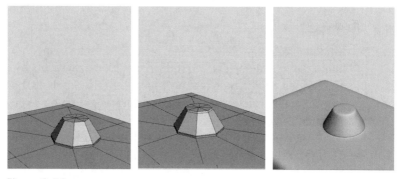

Figure 3-55

Notice the differences between the two images in Figure 3-56. The one on the left represents the extruded shape, and the one on the right is the same shape with one of the base edges removed.

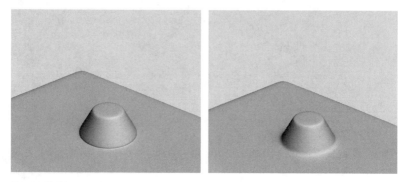

Figure 3-56

Circular Depression

You can also create a circular depression. Start by creating a rectangle and slicing the polygon with the Cut tool, as shown in Figure 3-57. Scale up this rectangle to get a more elliptical hole when we extrude down.

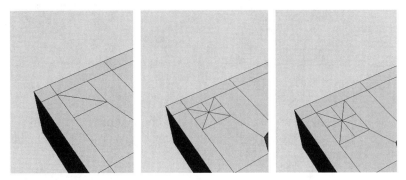

Figure 3-57

With the face scaled we can cut the ellipse inside the rectangle, cutting from vertex to vertex. Select the circular polygon and extrude down to generate new tension where the extrusion stopped.

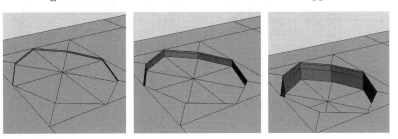

Figure 3-58

By making the hole manually, we can set the shape and the border in many ways.

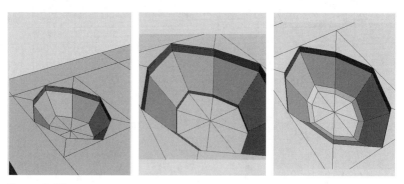

Figure 3-59

The above step gives us the smoothing shown at the left in Figure 3-60, but we can chamfer the lower edge and get a much sharper result.

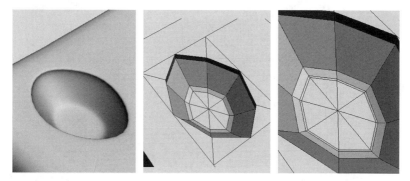

Figure 3-60

Figure 3-61 shows the results of creating a bump and a circular depression after three levels of subdivision and shading with a high specular value.

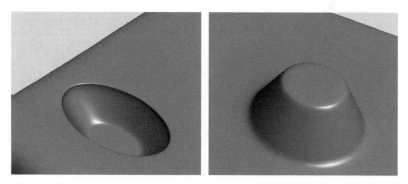

Figure 3-61

Cracks

Cracks are an important part of inorganic modeling. With polygons you can set a variety of cracks in just about any type of object. Figures 3-62 to 3-67 show how to create a crack in an object.

Starting with a 12-sided cylinder, we approximate three edges, as shown on the right in Figure 3-62. Notice that this modification changes nothing when rendered.

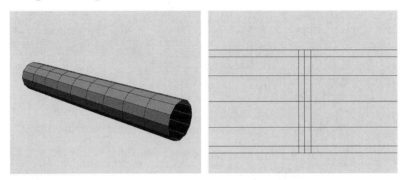

Figure 3-62

Pushing down the middle vertices makes a very smooth crack appear, as the tension there is very low.

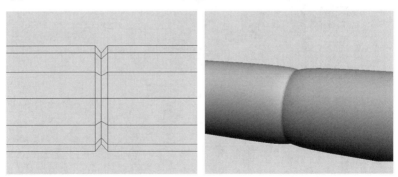

Figure 3-63

Figure 3-64 shows two edges after a chamfer operation. The tension generates a sharp crack.

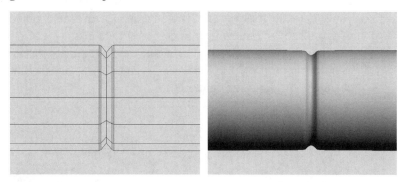

Figure 3-64

All the edges are involved now and there is more tension.

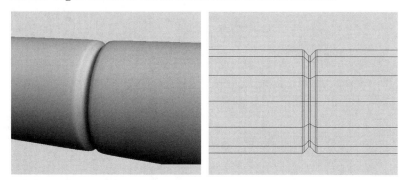

Figure 3-65

Figure 3-66

The vertices are moved closer and the crack gets thin.

Figure 3-67

Body Cracks

In this section we discuss how to efficiently make holes in your mesh and get a nice, smooth mesh without errors.

Create a rectangle structure using the Cut tool and then select the middle edge and chamfer it. Instead of one edge, you'll have two. Cut in the middle of the center polygon as shown at the right in Figure 3-68.

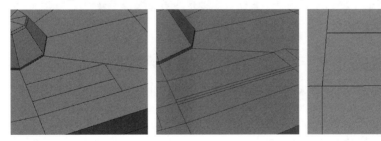

Figure 3-68

Now we'll create the rounded corner structure. Make cuts as shown at the left and center in Figure 3-69, and notice everything outside the crack is as much quad as possible. Select the interior polygons of the crack, extrude down a bit, and then extrude again and again. The edges generated by the first extrusion create good tension on the inside part of the border's crack.

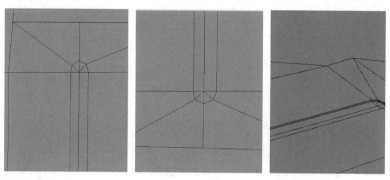

Figure 3-69

The general structure is done. However, you may also want to cut an extra border outside the crack border loop, as shown in the center in Figure 3-70, to improve the local tension.

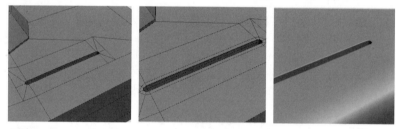

Figure 3-70

Thickness

Primitives and polygons by default don't have any thickness. If you delete half of a polygon sphere, you'll notice absolutely no thickness. 3ds Max 6 has a tool named Shell Modifier that allows you to give thickness to your object. In this section we show how to add thickness to your mesh without using any special tool or script.

First, pick a sphere and delete half. Duplicate the object and scale it down a bit.

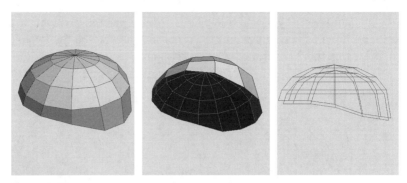

Figure 3-71

Then flip the normals of the interior object and start welding the vertices until the entire object is closed and has no holes. When finished, apply smoothing; you'll notice almost no thickness.

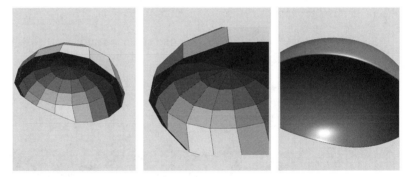

Figure 3-72

Select the welded edges and chamfer until you get a desired thickness. You may need to move the edges down. To improve the tension, select the exterior border edges and chamfer again.

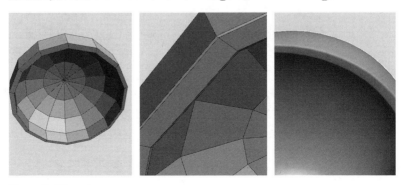

Figure 3-73

Another way to add thickness to your object is to duplicate it and flip it as in the previous exercise and then attach the two pieces together. This time, select the upper border edges, extrude them down a little bit, and merge the vertices.

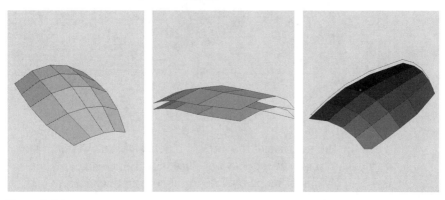

Figure 3-74

Do the same on the other side and the back and front. Now select all the border edges and chamfer.

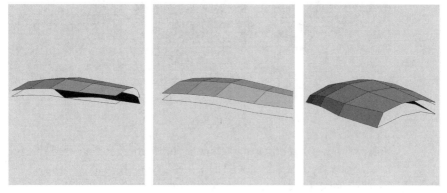

Figure 3-75

The chamfer borders will have more tension and the thickness will look more rigid.

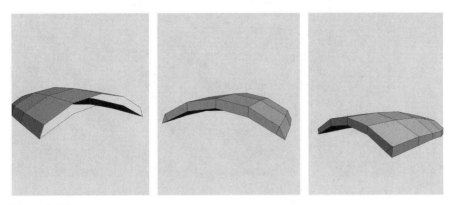

Figure 3-76

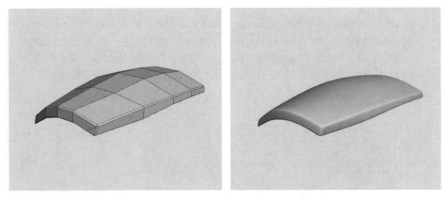

Figure 3-77

It's important to remember that it is very common to have two or more ways to do the same thing in 3D. This is really great because it allows you to choose the best (and possibly quicker) way to reach the desired result.

Holes in Curved Surfaces

Another inorganic modeling technique is making a hole in a curved polygonal surface. Figures 3-78 to 3-82 demonstrate this process.

The first step is to align the edges to sketch a square and then cut as shown at the center and right.

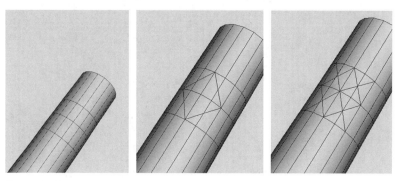

Figure 3-78

Then weld excessive vertices to clean up the mesh, select the polygons around the hole area, and delete them. With the hole defined, cut around it to rebuild the adjoining polygons. There are too many triangles here, which add unnecessary tension. Remove the edges to form the mesh as shown on the right in the following figure.

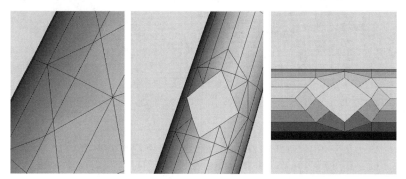

Figure 3-79

With the correct topology established around the hole, you can cut using the same polygon loop to improve the local tension and get a nice, smooth hole in curved surfaces. Notice that this is a perfectly round hole, but if you wish you can move the vertices around to modify its shape.

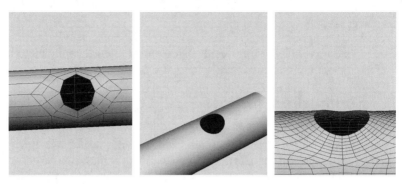

Figure 3-80

Now that the hole in the curved surface has the correct topology, you can attach another piece, as shown in Figures 3-81 and 3-82 below. Pay attention to the number of vertices of the objects you are attaching. Notice that in this exercise both the hole and the new cylinder have eight vertices to be merged.

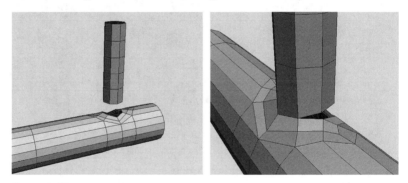

Figure 3-81

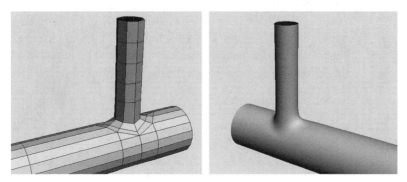

Figure 3-82

Advanced Techniques

Here we discuss more advanced and refined techniques to improve mesh control and correct topology under specific circumstances.

Unmatched Vertices

Unmatched vertices occur when you need to weld two meshes that do not have the same number of vertices. Earlier examples showed how to weld matching vertices when attaching two objects. In this section we see how to proceed when the number of vertices of each object differs.

In this example we have two cylinders, one with eight segments and another with 10 segments. We start welding the vertices, as shown in Figure 3-83.

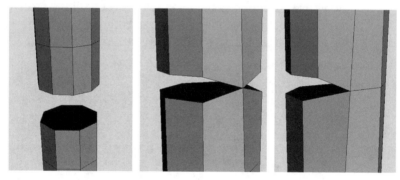

Figure 3-83

At the end of the welding process, two vertices will be unconnected because the lower cylinder has only eight vertices. This is a common problem when joining two pieces of geometry. We can insert a vertex at the edge or create a vertex by cutting in the path of the upper cylinder's edge. This technique is commonly used when you separately model parts of the body that must be joined in a later modeling session, like hands, heads, or limbs.

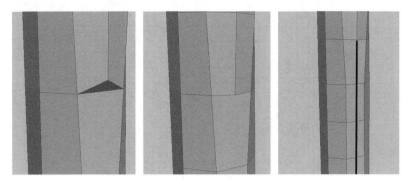

Figure 3-84

90 Degree Cut

Sometimes when cutting in order to add more edges and tension to
the mesh, we need to cut the mesh at 90 degrees or change the
course of the flow.

Notice in the following figure that cutting the plane to change
the direction results in a triangle in the mesh that can be avoided.

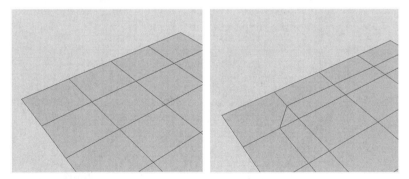

Figure 3-85

Simply cut the marked edge, as shown in the center of Figure 3-86,
and move the vertex in the direction of the new cut.

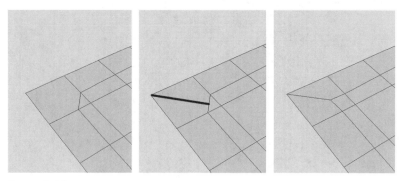

Figure 3-86

How to Fix Boolean before Subdivision

Sometimes using Booleans is inevitable or simply less time consuming. Here we discuss some techniques to correct the mesh after performing a Boolean operation.

When subtracting using curved and rounded surfaces, use a low number of segments to make the mesh easier to repair. In Figure 3-88, the sphere on the left has 16 segments and the sphere on the right has eight segments.

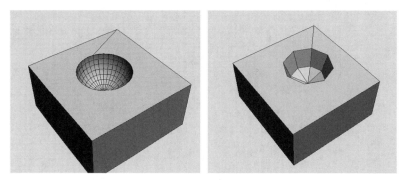

Figure 3-87: Fixing Boolean with curved subtraction.

If we subdivide this mesh as it is, it will be a complete mess since the top polygon has been reconfigured after the Boolean operation. We need to construct a structure over the face that was forced to accept the new element (the carved sphere in this case).

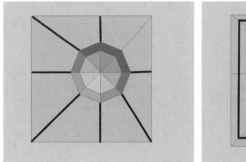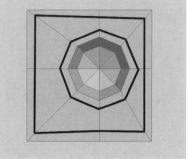

Figure 3-88: It is easier to extend the edges of the sphere with eight segments and cut around to improve the tension.

Now when we subdivide we can see it works much better. The same procedure can be applied to a number of other Boolean operations; simply cut new topology around the area affected by the Boolean operation in a way in which the new tension works to support the previous operation, and everything works as one.

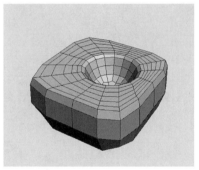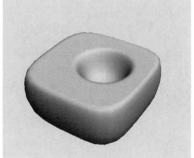

Figure 3-89: Object after subdivision.

Chapter 4

Visual References

Why We Need References

Collecting reference material is the first step toward creating a high-quality model. When working on complex models, the reference (also called a blueprint, model sheet, or chart) shows your modeling object from a variety of orthogonal views, generally front, top, and side.

After the blueprint is set up in the viewports, the modeling process starts with the placing of a primitive or a polygon. Usually when starting with a primitive, the vertices are reshaped to fit the blueprint and half of the object is deleted when the object is symmetrical. Once the modeling is finished, the modeled half is mirrored and the vertices are welded.

How to Create References

In this section we discuss common techniques for creating a reference sheet and making adjustments for polygonal modeling.

First, we sketch the basic shape of the object from the side view. It's important to note that depending on the object's complexity, more details may be needed and more attention given to the guidelines for projecting.

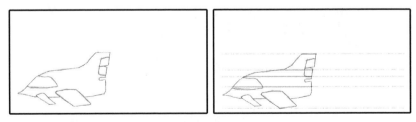

Figure 4-1: A sketch to be used for reference.

After drawing the side proportions of the model, we can trace the horizontal lines. These lines are traced based on points of the model that we can use as reference points to draw the other views.

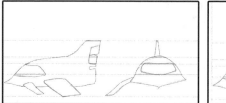 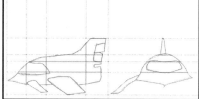

Figure 4-2

The horizontal reference guides will help us to sketch the front of the ship.

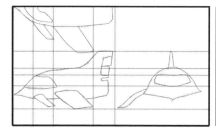 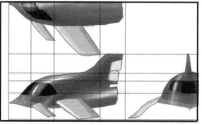

Figure 4-3

With the side and front sketched, we can trace the vertical guides to create the top of the ship. After finishing the base of the sketch, we can start coloring and add some shading for a better visualization on the concept sheet.

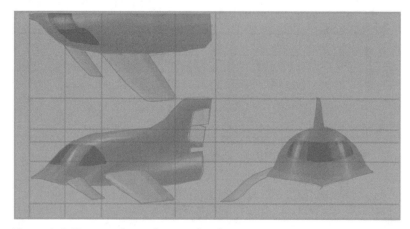

Figure 4-4: The complete reference sketch.

Depending on the color scheme of your 3D application, you may want to lower the brightness and the contrast of the concept drawing to make it easier to see the contrast between the selected edges and vertices and the reference sheet during the modeling session.

Projecting Complex Forms

Notice the lines in Figure 4-5. These parallel lines are used to keep the proportion of the drawings correct from one orthogonal perspective of the model to another.

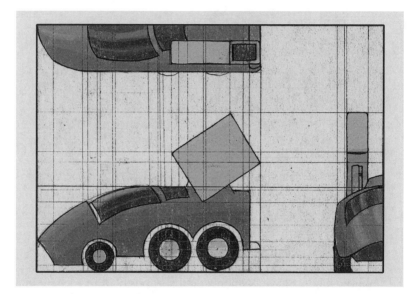

Figure 4-5

Additional References

When working with complex objects, it is highly recommended that you use additional references as a complement to the basic reference sheet, including side, front, and top views, or even for parts of the object that will be behind glass, for example. When modeling characters, you should collect additional references from the real world, even if you are creating a fantasy character. Work done by Pixar, DreamWorks, Blue Sky, and so forth can be used as reference for cartoon characters.

Blocking

Depending on the intricacy of the object, such as the number of moveable parts or sectors, or the complexity of the character's limbs or parts, you may need to model some of the character in blocks to make it easier and more accurate.

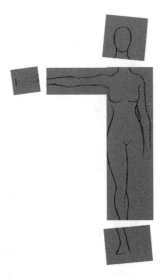

Figure 4-6: Modeling in blocks.

For the human project presented in Chapters 5 through 9, parts of the models have been modeled separately from each other and then joined together and merged into a single model. When you block out and separately model parts of the object, you gain a bit more freedom to start from scratch using a box or a single polygon rather than continuing to extrude an already modeled set of polygons.

Chapter 5

Human Project: Male Head

The Head

The head is usually the first thing users want to model. It is often considered the most difficult object to model in 3D. The head may not be simple to model, but it isn't the hardest either. You can model a human head from several starting points using different shapes and methods. It really depends on your needs, what you will do with the head, whether it will be animated or a still image, and so on. However, when modeling you must keep your focus on making a clean and functional mesh where you can deform, push, and pull as much as is required for the character.

Figure 5-1 shows the reference sketch used in this head modeling session.

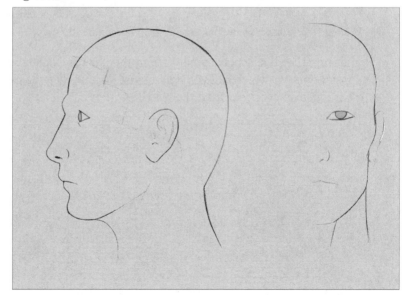

Figure 5-1: Head reference model.

The Male Head Shape

This section shows how to create the shape of a head for a male figure.

For this head, we use box modeling, starting with a 4x4 segment box and then deleting the other half. Since human heads are symmetrical, we model half, mirror it, and weld the vertices. (3ds Max has a symmetry modifier that automatically welds the vertices while you adjust in real time.)

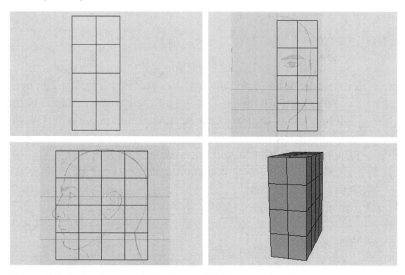

Figure 5-2: Using box modeling to model a human head.

Position the cube's 4x4 segments to fit the head and delete half. It doesn't matter which half you delete; just do it so that you can see the edges and vertices from the side view (left or right).

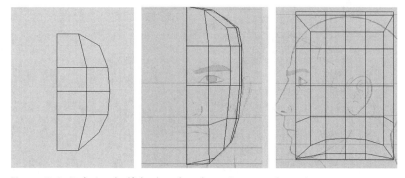

Figure 5-3: Deleting half the head and starting to reshape it.

The first thing to do when modeling a head is to shape it into an oval from the top view, the front view, and then the side view. It's one of the quickest ways to start without getting confused about the vertices.

Select the edge that's marked in Figure 5-4 and remove it. Depending on the software you're using, you'll probably have to remove stray vertices.

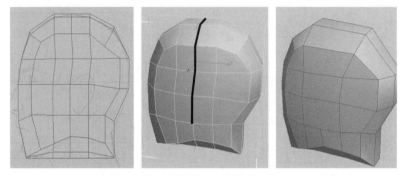

Figure 5-4

Then cut the marked area where the ear will be positioned, and remove the dashed line.

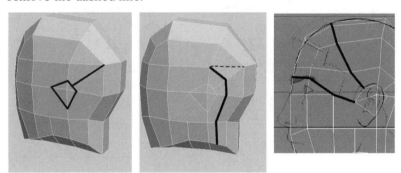

Figure 5-5

At this stage we've made the basic shape of the head, so now we can tweak it for just about any kind of humanoid-like head.

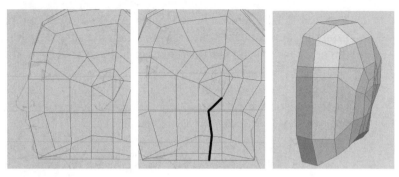

Figure 5-6

The head should look like Figure 5-7 when viewed in the viewports. Although we've just started, the head is beginning to take shape. It does not have to fit the reference exactly, but the proportions must be matched during the process.

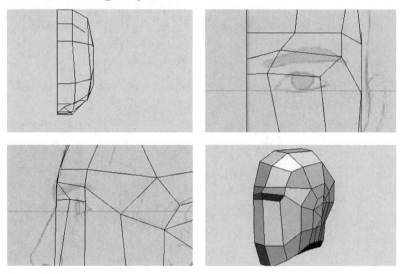

Figure 5-7

Now it's time to define the eye and nose area. Creating a good structure and a line flow that works is critical here.

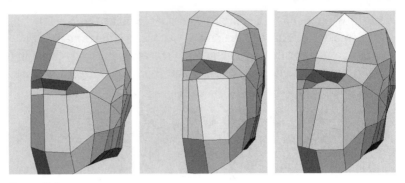

Figure 5-8

Figure 5-9 shows where to cut the eye area and gives the main scheme for the nose and face area.

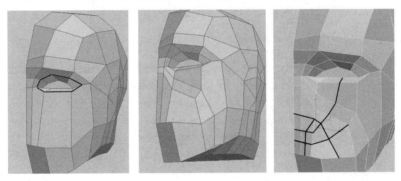

Figure 5-9

Do not extrude the nose; just push the two front vertices to give the shape. Remember, nothing substitutes for practice and keeping everything quad while you cut.

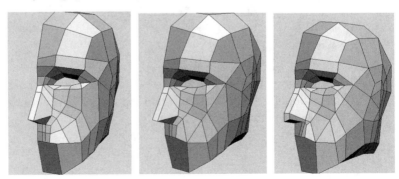

Figure 5-10

When defining the mouth area, try to make the line flow as round as possible. This will make it easier when animating phonemes. As you gain experience, you will find your own way to do this, but for now cut the mouth and cheek as shown in Figure 5-11 to create lines and move vertices.

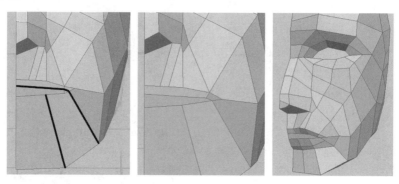

Figure 5-11

Now it's time to define the mouth a bit. Be sure to delete the polygons in the ear and eye socket areas so we can smooth them. The areas will be processed as holes during the smooth operation and will not generate tension as they would with polygons there.

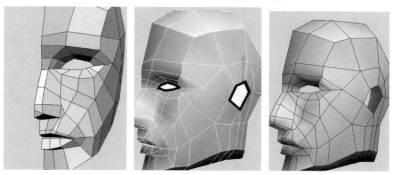

Figure 5-12

Now it's time to refine the area eye. After we open the hole, create and position the sphere as shown in Figure 5-13. Be sure to use all the viewports that are necessary.

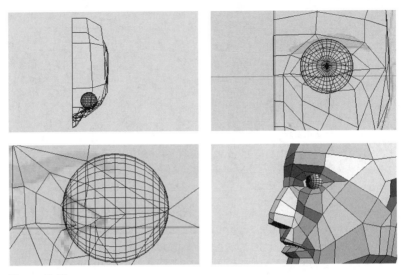

Figure 5-13

The following figure shows the smoothed result of the head at this stage. It's recommended that you create some lines around the eye socket to generate appropriate tension and to make it easier to control the detail.

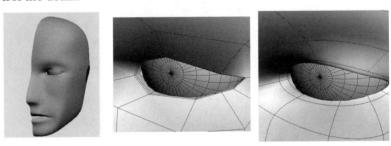

Figure 5-14

Cut the marked area at the left of Figure 5-15 to define the nose. Then cut as shown in the center image (note that everything is quad) and select the marked polygon, extrude up, scale down a bit, and extrude up again.

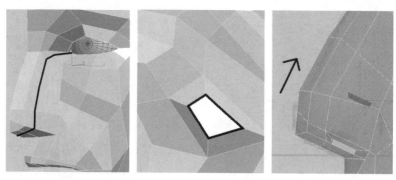

Figure 5-15

After cutting the region of the nose that's marked at the left of Figure 5-16, it's time to work on another part of the head.

Select the neck as shown and extrude down.

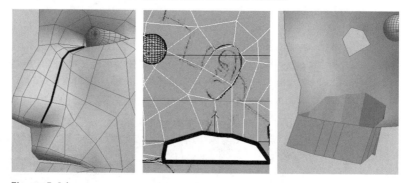

Figure 5-16

Select the polygons of the neck that were generated on the mirror line and delete them. Then cut the marked areas.

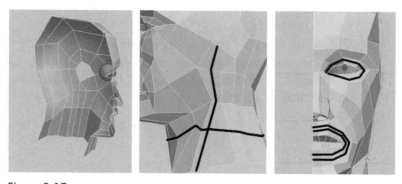

Figure 5-17

It's looking more like a head now, but it still needs a lot of work. Cut the area marked below; this is an important area for the line flow of the head. You'll want to mirror the geometry from time to time to see how your model looks.

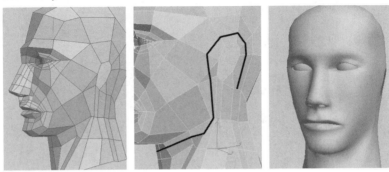

Figure 5-18

The top of the head is less important, and you don't have to do exactly as shown in Figure 5-19.

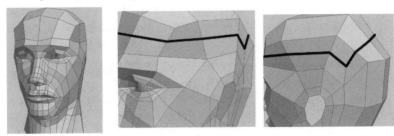

Figure 5-19

Figure 5-20 shows more cuts. Just follow the lines defined in earlier steps. These new edges will generate more tension and help with detail and shape control.

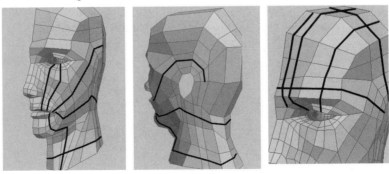

Figure 5-20

More edges are created in Figure 5-21 for better detail and shape control. Just follow the line flow and the loops.

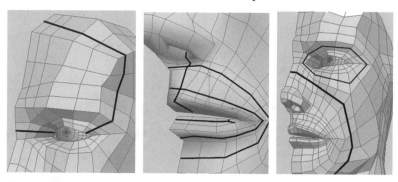

Figure 5-21

It is important to note that we are moving vertices and changing the shape of the model throughout the modeling process. This process usually takes a few hours just to model a refined rough base mesh.

Cut the area marked in Figure 5-22 to create finer control around the eye and push back an entire row of vertices to define the eyelid. The marked edges for the nose area generate tension. Cut more polygons following the lines if you need more control.

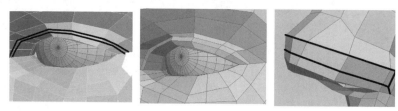

Figure 5-22

Cut the nose to improve control around the nostril as shown in Figure 5-23. At this stage we have a head with sufficient edges and tension. From this point it is just a matter of moving vertices and using Soft Selection to adjust the volume of the head.

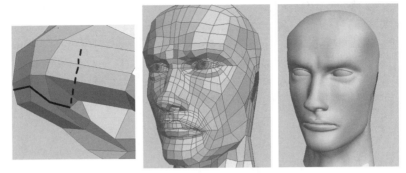

Figure 5-23

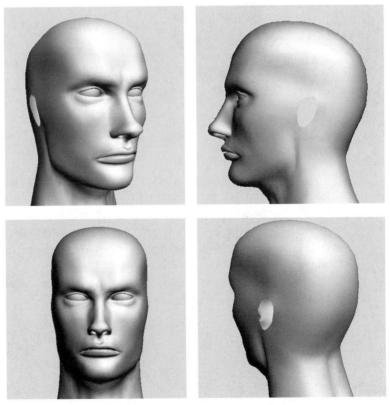

Figure 5-24: The current head model. More work is needed to fix some areas, but we'll refine the head when the ear model is attached.

The Ear

The ear is probably the most intricate part of the human anatomy to model. As with almost anything in the 3D world, there is more than one way to create an ear. As you gain experience, you will find the easiest way for you to perform this task.

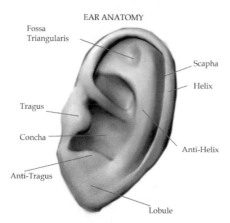

EAR ANATOMY

Fossa Triangularis

Scapha

Helix

Tragus

Concha

Anti-Helix

Anti-Tragus

Lobule

Figure 5-25: The anatomy of a human ear.

For this ear modeling exercise, either we can start with a single quad polygon and use extrusion or we can create a plane primitive with a 1x1 segment. In 3ds Max you can create a poly box with 1x1 segments, delete the five faces, and position the face as shown in Figure 5-26, or you can draw corner splines, extrude, and delete the back part.

Starting with a single polygon, select the edge, and start extruding until we get the ear reference covered.

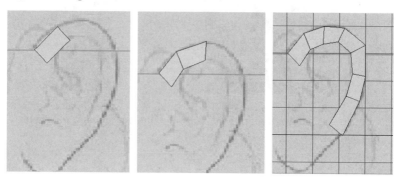

Figure 5-26

Then extrude the edge as shown below and weld the vertices.

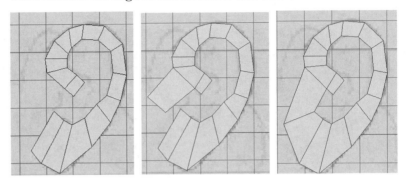

Figure 5-27

Now we can cap the hole and start cutting the polygon. Keep in mind that you should keep everything quad as much as possible while following the flow of the ear's anatomy.

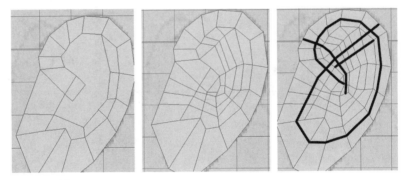

Figure 5-28

At this stage you will notice the ear is pretty flat. You can choose whether to cut now or later in order to add some volume.

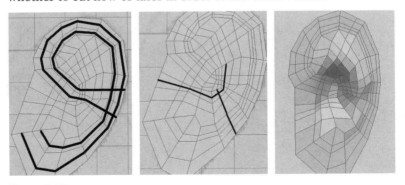

Figure 5-29

Select the area marked in Figure 5-30, extrude in a bit, then scale down.

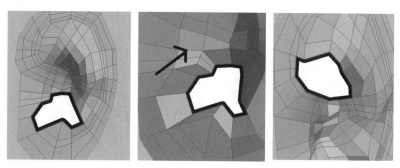

Figure 5-30

Now we can see how it's coming along in the smooth version. Select the marked region and extrude a bit and scale down but not too much.

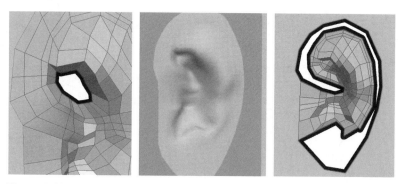

Figure 5-31

We now have the base of the ear done. Select the marked vertices and push forward to improve the roundness of the helix.

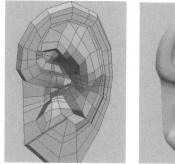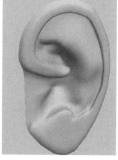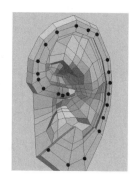

Figure 5-32

Weld the marked vertices of the image on the left to blend the region of the helix and the concha. Select the vertices as shown at the right and push back a bit to define the scapha.

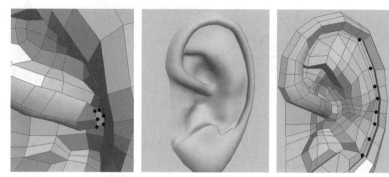

Figure 5-33

Then push back the vertices as shown at the left in Figure 5-34 to prepare the fossa triangularis. Select the marked vertices on the right on the anti-helix area and push forward (with some Soft Selection, Cluster, or whatever tool you have at your disposal).

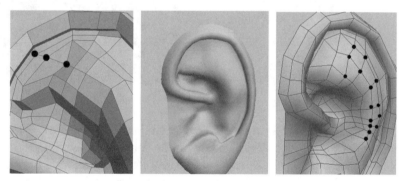

Figure 5-34

Cut the marked region to get more control over specific areas. We now have more control over the fossa triangularis and the concha area near the tragus.

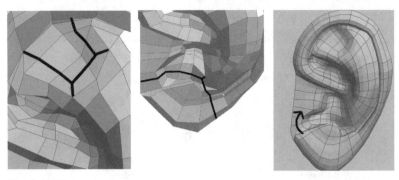

Figure 5-35

Now it's time to define the tragus and the hole. Cut the marked region in the center of Figure 5-36 and select that group of polygons. Extrude in and scale down a little bit.

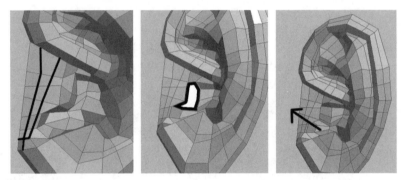

Figure 5-36

At this point we have something similar to Figure 5-37. (The image at the left shows the view from the back with the normals flipped to the other side.) Now we cut the marked area and weld the vertices between the helix and tragus to blend them a little bit so that the helix doesn't protrude too much.

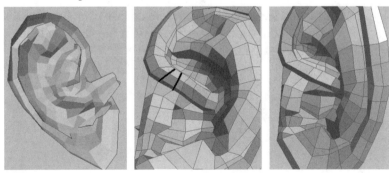

Figure 5-37

Cut some more and eventually smooth the whole piece to see how it's going. In the beginning, sometimes it is hard to get this sense without smoothing.

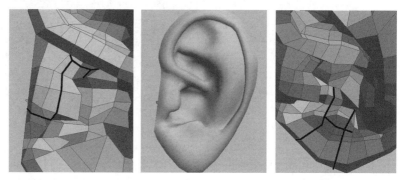

Figure 5-38

Push some vertices in the anti-tragus area to make it more rounded, and cut a little more, following the flow to improve the control in this specific area.

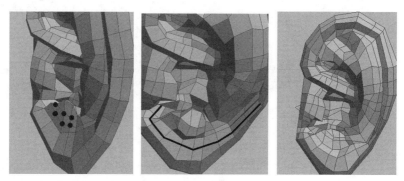

Figure 5-39

We can push back more vertices on the scapha area to define it better. This is just a matter of preference. Then select the outside edges of the ear.

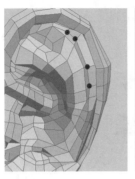
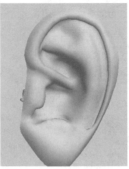
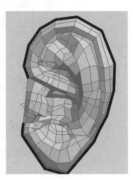

Figure 5-40

Figure 5-41 shows the ear from the back. Extrude the edges, scale down a bit, and extrude again, scaling down until you reach something similar to the image at the right.

Figure 5-41

Cut in loops to obtain more control over the back surface and take care of areas that intersect. Push and pull vertices until the shape closely resembles the human ear. Then we are ready to weld the ear to the head.

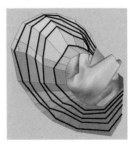
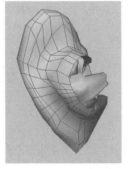
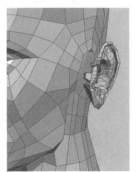

Figure 5-42

Save the ear and import or merge the head and ear meshes in one scene. Then position the ear where it should be. You may also want to scale up the border of the ear hole on the head to clearly see the vertices that need to be merged.

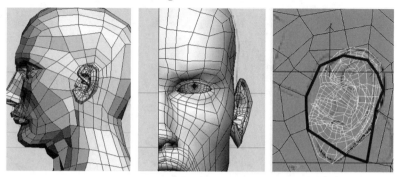

Figure 5-43

Now it's time to deal with unmatched vertices, which were discussed in Chapter 3. Then we can cut one more loop around the head hole where the ear goes to hold the tension. (You may want to hide the ear geometry during this process.)

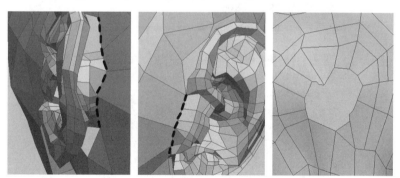

Figure 5-44

With this stage finished, we can tweak a little more to get the desired result. Now we use the Soft Selection-like tools to improve the volume of what we have modeled.

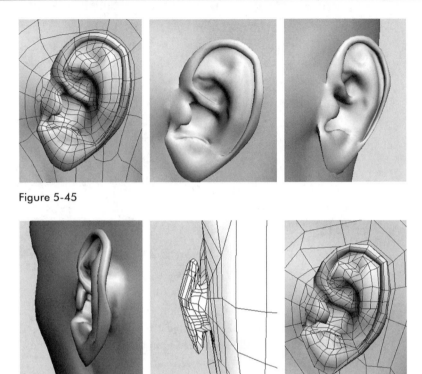

Figure 5-45

Figure 5-46: Back and side view of the ear.

Now we have a base mesh cage. From this point we can add more edges (and more control) following the cage we've created.

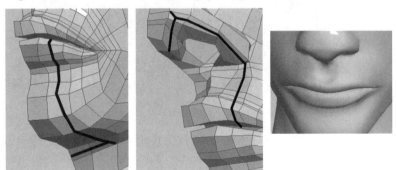

Figure 5-47

Final Words about the Male Head

Figures 5-48 to 5-50 show the complete head model and close-ups of the ear and eye areas.

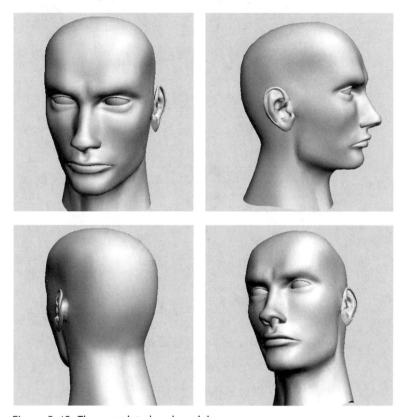

Figure 5-48: The complete head model.

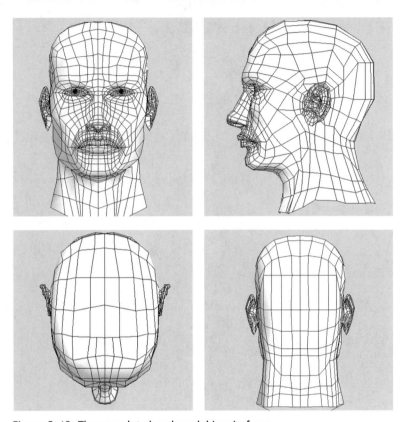

Figure 5-49: The complete head model in wireframe.

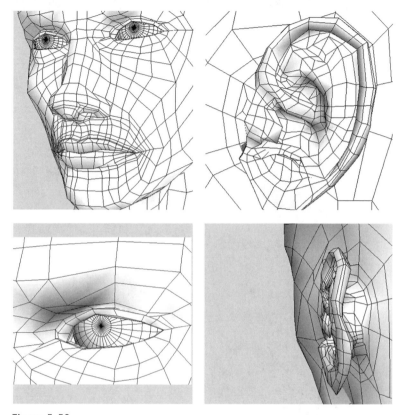

Figure 5-50

Take a look on the structure of the edge loop and flow of the face in Figures 5-51 to 5-53. This scheme makes it much easier to animate and reshape the head.

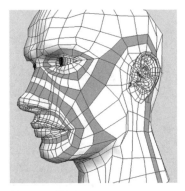

Figure 5-51

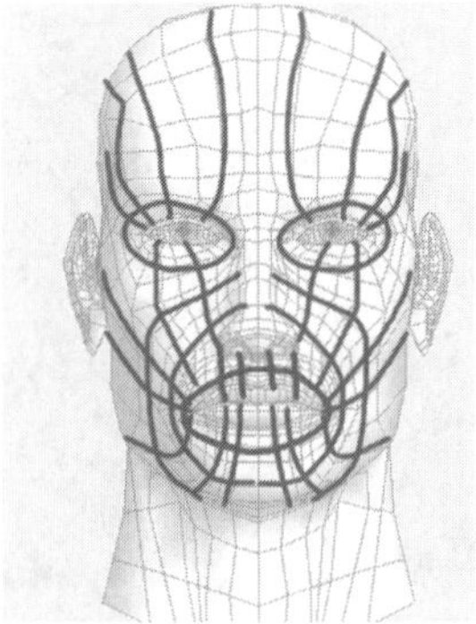

Figure 5-52

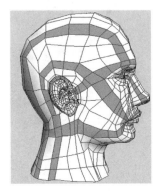

Figure 5-53

When you model a generic male head like the one in this chapter, you can reshape it using Soft Selection or by moving the vertices until you get the desired shape of the nose, mouth, eyes, ears, etc. Of course, the final look of your head will be determined mostly by the texturing, shading, and lighting of your scene, but never underestimate the importance of a good model.

Chapter 6

Human Project: Male Body

Torso and Limbs

This chapter describes the overall process of modeling a male human body. The topology and workflow shown can also be used for multiple purposes related to humanoid body modeling, with correct deformation structure and proportions.

Figure 6-1 shows the reference sheet we use in this chapter.

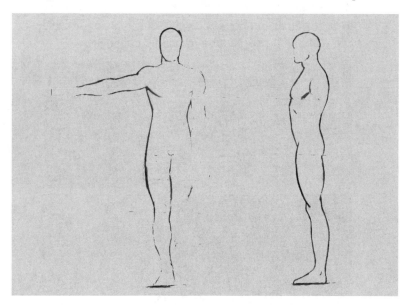

Figure 6-1: Male body reference.

For this lesson on torso and limb modeling we start with half of a box. As shown in the previous chapter, just create a symmetrical box. Select the vertices of one half and delete. Then position the box to match the reference as much as possible.

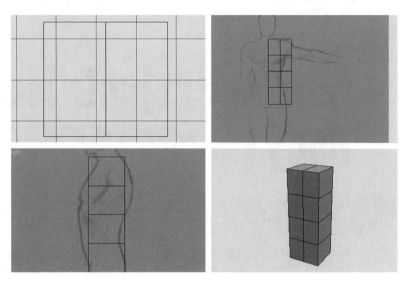

Figure 6-2

We reshape the box to fit the reference without making any changes to the original number of polygons (like cutting or welding). We're just making the shape for a basic low-poly body.

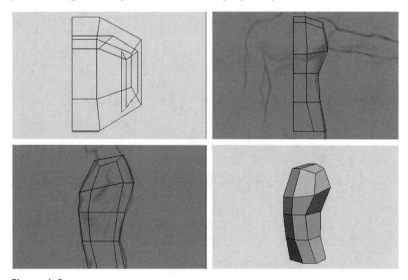

Figure 6-3

Cut as shown in the center of Figure 6-4 and select the polygon for the arm. Extrude it one level, then cut as marked at the right. This is the start of the basic arm.

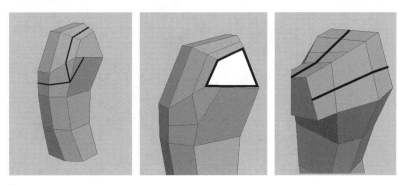

Figure 6-4

Cut the marked area and move the eight-sided n-gon in the direction marked in the center image below, then cut some loops around the arm area. These are pretty important because they are the first steps in determining the basic workflow of the mesh. Like most things in art (and in life too), if you don't have a good foundation, it becomes harder to make something more sophisticated.

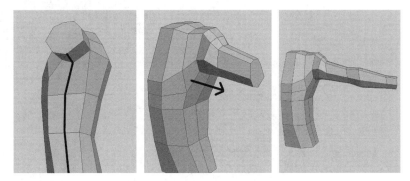

Figure 6-5

With the upper body finished, we create a cylinder. Cut the marked area below the torso to create an eight-sided shape to merge with the eight-sided cylinder that will be the leg.

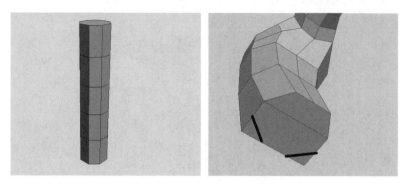

Figure 6-6: Left, eight-sided cylinder for the leg. Right, cut the bottom of the torso to create eight sides.

After some tweaks, we have a rough torso and leg in the viewport. Low-poly game modelers would want to be careful about adding polygons here so the mesh doesn't slow down the game too much.

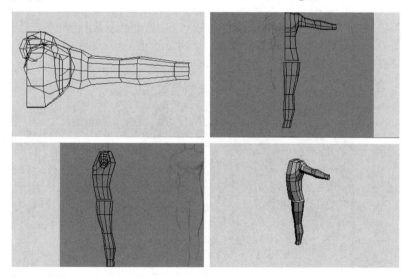

Figure 6-7

Now we select the marked polygons and delete, as shown in Figure 6-8. The vertices from the torso and the leg should match perfectly after the attach operation. We also need to cut in a loop near the center to get more control in the front and the back of the geometry.

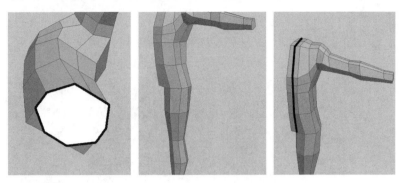

Figure 6-8

Create some more edges with the Cut tool to improve the control cage of the whole mesh.

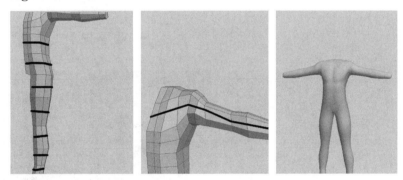

Figure 6-9

Notice the whole mesh after mirroring. It's very rough but has good topology. With efficient rigging, the mesh will deform smoothly.

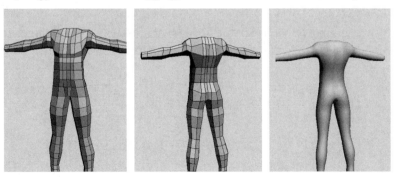

Figure 6-10

With the base mesh already done, we can start with more complex refinement, like adding basic muscle structure for even further definition.

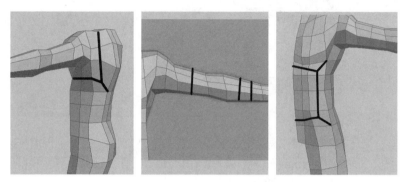

Figure 6-11

Cut closer to the middle where we are going to weld the abdominal muscles.

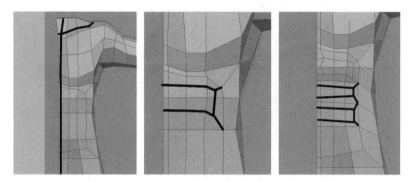

Figure 6-12

Improve control of the abdominal muscles a bit and then cut the pelvic area to obtain more control and redefine the correct polygonal flow.

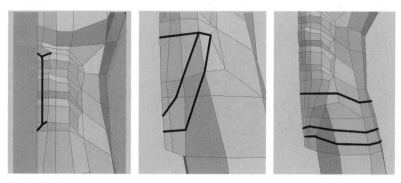

Figure 6-13

The following step adds more edges just by following the line flow. There is a triangular polygon that will generate unwanted tension, but as long as we cut the polygons, this triangular polygon will be replaced by a quad.

Figure 6-14

Select the marked polygons in Figure 6-15 and extrude up, cut the marked edges, and delete half. If the half is not deleted, it will produce undesired results when smoothing. Cut the marked back area to increase the tension around the spine.

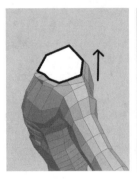

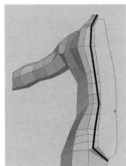

Figure 6-15

Notice the marked lines to cut. These follow the line flow and help us to obtain more control of the mesh cage and improve the definition.

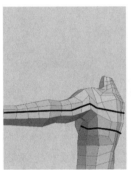

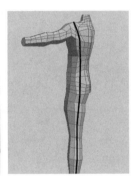

Figure 6-16

Here we have the choice of where to cut and where we want to have more or less tension.

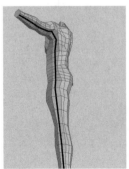
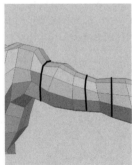
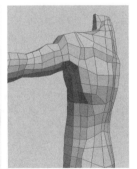

Figure 6-17

Now it's time to define the back area. Use as much reference as you can when adding muscles and other details, but don't overdo the cutting. If the model is going to be animated, having too many polygons will make it hard to rig and set up the bones/deformations and slow to animate. An alternative is to use displacement for these extra details as described in Chapter 10.

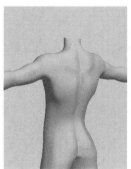 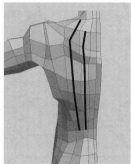 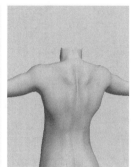

Figure 6-18

Cut the marked edges and remove the dashed lines to make the polygons quad. In the image on the right, a big triangular polygon and a few discontinued edges appear on the mesh. Don't interrupt the modeling flow to correct little errors or things that can easily be fixed later.

Be sure to mirror the geometry from time to time to check the symmetry.

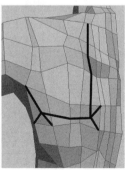 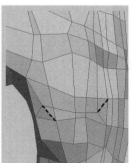 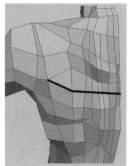

Figure 6-19

After tweaking some vertices, the shaded and mesh versions of the male back torso look like Figure 6-20.

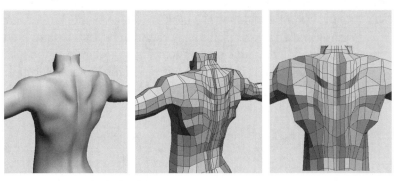

Figure 6-20: The male back torso.

Notice that at this point, there are not enough vertices and edges to produce well-defined muscles on the male torso. If your model is nice and clean, you can choose between leaving it as it is right now or increasing its definition with a number of details.

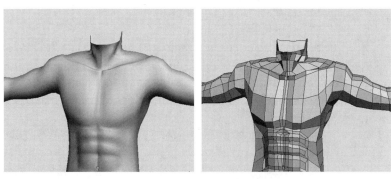

Figure 6-21: The male front torso.

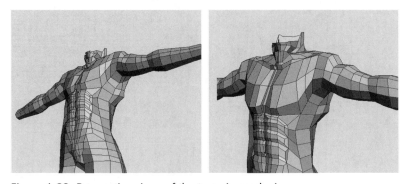

Figure 6-22: Perspective views of the torso in mesh view.

Now it's time to raise the bar a little bit for details. The model at this point can be used as a base mesh for sculpting (using displacement) or as a high-end game model, but for a high-resolution model it needs more details. We start by adding more control for the torso area and the arm joints, extruding the selected marked polygons.

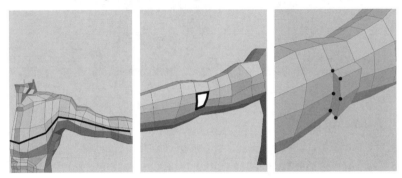

Figure 6-23

Weld the marked vertices and cut the marked edges; the actual edges aren't enough to generate sufficient tension and smoothing for the gluteus area. Notice also that the edges of the leg are pretty much the same as the reshaped cylinder, but the leg has much more detail than a simple cylinder.

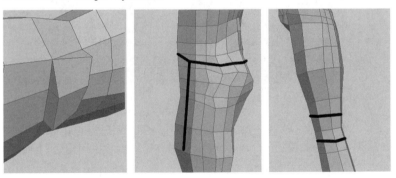

Figure 6-24

The new edges are very welcome, as they add detail, but remember that they must be planned carefully to follow the edge flow and edge loops in order to be topologically and anatomically correct.

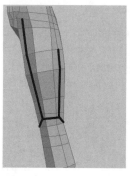
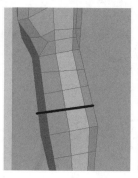
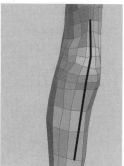

Figure 6-25

Now the line flow of the arms must be rearranged to fit the anatomical flow of real muscle topology. Cut the marked edges, weld the marked vertices, and remove the dashed lines in Figure 6-26. This way we keep everything quad and redirect the flow correctly for this purpose.

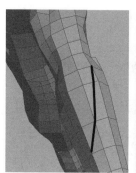
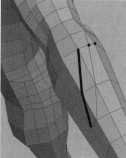
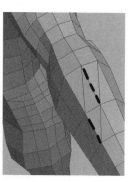

Figure 6-26

We do the same thing on the other side of the arm: Redirect the edges by cutting diagonally and removing the dashed lines.

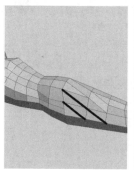

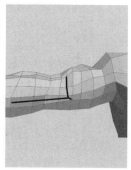

Figure 6-27

The triceps area needs some more cutting for a better refinement of the muscle. Figure 6-28 shows the triceps area after additional cutting and vertex moving.

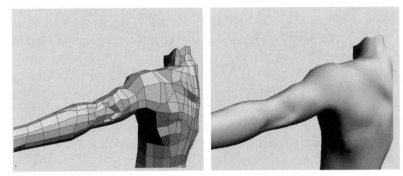

Figure 6-28: Mesh and shaded versions of the triceps area.

The marked areas in Figure 6-29 will be the base for the patella and the patellar tendon.

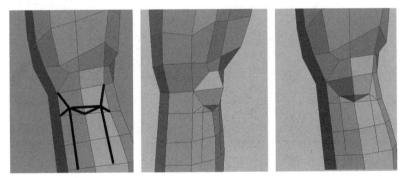

Figure 6-29

Now let's work on the hands and feet. When they're finished, we will put them all together and refine the whole mesh at once.

Hands

Modeling hands that look good can be a tricky task depending on your goal. Hands are parts of the body that often have a great amount of expression and deformation when animated. When a mesh has a lot of deformation, we must carefully plan the edge flow in order to match the original reference. At the same time, clean up as much as possible; you may find that rigging a character with a dense mesh (especially in areas that have too many vertices) can be a real nightmare. In this section we discuss how to plan and execute a human hand that can be used as the basis for any generic humanoid hand, balancing the accuracy of the original shape with mesh details.

We begin with a 4x4 box and a simple eight-sided cylinder. As is common when starting with a primitive, we reshape the primitive by moving the vertices to fit the reference image we have.

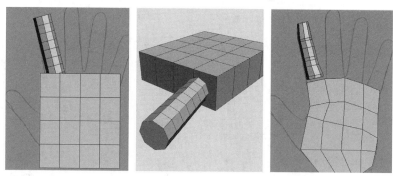

Figure 6-30

We then cut the marked areas. Cutting the cylinder will provide the base for the nail and cutting the box will give us the basic structure for attaching the fingers.

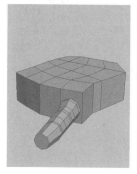
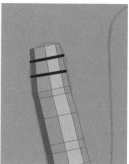
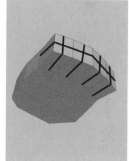

Figure 6-31

Then we continue to cut the palm and refine the finger. Notice that not capping the cylinder (n-gon sided) can produce undesired results with Catmull-Clark subdivision, as shown in Chapter 3. We push the marked edges to make the finger rounder at the tip.

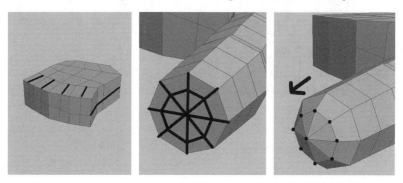

Figure 6-32

Now it's time to create the base of the thumb. In the following figure, we cut the marked edges, extrude the face, and scale it down a little bit.

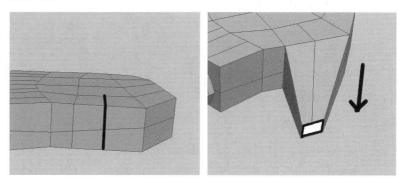

Figure 6-33

At this point, the thumb needs more edges. This can be done with a few extrusions or by cutting some loops. Notice the result in Figure 6-34 after one level of subdivision (see center image). Cut the marked area to continue the line flow, as shown at the right.

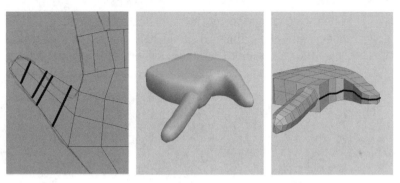

Figure 6-34

We reshape the vertices of the thumb and the areas where the fingers will be attached to make the hand rounder and match the natural organic flow of the hand.

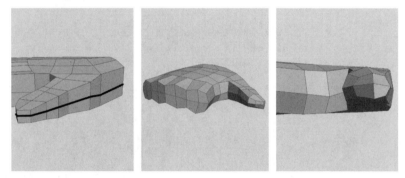

Figure 6-35

In viewing the shape from the bottom, we see that the palm is flat, but it's okay for now. More details will be added once we have the base mesh ready and working. Cut the marked edges of the finger joints.

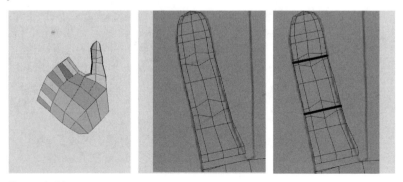

Figure 6-36

Cut the marked edges and delete the dashed lines. Notice that the parts of the finger that will be stretched are planned in a way that reduces the amount of work during the setup process.

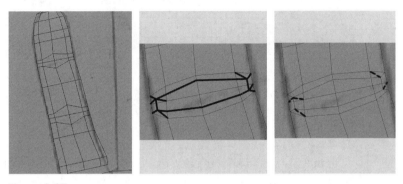

Figure 6-37

We now have everything nice and quad. Cut the marked areas to obtain more control over the finger joint and remove the dashed line.

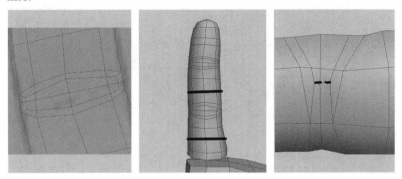

Figure 6-38

Try to keep the polygons four-sided as much as possible. Sometimes, however, you can't avoid triangles or you may find that they will be useful in some way to the deformation. In any case, keep the number of triangles to a minimum. After the work is done, push down the areas near the joint a bit to make it rounder and push down the nail area a little.

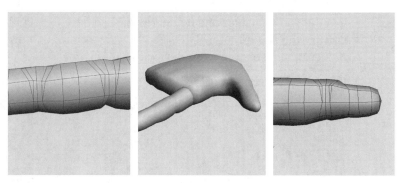

Figure 6-39

Cut in the marked area to start modeling the nail, then select the edges shown at the right and chamfer it. You can also produce the same result by cutting following the edge.

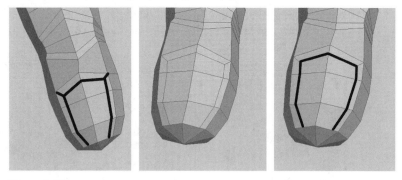

Figure 6-40

Push the vertices down a little near the nail, then connect the vertices of the end of the nail with the Cut tool.

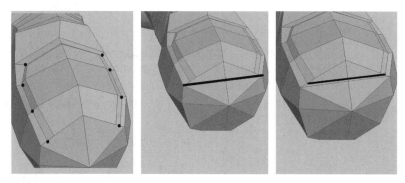

Figure 6-41

After making the last connection we can cut the nail to improve the tension and have better control on the cage. Depending on the software you are using, you may need to create some triangle meshes. Here we create the edges shown in the center, then remove the edges shown at the right.

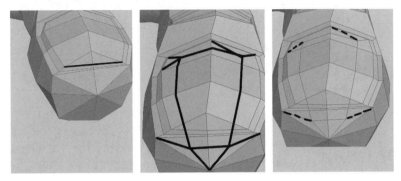

Figure 6-42

Cut the marked edges to reduce the triangular tension of the fingers. This gives us a nice, smooth finger to duplicate, tweak, and insert into the base mesh of the hand.

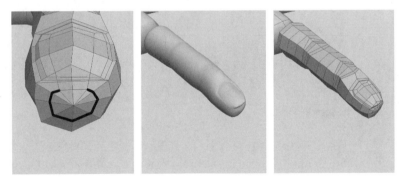

Figure 6-43

The following figure shows the finished finger being duplicated and ready to be inserted. Notice that the fingers are not exactly the same. Real fingers differ in size and shape, so you may want to tweak them before inserting them to add more realism.

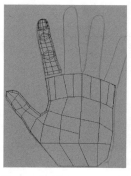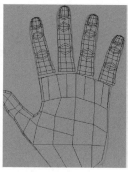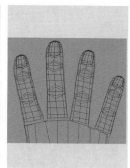

Figure 6-44

We have cut the finger and added tension, but we haven't changed the number of sides of the original cylinder. This was done intentionally to help us easily match the vertices of the fingers and the base palm mesh.

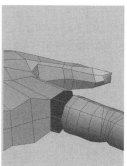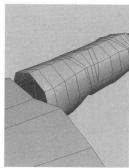

Figure 6-45

We repeat this process for each finger, removing the polygons of the finger and the hand in the areas where the vertices will be merged.

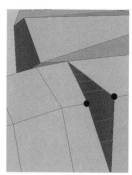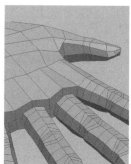

Figure 6-46

Once we are done, we get a clearer picture of the final shape of the hand. With the fingers finished, it's time to add details to the palm and the thumb.

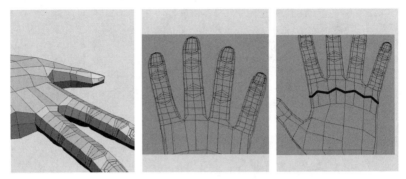

Figure 6-47

Cut the palm in the area shown below and continue the line flow. This area clearly needs more detail.

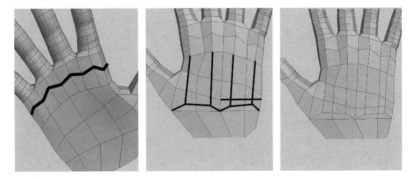

Figure 6-48

Figures 6-49 and 6-50 show the edge structure for well-defined tendons in the hand. Depending on the kind of model you're creating, you may want to spend more time to make this area well defined and plan how to insert modeled veins inside the current topology.

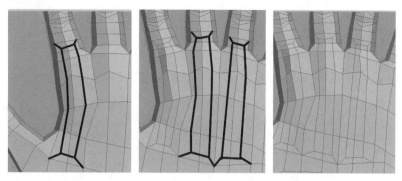

Figure 6-49

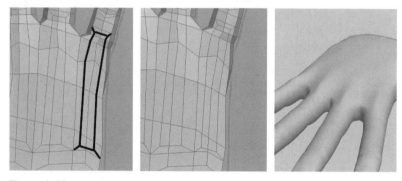

Figure 6-50

Push the marked vertices up a little bit and notice the difference in shaded mode.

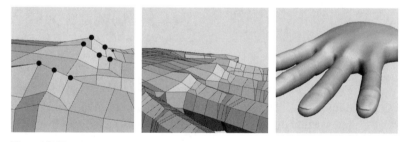

Figure 6-51

Cut a loop near the area where we've welded the fingers; this is an important area for deformation and shape definition of the hand.

Figure 6-52

Take a look at the hand in shaded mode. The fingers seem to be much more finished than the rest of the hand.

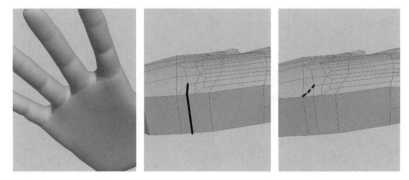

Figure 6-53

Now it's time to add detail to the palm. After some quick triangle polygon corrections we add more edges to the palm to make it more topologically correct.

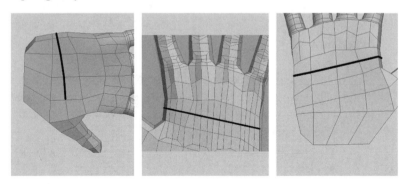

Figure 6-54

This area of the palm has a flow completely different from the actual flow, so we need to change this by adding new edges using the Cut tool and removing the old ones.

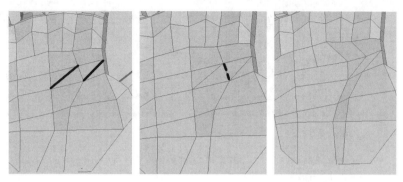

Figure 6-55

Then we add more edges, always checking for triangular meshes formed when cutting the polygon. As we refine the mesh, more edges and vertices are added. If the base structure isn't correct, it will be much harder to fix after a number of vertices have been moved and tweaked.

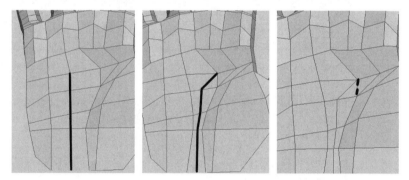

Figure 6-56

When cutting the marked area, keep everything as much quad as possible. Notice that when the new edge is generated by the cut, a triangle has appeared, but in this case it's easily removed by welding the marked vertices.

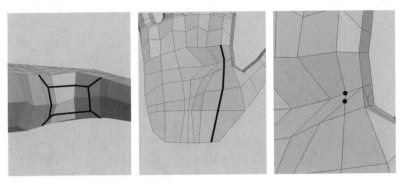

Figure 6-57

Now this is looking much more like a palm should look, but it still needs more work on some areas. Cut the marked edges.

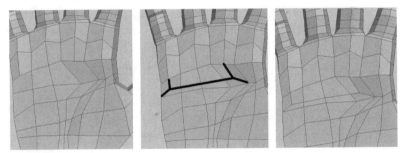

Figure 6-58

When we cut the marked areas, notice that many control edges have been added to improve the bulge during the rigging process of the hand.

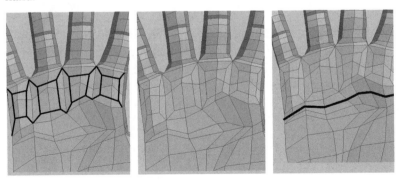

Figure 6-59

We continue to cut the palm to add more tension, planning every step and following the correct line flow.

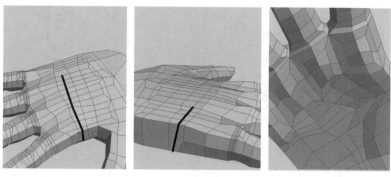

Figure 6-60

With the new edges we got a more defined bulge area of the palm as shown in shaded mode. Try to avoid triangles and areas where there are big size differences between the polygons.

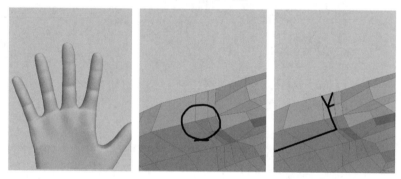

Figure 6-61

Remove the dashed lines shown in Figure 6-62 and continue the line on the side of the palm. If you get two triangles, weld the vertices; it will be easier to make one triangle disappear than two.

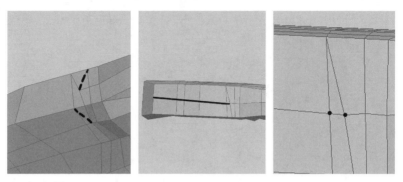

Figure 6-62

In comparing the shaded mode and the wire mesh, we can clearly see the hand structure and how the polygons we have planned and tweaked behave when subdivided.

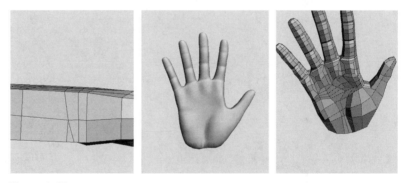

Figure 6-63

The hand is almost finished, but the thumb still needs work. Cut the marked area to improve the tension and define the base mesh for further refinement.

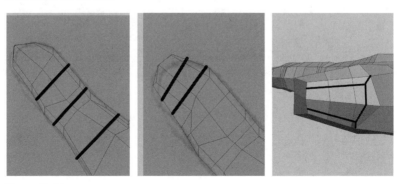

Figure 6-64

With the base mesh well defined, we can make a cut similar to the other fingers' nails.

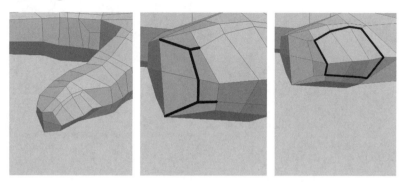

Figure 6-65

Now our hand is complete.

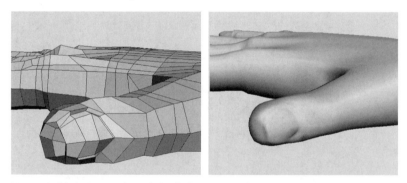

Figure 6-66: Wire mesh and shaded versions of the hand.

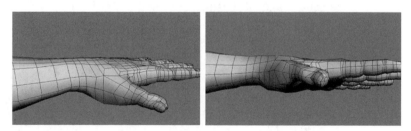

Figure 6-67

The Foot

In this foot modeling exercise we discuss techniques for creating a basic foot shape for a shoe, boot, and so on. The foot modeled here does not have toes; those are modeled in Chapter 8.

We start with an eight-sided cylinder and push the three front vertices forward.

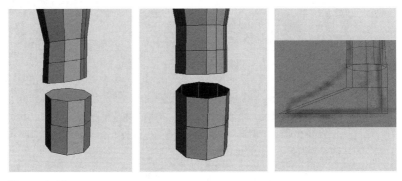

Figure 6-68

Cut the marked edges and reshape the vertices generated to fit the reference. Notice in the perspective view that we've matched the shape only from the side perspective. Adjust this by scaling the back vertices a little.

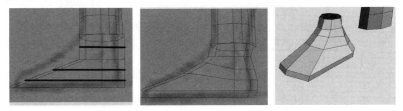

Figure 6-69

Then we can cut some more edges to reduce the tension of the big stretched polygons at the front of the foot.

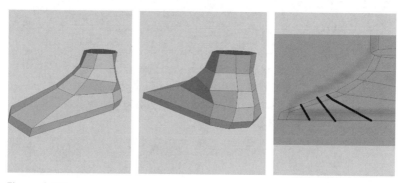

Figure 6-70

We then cut near the medium malleolus to add some necessary base lines. Notice that as we cut this area, the original eight-sided cylinder will no longer be eight-sided. This is okay because the leg will allow us to continue this flow.

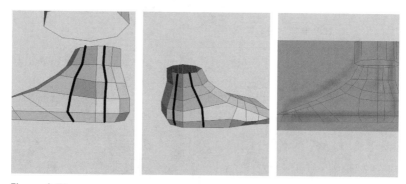

Figure 6-71

We continue adding more edges to improve the control cage.

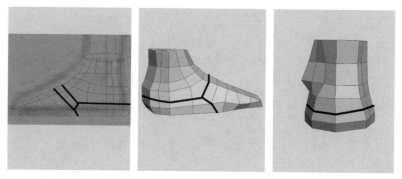

Figure 6-72

Now the foot is taking better shape as shown in shaded mode and wire mesh.

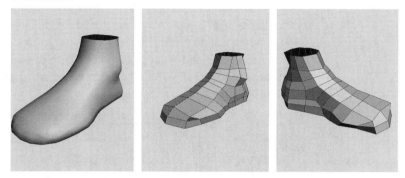

Figure 6-73

The view from the bottom of the foot reveals we have done almost nothing there.

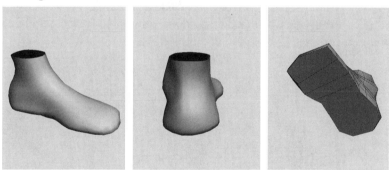

Figure 6-74

We need to cut the sole to make the tension more natural and self sustained.

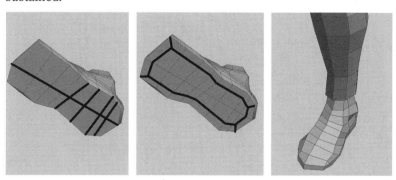

Figure 6-75

Putting It All Together

At this point we have all the separate body parts nearly finished. Now we can join them all together and start refining until we get a well-defined male body. Later chapters show how to refine the models, but you can choose what level of detail you want for your model.

The first thing to do when joining parts modeled separately is to check out the proportions.

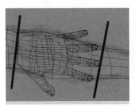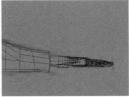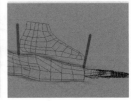

Figure 6-76

Then we move the parts as close as possible and start welding vertices. See Chapter 3 if you don't remember how to weld unmatched vertices.

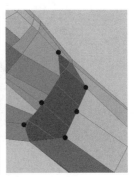

Figure 6-77

Here we weld the wrist, attaching the hand to the arm.

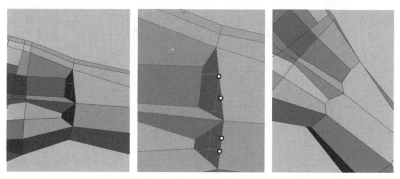

Figure 6-78

The complete arm is shown in Figure 6-79.

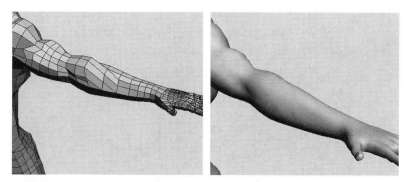

Figure 6-79

Now we can attach the foot to the leg and start welding just like we've done with the hand.

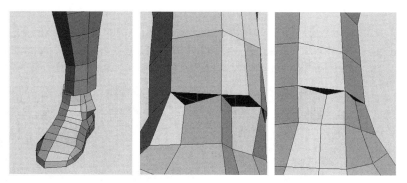

Figure 6-80

You may want to continue the line flow of the foot by cutting the marked area and then welding the marked vertices.

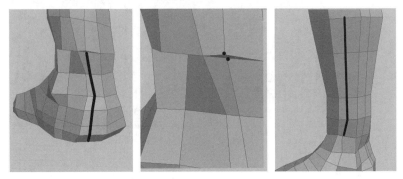

Figure 6-81

With these parts ready we can start adding the final edges for finer control of muscles and definition areas.

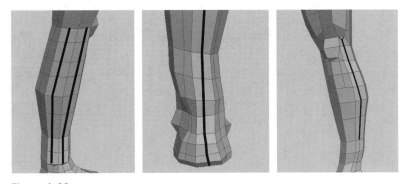

Figure 6-82

Here we cut on the tibialis area. Notice the front marked edges; they provide a base mesh for toes. Then we add more control vertices for the quadriceps and start changing the structure of the pelvis.

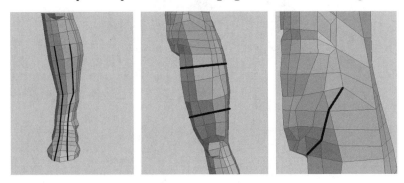

Figure 6-83

Notice that we must cut, remove, and weld some specific sub-elements to change the current flow of the edges. Remove the dashed lines, cut the marked edges, and weld the marked vertices shown in Figure 6-84.

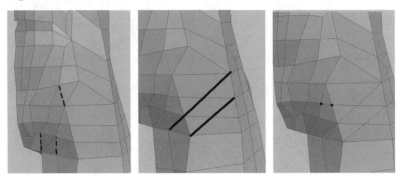

Figure 6-84

Remove the dashed edges at the left and cut the marked area in the following figure. Then remove the dashed lines at the right. Notice that this procedure will lead us to a quad mesh as much as possible. It is okay to leave some tris as long as they are oriented so that they won't cause problems.

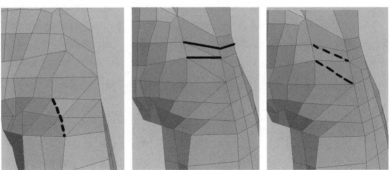

Figure 6-85

Then we start adding more vertices that follow the edge flow to improve the tension and control areas.

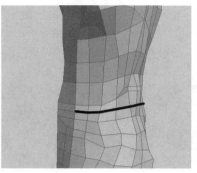
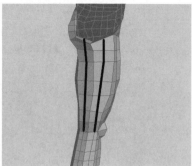

Figure 6-86

The wrist needs more control for deformation purposes as well as some continuous edges for better definition of extensor muscles.

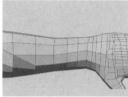
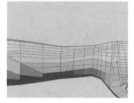

Figure 6-87

Notice that after we joined the hand with the arm, some edges are made as long as possible.

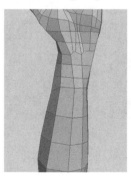
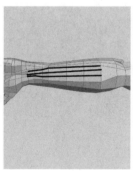
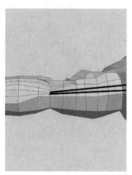

Figure 6-88

Remove the dashed lines shown below to reduce the number of tri-angles on the hand.

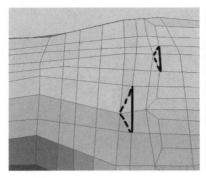 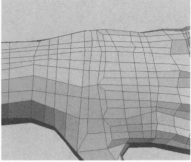

Figure 6-89

Figure 6-90 shows the arm in shaded view and wire mesh.

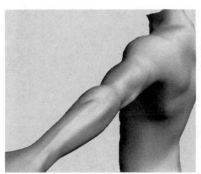 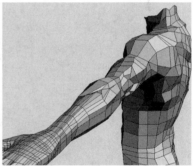

Figure 6-90

We continue making refinements of the line flow from the pectoralis muscle to the arm and the ulnar bone.

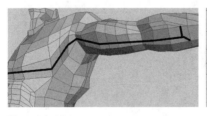 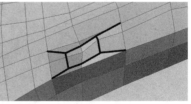

Figure 6-91

Make some additional cuts to refine the muscles of the inner thigh.

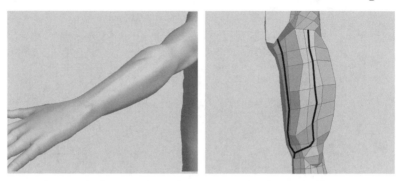

Figure 6-92: Left, the arm after refinements. Right, the inner thigh.

The remaining figures in this chapter illustrate the body parts modeled thus far.

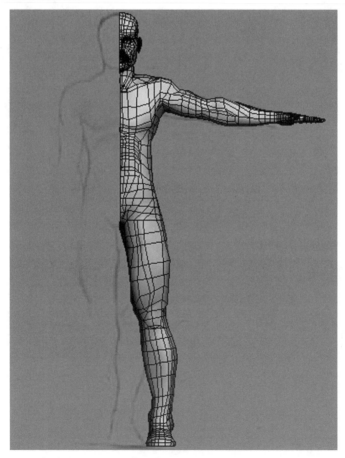

Figure 6-93: Body half in wireframe.

Mirror and weld when you are finished with the model.

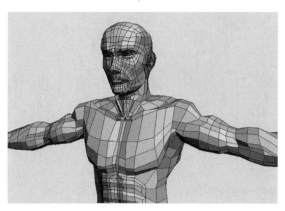

Figure 6-94: Front view of head and torso.

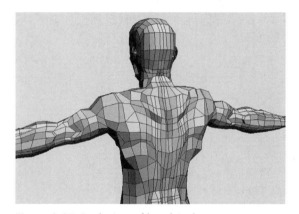

Figure 6-95: Back view of head and torso.

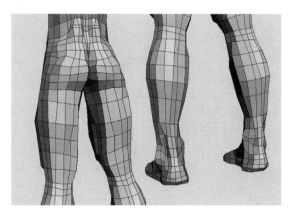

Figure 6-96: Back view of legs.

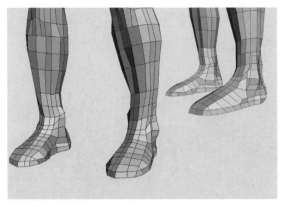

Figure 6-97: Lower legs and feet.

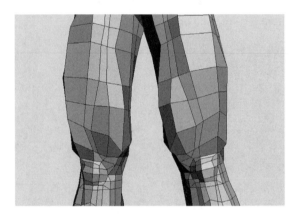

Figure 6-98: The thighs.

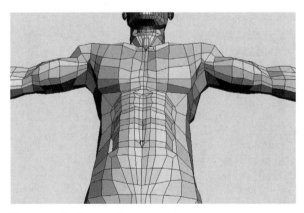

Figure 6-99: Perspective view of torso.

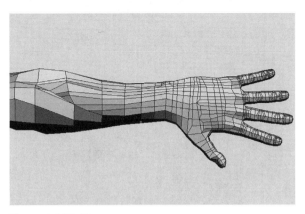

Figure 6-100: The arm.

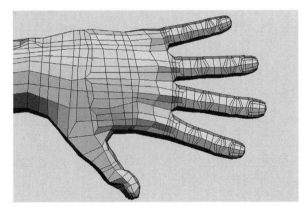

Figure 6-101: The hand.

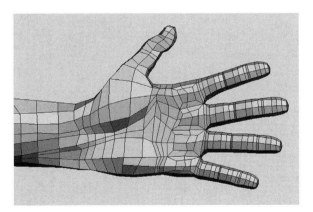

Figure 6-102: The palm.

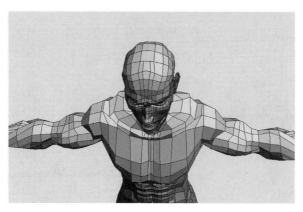

Figure 6-103: Perspective view from top.

Chapter 7

Human Project: Female Head

The Female Head Shape

We used box modeling to create the male head, but with the female head we'll start with a single polygon. This allows us to show a variety of different techniques and methods for successfully building a polygonal cage.

Figure 7-1 shows the reference sheet we will use for the female head.

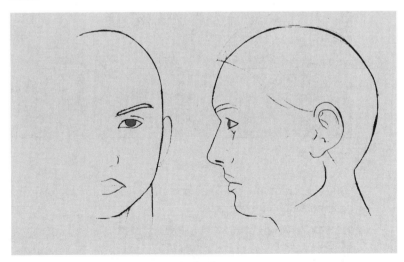

Figure 7-1: Reference sheet for female head.

We start with a single polygon, placing it near the eyebrow and extruding the edge.

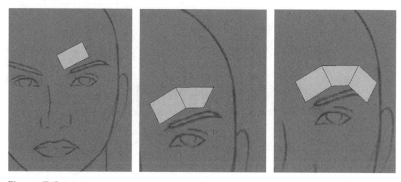

Figure 7-2

We continue this process until we get the ring with 10 faces as shown at the left in Figure 7-3. Weld the final vertices to the beginning polygon, then select the marked edges and push back to fit the reference sheet.

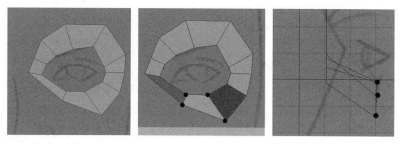

Figure 7-3

Continue the same process to reshape the flat polygonal ring to a base edge loop for the eye.

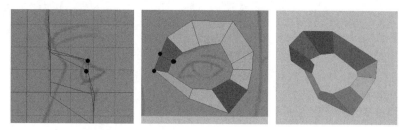

Figure 7-4

Next we extrude the upper edges down to fit the polygons to the eye contour. The lower edges are selected and extruded up.

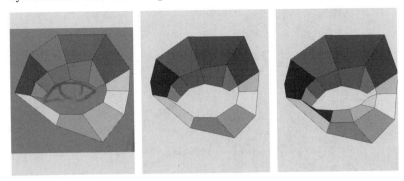

Figure 7-5

After this is done we need to make some adjustments. Merge the marked vertices, extrude the edges down and merge the corresponding vertices, then cut the marked edges as shown in Figure 7-6.

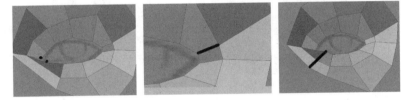

Figure 7-6

Now we expand the polygons using edge extrusion. Always remember to weld the extra vertices generated by edge extrusion.

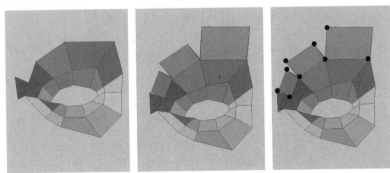

Figure 7-7

We extrude up and cut the marked edges.

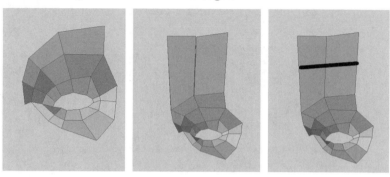

Figure 7-8

Reshape the new faces to fit the reference.

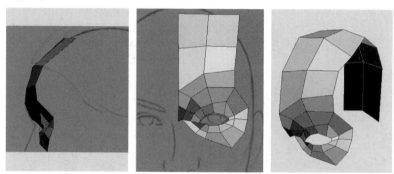

Figure 7-9

Then we continue to extrude the edges to match the already existing polygons.

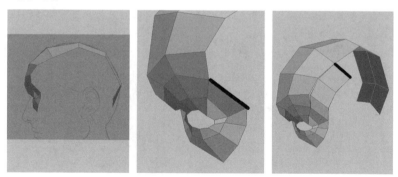

Figure 7-10

We extrude the eye's corner edge, weld marked vertices, and then generate a new four-sided polygon that can be extended as shown below.

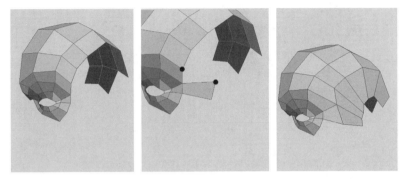

Figure 7-11

Notice in the front view that the faces that were just added conform to the front reference. We select the marked edges and continue, always checking our front reference.

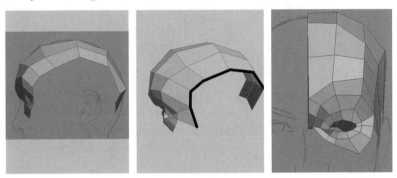

Figure 7-12

Now we can begin to model the rest of the face front with the same process of edge extrusion.

157

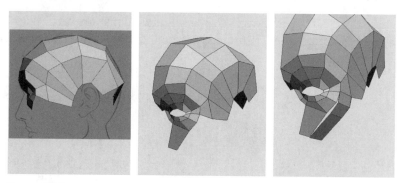

Figure 7-13

We cut the marked edge and extrude to the side.

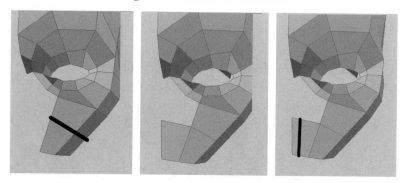

Figure 7-14

Extrude up the marked edge and weld the vertices, then cut again. This gives us two matching polygons to use to extrude the edge and weld the vertices.

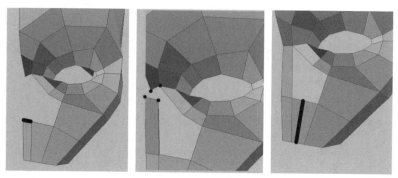

Figure 7-15

With the polygons around the nose starting to take shape, we select the marked vertex.

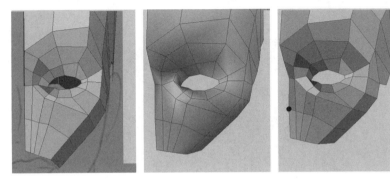

Figure 7-16

Push the vertex forward to match the nose in the reference sheet. We can then continue extruding lateral and discontinued edges to complete the maxilla (upper jaw) shape.

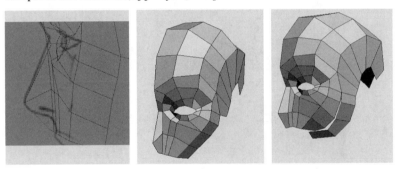

Figure 7-17

Select the marked edge and extrude to fit the maxilla to the chin in the reference.

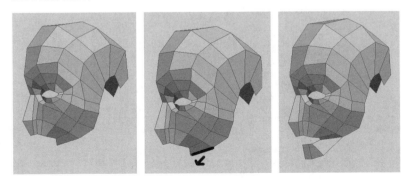

Figure 7-18

Use the same process and close the lower part of the maxilla and the chin.

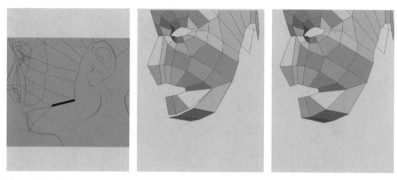

Figure 7-19

Now we can close the back of the basic head using the edge extrusion technique.

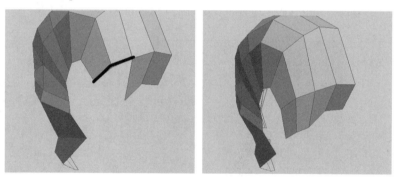

Figure 7-20

We extrude the back of the neck once and cut to give us more vertices to control when we reshape the head later.

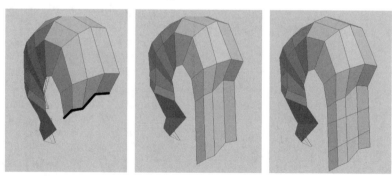

Figure 7-21

Cut the marked edge, following the flow to improve the tension of the targeted polygons. Then remove the triangle polygon generated by this process by cutting the marked area and removing the dashed line.

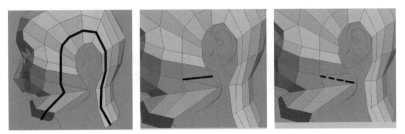

Figure 7-22

By extruding and welding the near vertices we start to build the neck and the bottom of the maxilla.

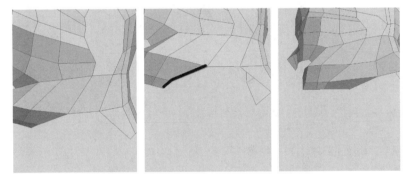

Figure 7-23

Select the marked edges and extrude them down; these will be the base mesh for the neck.

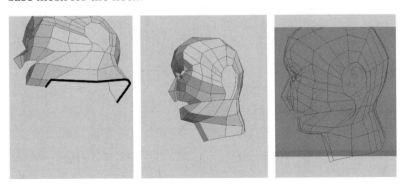

Figure 7-24

The last polygon on the border of the ear hole needs to be closed. Simply extrude the marked edge and weld the vertices.

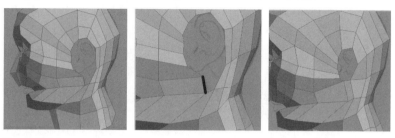

Figure 7-25

Now we cut the marked edges and remove the dashed lines to prevent future topology problems we may have with the ear.

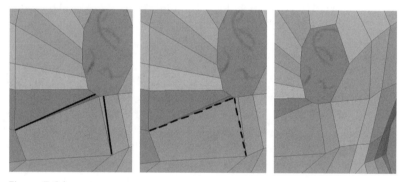

Figure 7-26

With the base mesh of the head already closed, we start adding edges following the earlier established flow.

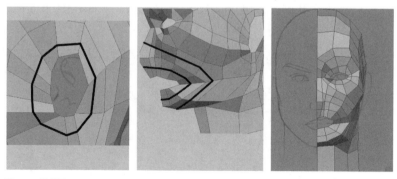

Figure 7-27

Watch the reference when moving vertices so that the volume of the head is correctly defined.

Figure 7-28

For the eye we need a sphere to fit the polygons, just like we did with the male head.

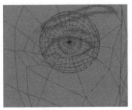
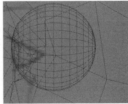
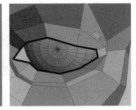

Figure 7-29

Select the border edges around the eye and chamfer or extrude them back a little.

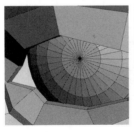

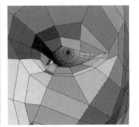

Figure 7-30

Notice that the extra edges around the border of the eye add tension.

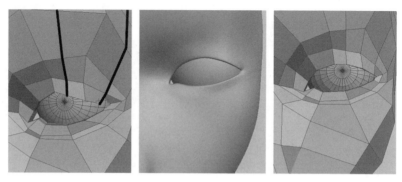

Figure 7-31

We continue refining the head, moving on to define the base of the mouth using a process similar to what we did with the loop around the eye at the beginning of this chapter.

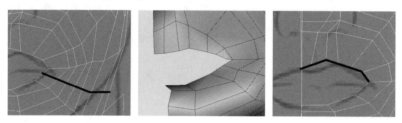

Figure 7-32

Select the lower edges and extrude up, welding the vertices at the corner of the mouth.

Figure 7-33

The interior edges are selected again and pushed back.

Figure 7-34

Then we cut the middle of the lips on the marked area and chamfer an internal edge. We can also cut around the previous cut.

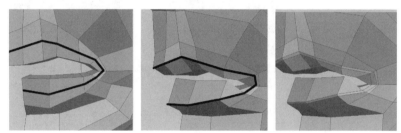

Figure 7-35

We add more edges for finer control.

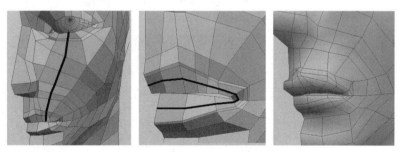

Figure 7-36

Now let's go back to the eye. Cut one more loop around the loop that already exists and the upper eyelid, and push the marked vertices back a bit. If you are modeling an Asian female, you may want to skip this step or make it very soft.

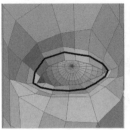
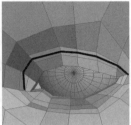
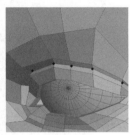

Figure 7-37

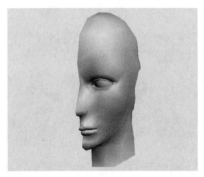

Figure 7-38: Shaded view of eyes.

The eyes are now finished, but the nose and lips still need more work.

Below the nose we cut the marked edge to have more definition. Pay attention to the quad polygon flow in this area.

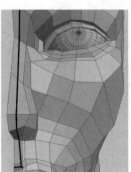
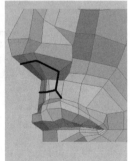

Figure 7-39

We cut one more time for the nostril and remove the unwanted edges, making sure everything is quad. Then select the marked polygons and extrude up a bit.

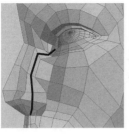
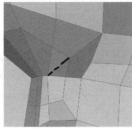
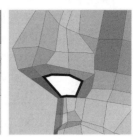

Figure 7-40

With the polygons still selected, scale down a little bit and extrude up two or more times.

Figure 7-41

The Ear

For the female ear we start by modeling from the n-gon of the ear hole. This method is different from and a bit more complicated than the method shown in Chapter 5 because it requires more practice and planning of the ear structure and the line flow.

To start the ear modeling process, we cap the hole of the ear, then extrude the polygon up and scale it down.

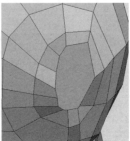

Figure 7-42

Weld the target vertices and extrude again. Then cut the marked edges for finer control and continuity of the back of the head.

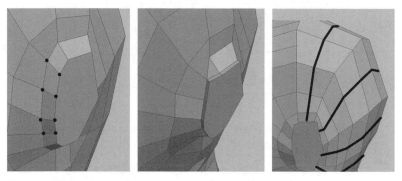

Figure 7-43

The ear now looks closer to its final shape, but if we subdivide the whole mesh it will produce undesirable results because the ear shape is a big n-gon without edges to hold the tension.

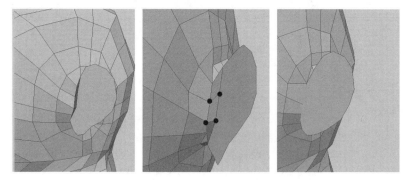

Figure 7-44

We need to start cutting the n-gon and define the general structure of the ear flow.

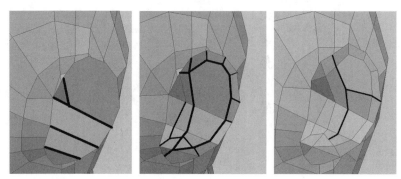

Figure 7-45

Then we pull and push the vertices so the ear volume conforms to our reference and cut some more edges to improve the control.

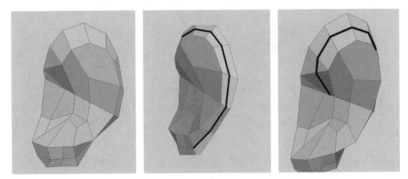

Figure 7-46

Scale up the marked edges to get a rounder shape, and then extrude the marked polygons back.

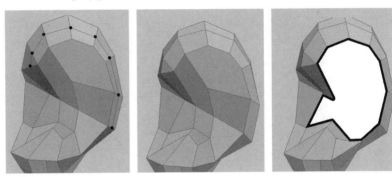

Figure 7-47

Finishing this step establishes the base for the anti-helix.

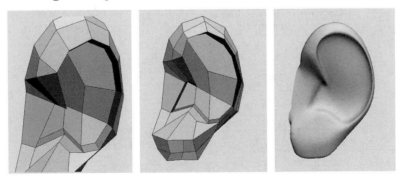

Figure 7-48

Now we need to add more control to define the anti-helix, helix, scapha, and tragus.

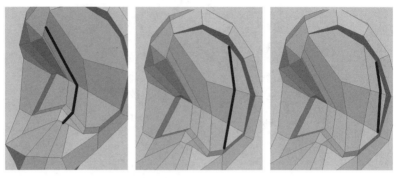

Figure 7-49

Keep an eye on the edges while you're cutting to make sure everything stays quad and so the subdivision process runs smoothly.

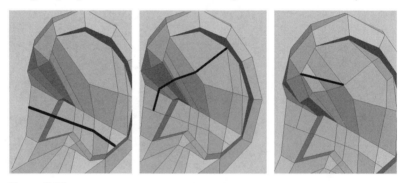

Figure 7-50

We define the anti-helix structure and then remove the dashed lines to avoid triangle polygons. Even if the ear doesn't have much deformation, avoiding triangles can prevent undesired artifacts.

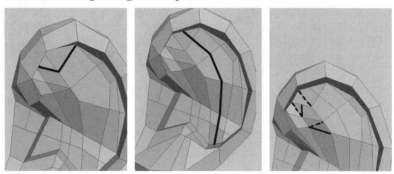

Figure 7-51

Move the marked vertices, and the ear approximates to the final shape.

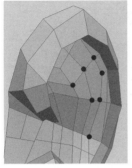  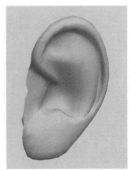

Figure 7-52

Push to make the volume a bit more precise while cutting the marked areas in order to hold the tension.

  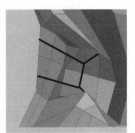

Figure 7-53

Select the marked polygon to extrude in and create the ear hole.

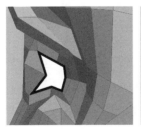  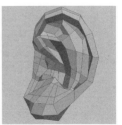

Figure 7-54

Then cut a ring around the ear to hold the tension.

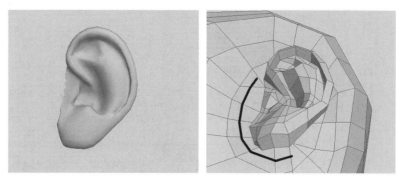

Figure 7-55

Now that the ear is finished we start refining the area around it to make sure the ear will blend perfectly with the head.

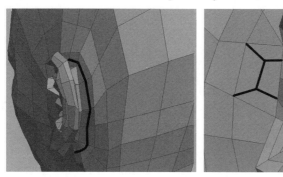

Figure 7-56

Figures 7-57 to 7-60 show various views of the completed ear and head after mirroring.

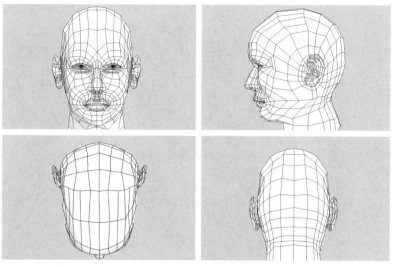

Figure 7-57: Viewing the ears in all viewports.

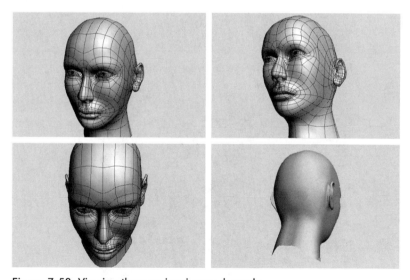

Figure 7-58: Viewing the ears in wire mesh mode.

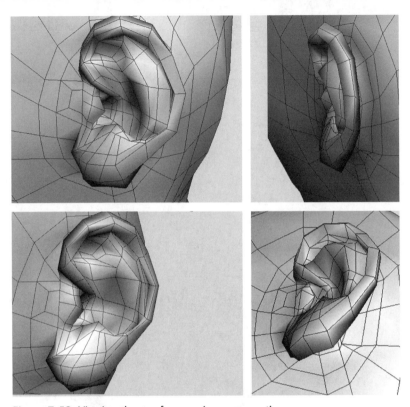

Figure 7-59: Viewing the ear from various perspectives.

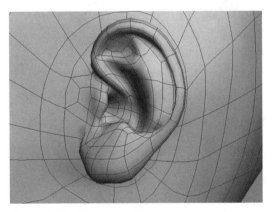

Figure 7-60: Close-up of the ear.

Chapter 8

Human Project: Female Body

Torso and Limbs

Modeling a female body isn't a complicated task; however, it requires a great deal of planning on the mesh control cage. In this chapter we start by modeling the torso and limbs, then model the hand and foot, and finally put it all together with the head.

Figure 8-1 shows the reference sheet for the body.

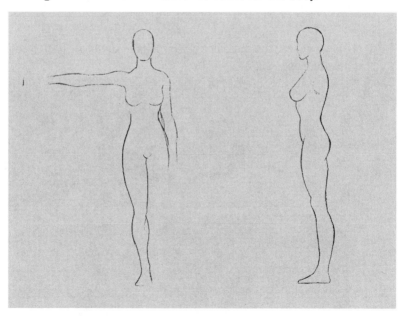

Figure 8-1: Reference sheet for female body.

We start with a 2x5 box as shown in the following figure.

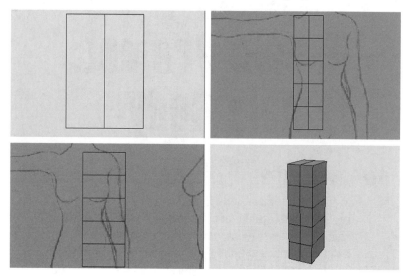

Figure 8-2

As we did for the male body, we reshape the basic box to conform to our reference shape.

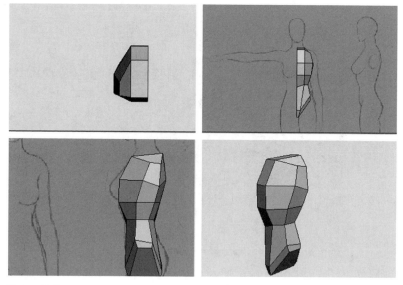

Figure 8-3

To make the arm, select the marked polygon and delete it, then place a box according to the reference sheet.

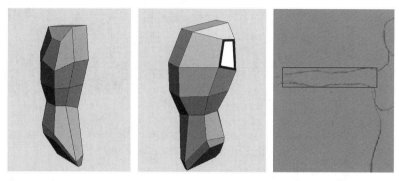

Figure 8-4

Cut the box into eight segments and delete the polygon on each end.

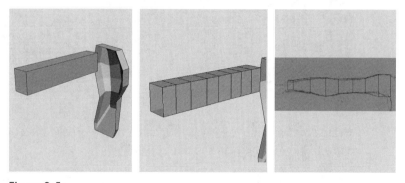

Figure 8-5

Adjust the vertices to fit the arm reference and weld it to the body.

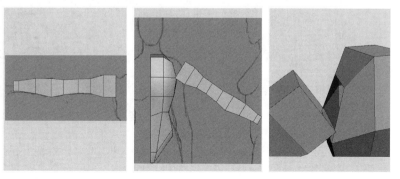

Figure 8-6

Now we have the base of the torso and arm for this model.

Figure 8-7

Cut the marked polygons to generate the base for the breasts, then select the marked edge at the right of Figure 8-8.

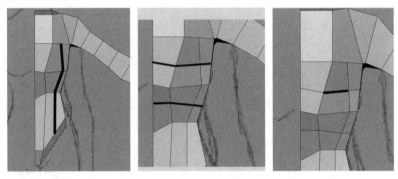

Figure 8-8

Scale down and move forward to match the reference (use the side view to align). Then cut the marked polygon.

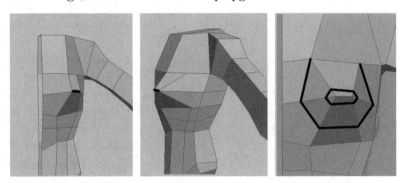

Figure 8-9

We just need a few more cuts as shown at the center of Figure 8-10 to have a base mesh for the female torso.

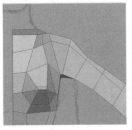
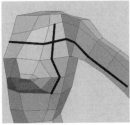
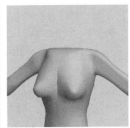

Figure 8-10

As shown in Figure 8-11, cut the marked edges and remove the dashed lines on the left, cut as marked in the center, and weld the marked vertices on the right.

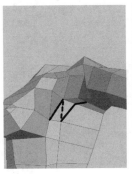
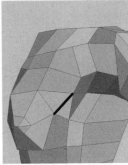
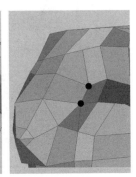

Figure 8-11

Remove the dashed lines and cut one more ring inside the nipple, then remove the dashed lines. Notice how all the tris become quads.

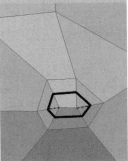
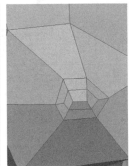

Figure 8-12

Cut the marked area shown at the left to hold the tension for the breast. Notice in the center and at the right that we need more cuts and tweaks to give the pelvis a rounder shape (notice the eight-sided shape of the n-gon).

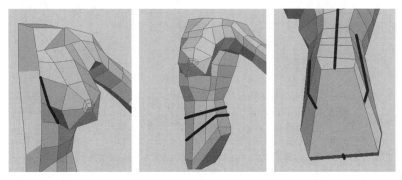

Figure 8-13

We also need to delete the marked polygon so we can attach the leg. For the leg we must have an eight-sided cylinder with seven segments and no cap at either end (we'll attach the foot later on).

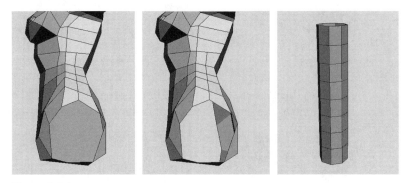

Figure 8-14

The basic leg is created by simply moving the vertices to fit our reference.

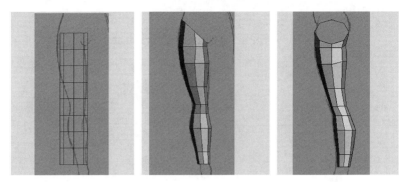

Figure 8-15

The next step is attaching the leg to the pelvis and welding the eight matched vertices.

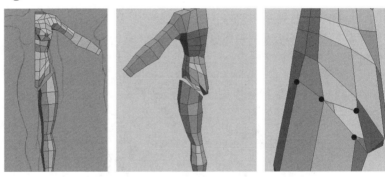

Figure 8-16

Low-poly game modelers would want to be careful about adding polygons here so the mesh doesn't slow down the game too much.

Now let's start refining the back.

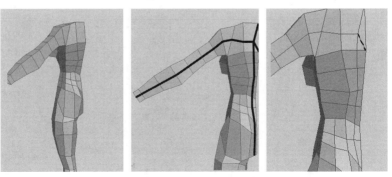

Figure 8-17

Select the marked polygons, extrude them up, and scale down. Delete the face generated in the mirror line by the Extrude tool.

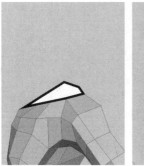 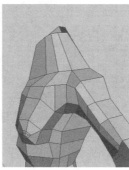 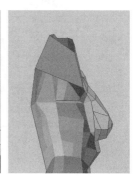

Figure 8-18

We add more edges, just following the flow.

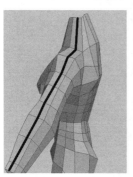  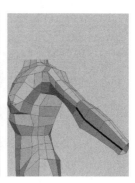

Figure 8-19

Cut the marked edges to improve the tension in the respective areas.

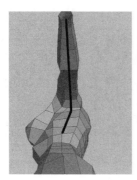 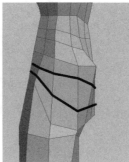 

Figure 8-20

Then add one continuous edge on the back to hold the tension on the spine area.

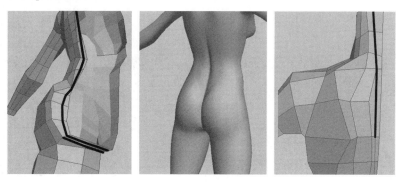

Figure 8-21

Now we start changing the flow of the abdomen by cutting the marked lines and removing the dashed lines.

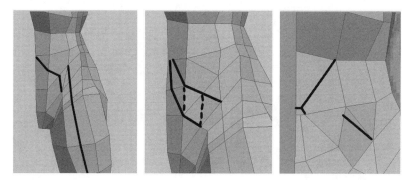

Figure 8-22

Notice the loop structure for the abdomen; select the polygons in the umbilical region and extrude them back a little bit.

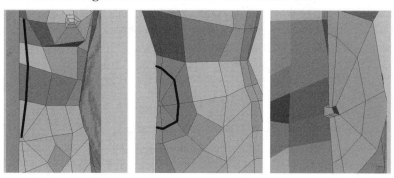

Figure 8-23

We start the next step of refinement near the clavicle bone. Cut the edge marked at the right of Figure 8-24.

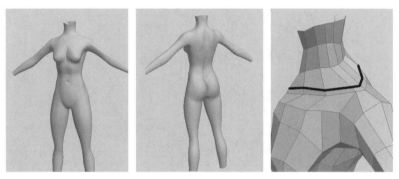

Figure 8-24: Shaded version of the mirrored and welded version of the female body.

Cut the marked edge and remove the dashed line, pushing up the marked vertex a little.

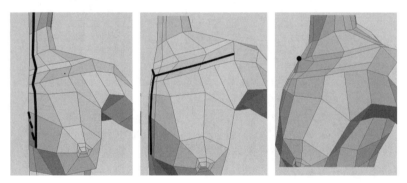

Figure 8-25

After subdividing, we get the result shown in Figure 8-26 for the clavicle. We redefine the loop for the neck as shown in the center. The image at the right shows the subdivided geometry of the clavicle and the neck.

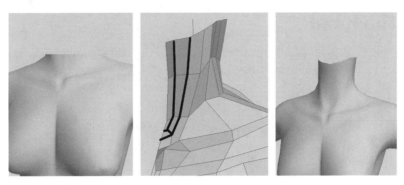

Figure 8-26

Now we can refine both the arm and the leg; cut the marked edges and notice that the edges must be continued and follow the actual flow.

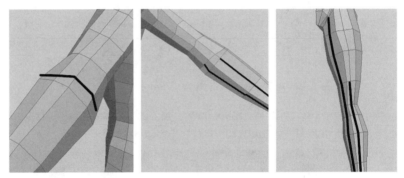

Figure 8-27

The Hand

The female hand is very similar to the male hand topologically, but we usually don't need as dense a mesh.

Figure 8-28 shows the reference sheet for the female hand.

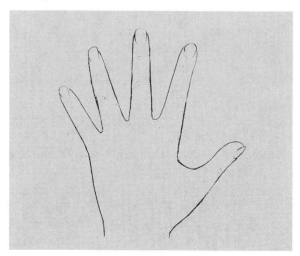

Figure 8-28: Reference sheet for the hand.

As we did with the male hand, we start with a simple 4x4 box and reshape the palm to fit our reference sheet.

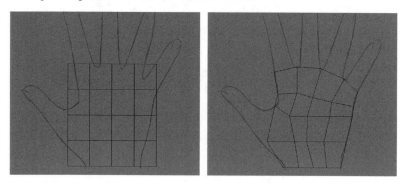

Figure 8-29

Then extrude the thumb and cut at least four edge rings to reshape the thumb so it matches the reference sheet.

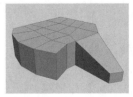
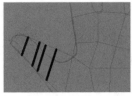
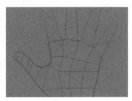

Figure 8-30

We need one extra vertical cut on the thumb.

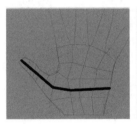
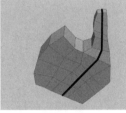
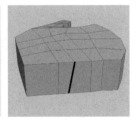

Figure 8-31

A horizontal cut completes the main thumb edges and holds the tension for the base of the palm.

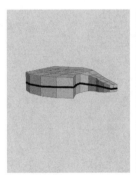

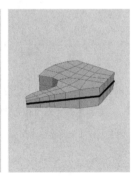

Figure 8-32

Makes cuts as shown in Figure 8-33 to generate the new vertices that will match the fingers.

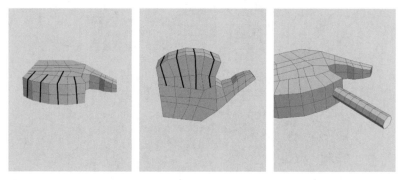

Figure 8-33

In this case, the cylinder has no cap, so we merge all the vertices as one.

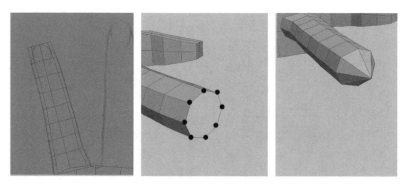

Figure 8-34

To form the fingertip, cut a ring at the top and remove the dashed lines. Now all the polygons are quads.

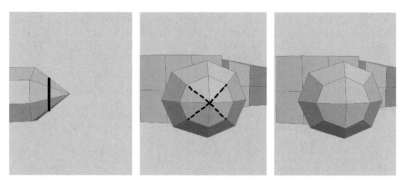

Figure 8-35

After the vertices are reshaped to fit our reference, we must add new edges to improve the control over the joints of our finger. Using the side view, push it up a little to reshape the bottom part.

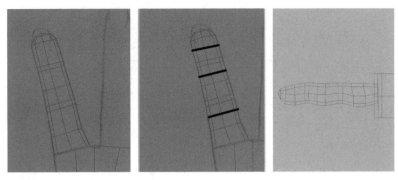

Figure 8-36

Add an extra edge in the middle, and the finger is ready for any deformation. Now let's start cutting the base edges for the nail.

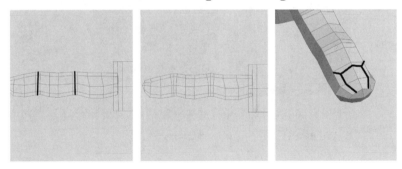

Figure 8-37

Select the four polygons of the nail and extrude a little bit, then weld the marked vertices.

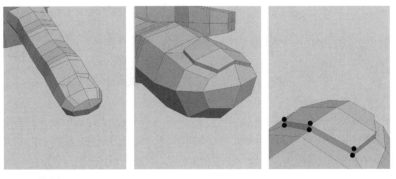

Figure 8-38

Now we select the marked polygons and extrude two times; this gives us a nail that is a bit longer than the one for the male.

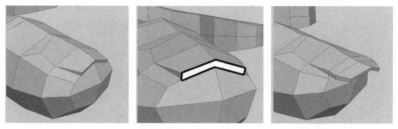

Figure 8-39

Then we add a few more edges to improve the tension and preserve the original shape around the nail.

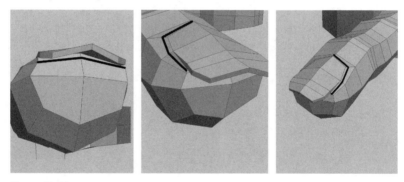

Figure 8-40

Push the marked vertices down a little. We're almost done with the finger.

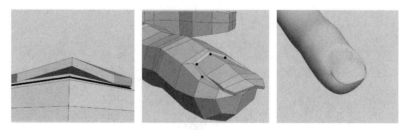

Figure 8-41

Push the vertices a little more and the finger is ready to be duplicated.

Figure 8-42

Using the same process as with the male hand, make three duplicates of the finger and reshape them according to the reference. Delete the corresponding part of the palm and merge the fingers, as shown in Figures 8-43 and 8-44.

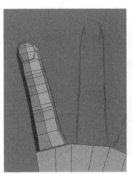  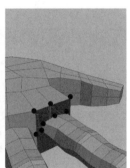

Figure 8-43

  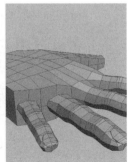

Figure 8-44

Cut two extra rings to improve the tension of the base joint.

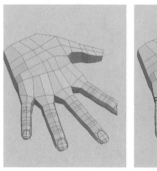
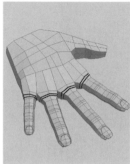
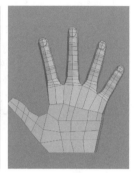

Figure 8-45

The hand is starting to take a good shape, but it needs more work on the palm and the thumb so we continue cutting the marked edges.

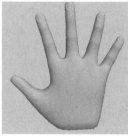
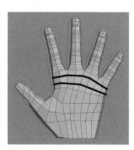

Figure 8-46

The topology refinement shown in Figures 8-47 and 8-48 is pretty similar to what we did with the male hand.

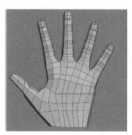

Figure 8-47

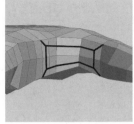
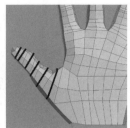

Figure 8-48

Cut the edges marked at the left, and select and chamfer the marked edges in the center to add more tension for the thumbnail.

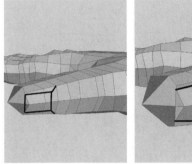
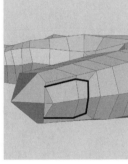
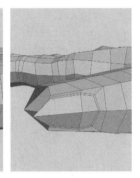

Figure 8-49

The base of the thumbnail is taking shape.

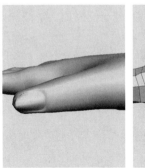
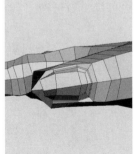

Figure 8-50

Now we need to add extra edges to bulge up the tendons of the extensor area a little bit.

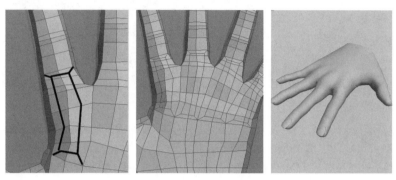

Figure 8-51

The completed hand is shown in Figure 8-52.

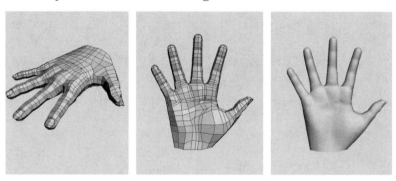

Figure 8-52: Wire mesh and shaded hands.

The Foot

We are going to model a bare foot including the toes here. Chapter 6 shows how to make the base shape for a boot or shoe.

Figure 8-53 shows the reference sheet for the foot.

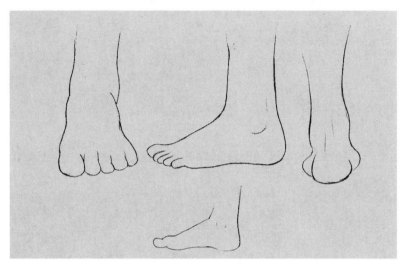

Figure 8-53: Reference sheet for the foot.

First, we'll create the toes, starting with an eight-sided cylinder. Remove the dashed lines to keep the front completely quad.

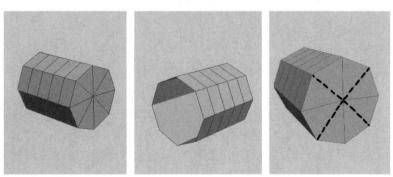

Figure 8-54

Move the vertices to fit the toe reference.

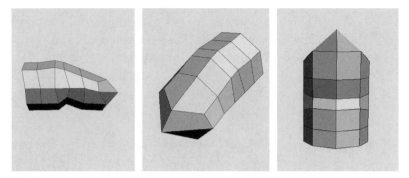

Figure 8-55

After checking the toe in the subdivided view, we start cutting the area for the nail.

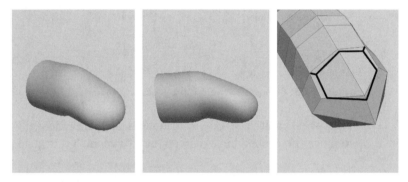

Figure 8-56

Chamfer the marked area so we get two extra edges, then reshape the nail to conform to our toe reference.

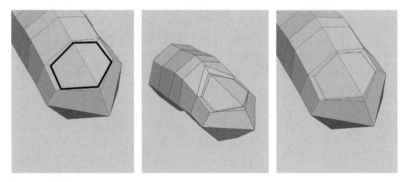

Figure 8-57

This toe will be used as a template for the others. Notice that the original toe must be duplicated and resized and the vertices need to be tweaked. For the base of the foot we use a box with 4x4x2 segments and reshape according to our reference sheet.

 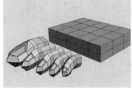 

Figure 8-58

The back polygons of the foot shape will be extruded in a way to follow the flow of the reference.

  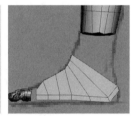

Figure 8-59

Now it's time to move the vertices to smooth the foot extensor's tendon and then cut as shown below to fit our eight-sided low-poly toe.

 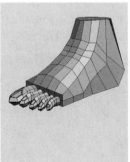 

Figure 8-60

With the hole opened, just weld and match the vertices of the toe and the foot.

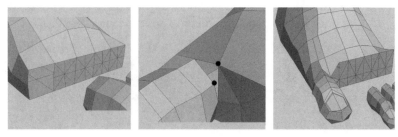

Figure 8-61

Repeat the process until all the toes are welded and integrated to the foot.

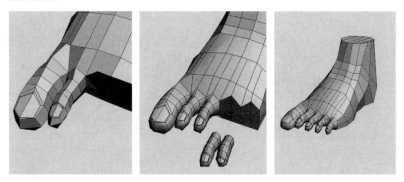

Figure 8-62

With the foot finished, we attach the foot to the leg and merge the matching vertices. If your focus is elegance, take care when refining the knee area so you don't add too many edges in the female leg.

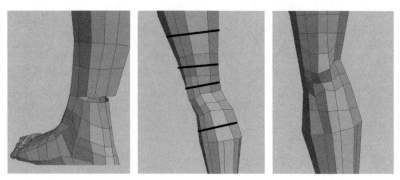

Figure 8-63

Figure 8-64 shows the female leg and knee section. From this point you can add more edges in specific areas to improve control and add muscles and details, but remember that this will increase the weight of the mesh for animation purposes. Be careful not to overdo it. Instead, you can use displacement maps for finer control.

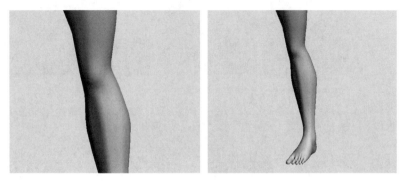

Figure 8-64

Putting It All Together

Figures 8-65 to 8-75 show the results of the modeling done in this chapter and Chapter 7.

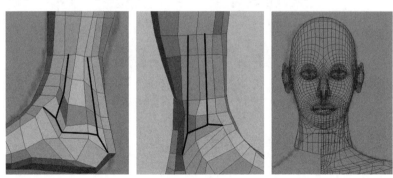

Figure 8-65: The ankle and head.

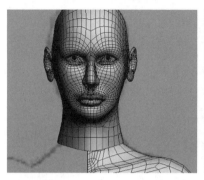
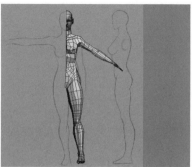

Figure 8-66: The head and body half.

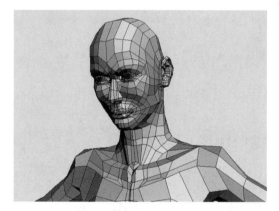

Figure 8-67: Front perspective view of the head and upper torso.

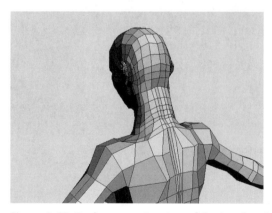

Figure 8-68: Back perspective view of the head and upper torso.

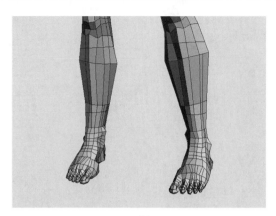

Figure 8-69: Front view of lower legs.

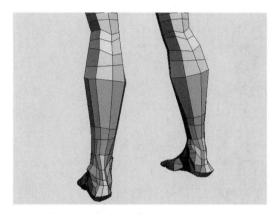

Figure 8-70: Back view of lower legs.

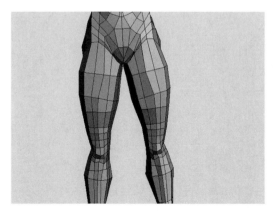

Figure 8-71: Front view of upper legs and pelvis.

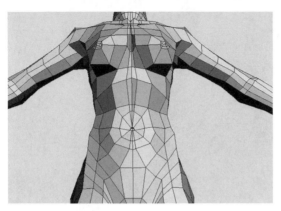

Figure 8-72: Perspective view of torso front.

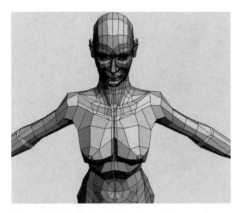

Figure 8-73: Perspective view of torso front.

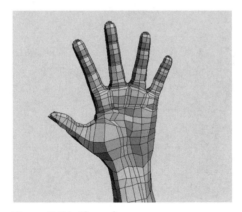

Figure 8-74: The palm.

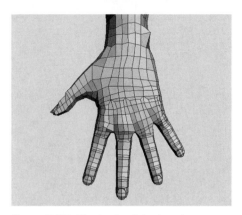

Figure 8-75: The back of the hand.

Chapter 9

Human Project: Anatomy Details

This chapter describes the process of modeling details of the human body that are not unique to the male or female figure. Here we cover polygonal modeling for teeth, eyes, and eyelashes.

Teeth

To model the teeth we use box modeling and the reference sheets shown in Figures 9-1 and 9-2.

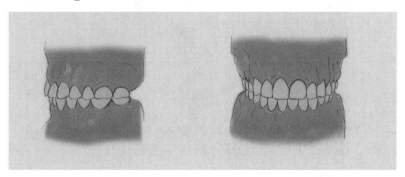

Figure 9-1: Reference for teeth.

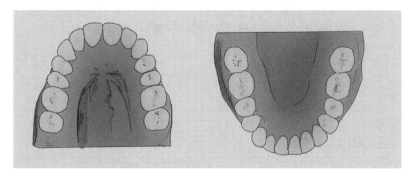

Figure 9-2: Reference for inner mouth.

We start by creating a box primitive, scaling down the top area, and placing the box to match our sheet.

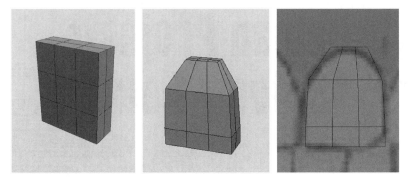

Figure 9-3

As we can see, after a few subdivision levels, the teeth conform perfectly to the shape of the reference. From the top view we curve the surface a bit.

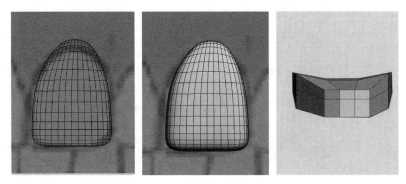

Figure 9-4

The next step is to duplicate the first tooth and place it according to the front view of the reference sheet.

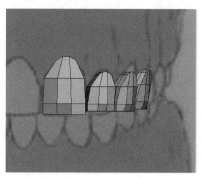 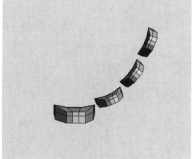

Figure 9-5

From the side view it looks correct. We now have half of the upper teeth. Remember that when working with symmetrical objects we can model half and mirror the objects, which saves a lot of repetitive work.

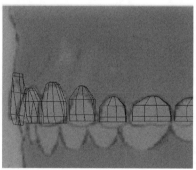 

Figure 9-6

We can tweak the shape of the back teeth later. Now we'll use box modeling to create the gums.

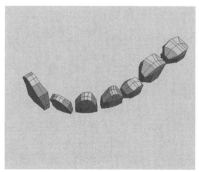 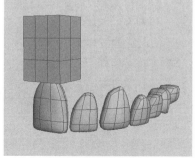

Figure 9-7

Start with a box, reshaping it based on our gum reference, and start extruding the marked polygon.

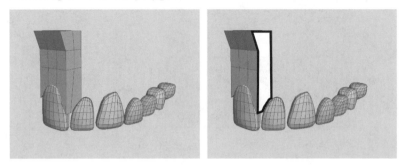

Figure 9-8

Remember to watch the rotation of the extruded polygon as it fits into the reference curvature of the gum.

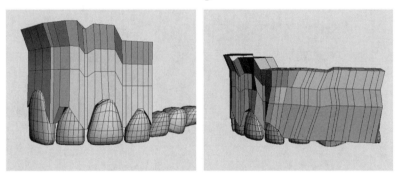

Figure 9-9

From inside it will look something similar to the image on the left in Figure 9-10. Now it's time to add more edges for more precise modeling and to hold tension near the teeth.

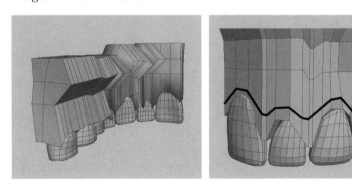

Figure 9-10

With the edges added, we can pull back the vertices so the gums jut out over the teeth a little bit.

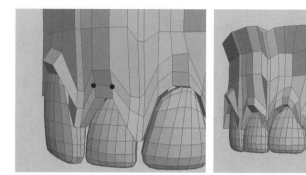

Figure 9-11

With the base shape of the gum finished, we start cutting in areas where the edges aren't enough to hold the tension during the subdivision process.

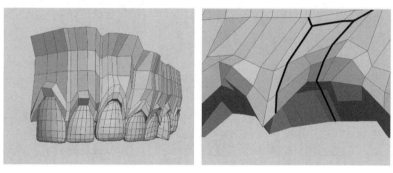

Figure 9-12

When cutting remember to keep quads as much as possible to avoid undesired artifacts when subdividing.

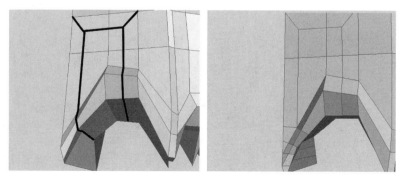

Figure 9-13

Cut the marked edge to improve the control of the curvature. The image at the right in Figure 9-14 shows half of the teeth and the gums in wire mesh. Notice how it's constructed.

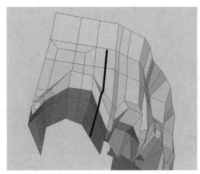
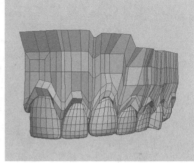

Figure 9-14

At this point we can start refining the back teeth.

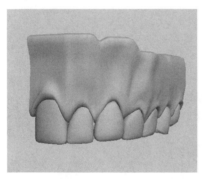
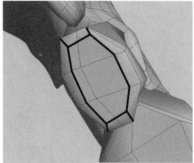

Figure 9-15

For finer control and detailing, add a few more edges and tweak the shape as desired.

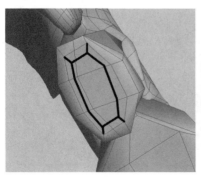
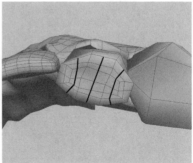

Figure 9-16

We now have a low-poly version of the teeth and a subdivided version.

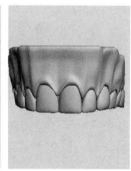

Figure 9-17

To create the bottom row of teeth, you could repeat the process for creating the upper row of teeth, but that is too time consuming and repetitive. Here, we duplicate and invert the upper row and then start scaling down the bottom teeth to fit our reference sheet.

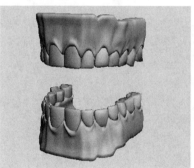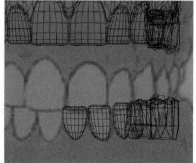

Figure 9-18

After finishing the process on one half, we can mirror the other half to complete the bottom row.

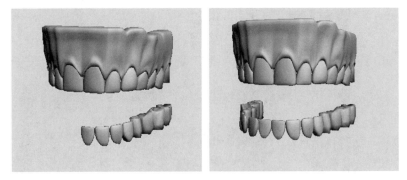

Figure 9-19

After the teeth are finished, the gum needs to be reshaped to fit the bottom teeth. Start by manipulating the mirrored upper gum to fit the bottom teeth.

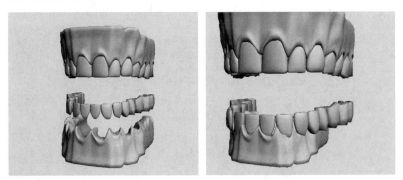

Figure 9-20

Figures 9-21 to 9-25 show the finished teeth and gums from a variety of perspectives.

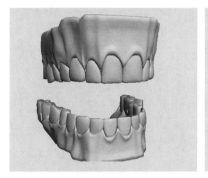
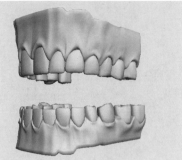

Figure 9-21: The finished teeth and gums.

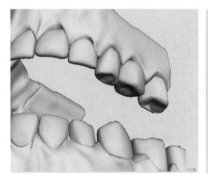
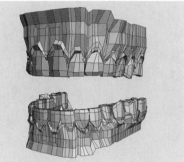

Figure 9-22

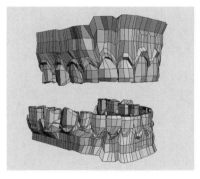
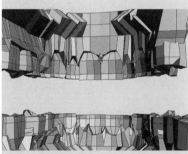

Figure 9-23

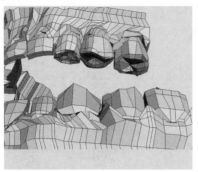
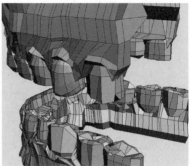

Figure 9-24

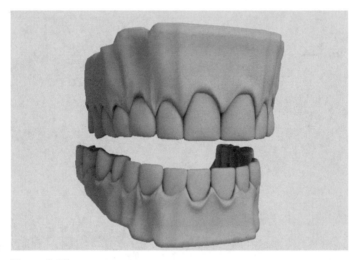

Figure 9-25

The Eye

The eyes are probably the easiest part of the character's face to model. In this section we discuss two different methods for easily achieving good eye modeling results.

Cartoon Eyeball Modeling

Here we discuss a quick method suitable for modeling cartoon eyeballs.

Starting with a sphere, we detach the first two sections as shown below. This will leave a hole in the eyeball.

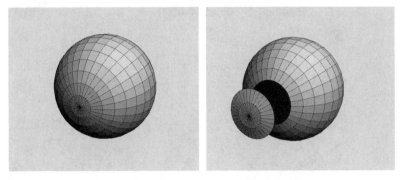

Figure 9-26

Then we cap the hole and extrude back the big n-gon.

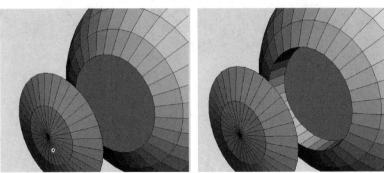

Figure 9-27

Scaling down gives us the iris. Now we can use the part that was removed earlier.

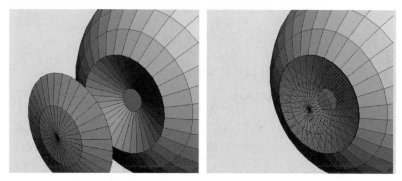

Figure 9-28

It's important to note that scaling down the n-gon will help later during the shading process, as the light will react much better on a non-flat surface.

Figure 9-29

Realistic Eyeball Modeling

To model a realistic eyeball, we start with a sphere that has 8, 16, or 32 segments.

For this lesson we'll use two separate spheres, one with 16 segments and one with 32. The sphere with 32 segments will be used to coat the internal eyeball for reflective purposes.

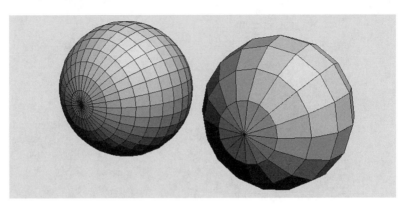

Figure 9-30

For the internal eyeball we select the marked ring and chamfer it to get two edge rings instead of one.

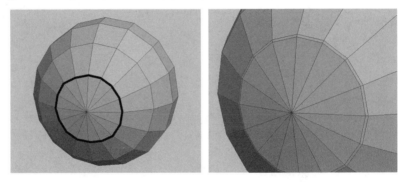

Figure 9-31

Cut the internal n-gon to avoid stretching the hole, keeping everything quad as much as possible.

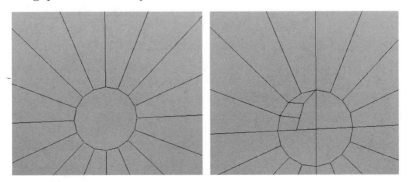

Figure 9-32

Then we extrude in.

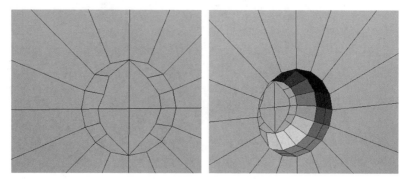

Figure 9-33

As shown in the previous eye exercise, we need to push the iris back to enhance the shader that you apply later.

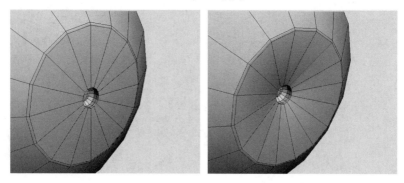

Figure 9-34

Figures 9-35 and 9-36 show the completed eyeball.

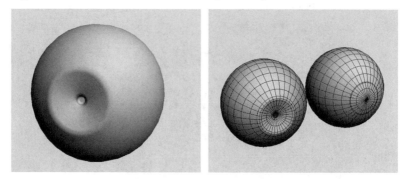

Figure 9-35

Figure 9-36

The Eyelashes

Eyelashes are not difficult to model, but they can be tricky. Here we will use our previously modeled female head to create and position the eyelashes.

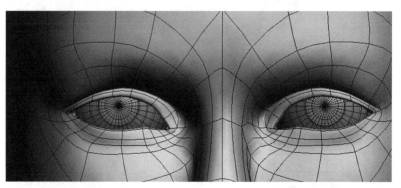

Figure 9-37: Wire mesh view of completed eyes.

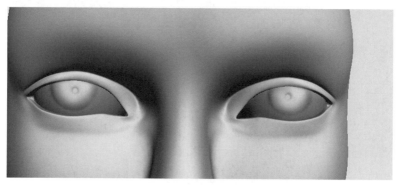

Figure 9-38: Subdivided view of completed eyes.

We start by creating a single eight-sided cylinder and placing it near the eye.

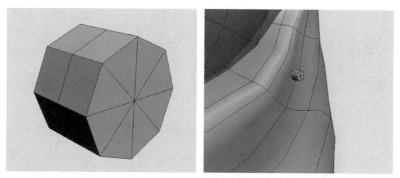

Figure 9-39

Extrude the cap polygons to make a curved shape and scale it down a bit every extrusion until it reaches the final point and then weld all the end vertices. Then duplicate the eyelash and tweak the rotation and scaling values while positioning the cylinders.

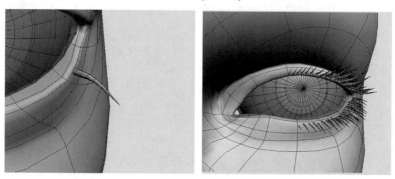

Figure 9-40

Figures 9-41 and 9-42 show the completed eyelashes.

Figure 9-41

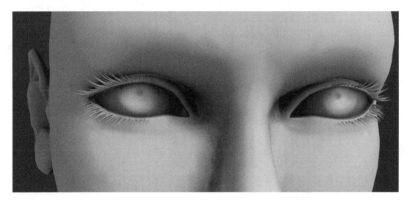

Figure 9-42: Rendered eyelashes.

Chapter 10

Ogre Head

In this chapter we model an ogre head that we will use in Chapter 11, "Introduction to ZBrush." We also discuss displacement and how it affects polygonal geometry.

Creating an Ogre Head

Figure 10-1 shows the reference sheet we will use to create our ogre head.

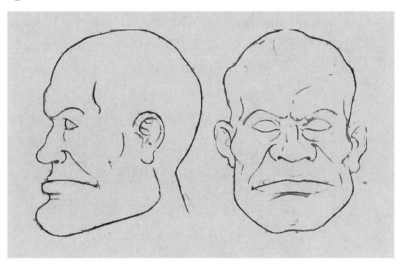

Figure 10-1: Reference for ogre head.

Start with half of a 4x4 box.

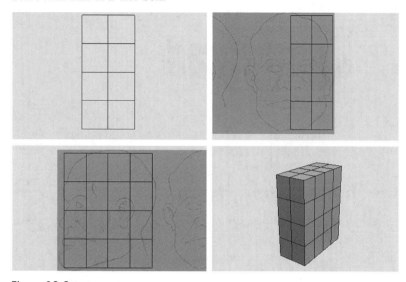

Figure 10-2

Reshape the vertices to fit the reference as much as possible.

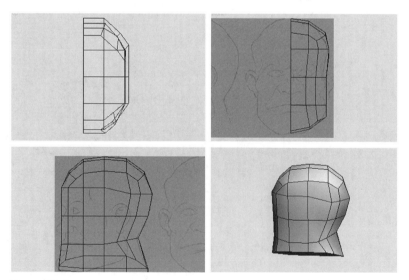

Figure 10-3

Next we position the vertices marked below to match their respective positions in the side view. This will help us to prevent "flat face." Then we remove the marked edges.

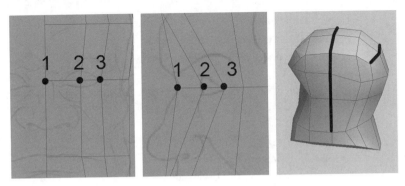

Figure 10-4

Cut as shown in Figure 10-5 to provide the base of the edge loop for the ear and the eye.

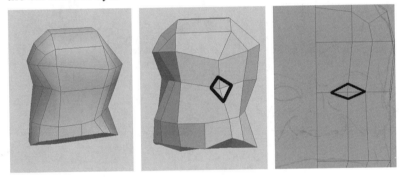

Figure 10-5

Add more edges as shown in Figure 10-6, always watching to be sure the topology of the head is correct.

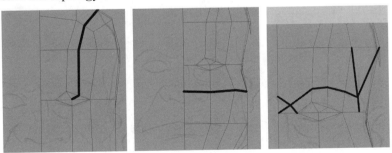

Figure 10-6

Remove the marked edges shown at the left in Figure 10-7 and rebuild the edges as shown at the right.

Figure 10-7

Complete the loop around the eye and add more edges.

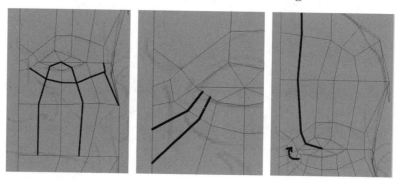

Figure 10-8

Cut the marked areas and notice the loops created: one internal and one external. Be sure to keep everything quad as much as possible.

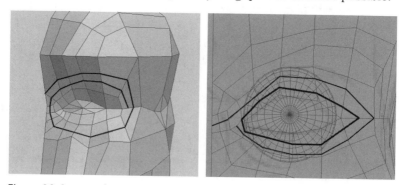

Figure 10-9

To define the eye area we'll use the same technique described in Chapter 9. Put the eyeball in position and reshape the area around it.

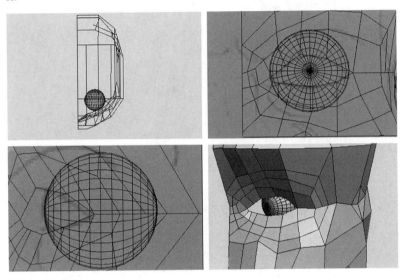

Figure 10-10

Delete the hole and create one more loop inside so that we have finer control there. The image in the center shows the two edges as a result of using the Chamfer tool and the image at the right shows an even finer chamfer of the interior edge.

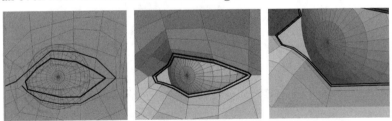

Figure 10-11

As we did earlier, push back the border edges. It doesn't matter if it enters the eyeball; just move the vertices to fit the volume of the shape you want.

Now we can go on the rest of the head and add more edges.

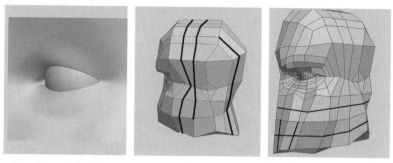

Figure 10-12

First we push the marked vertices to fit the nose in the reference.

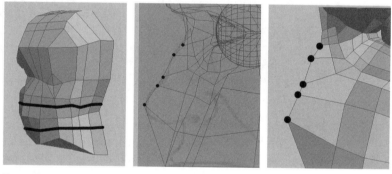

Figure 10-13

Then we add more edges and push back the vertices to fit the reference. The marked vertices in the center and at the right are the same vertices shown in the side and front views.

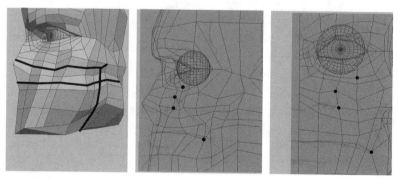

Figure 10-14

Add a couple more edges as shown at the left in Figure 10-15 and remove the marked edges shown in the center. Be sure to keep all quads to avoid undesired results in your mesh.

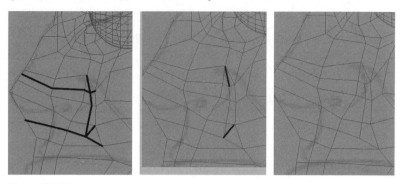

Figure 10-15

Cut the marked areas below to improve the control cage and notice how this reshapes the flow of the ogre nose at the right.

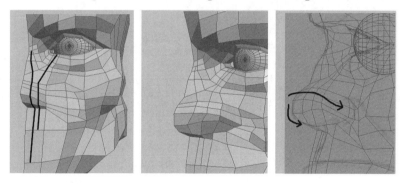

Figure 10-16

Cut around the nostril to give it some tension, then select the marked polygons, extrude in a little, scale down, and extrude again, following the same process we used in Chapters 5 and 7 for the male and female noses.

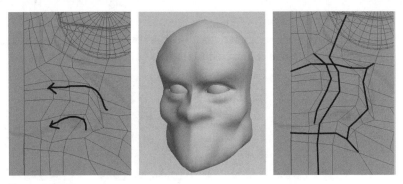

Figure 10-17

We add one extra ring to the nose, then select the marked polygons and extrude up.

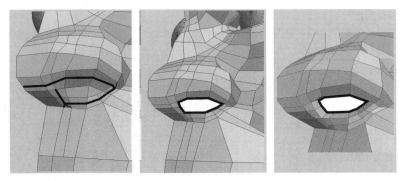

Figure 10-18

Take a look at the nose in the subdivided view. Now continue to cut the marked edges shown at right in Figure 10-19.

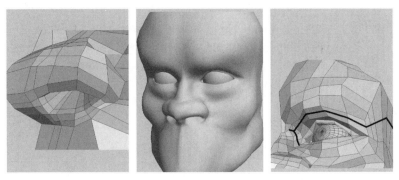

Figure 10-19

After some tweaking to increase the accuracy of our reference, we start working on the chin, creating more edges to make it rounder.

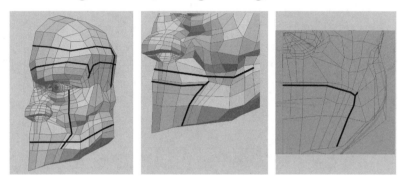

Figure 10-20

Delete the marked polygon at the left and continue refining.

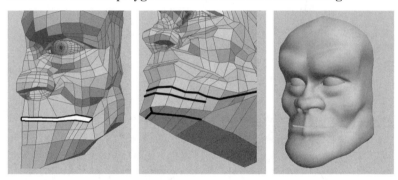

Figure 10-21

Then we cut some edges following the loop of the mouth to push forward and refine the lips.

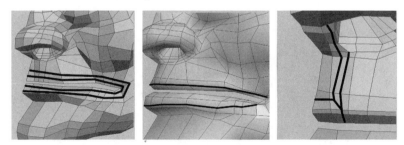

Figure 10-22

We need to add some extra edges to provide a refined base for the ear (center) and select the polygons (right).

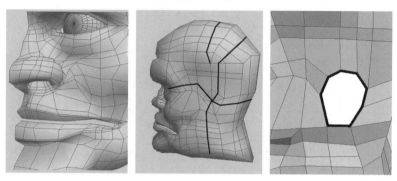

Figure 10-23

Cut in some local areas to obtain finer control and add details before displacement.

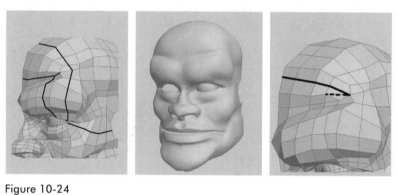

Figure 10-24

Select the bottom polygons at the base of the neck.

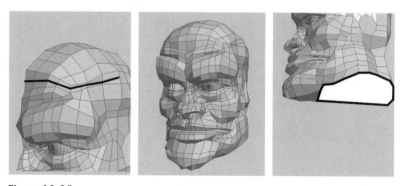

Figure 10-25

Extrude the polygons down, deleting the polygon we used to extrude. Then add a few more edges to give some definition.

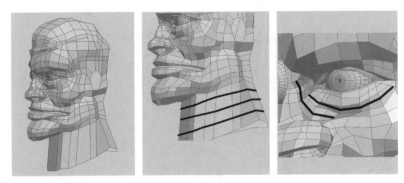

Figure 10-26

Cut the marked edges to provide a little more control for wrinkle definition.

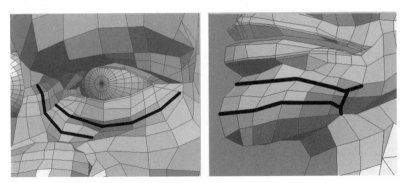

Figure 10-27

Figure 10-28 shows the steps for creating the neck and refining deformation areas for facial expressions.

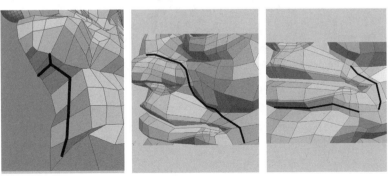

Figure 10-28

Figures 10-29 and 10-30 show the completed ogre head

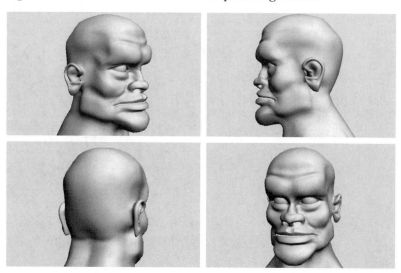

Figure 10-29: Finished ogre head.

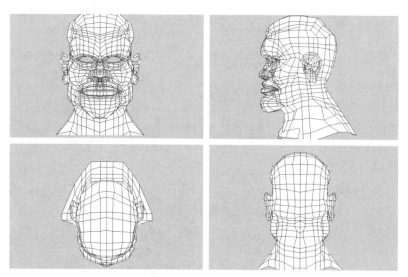

Figure 10-30: Finished ogre head in wireframe.

Introduction to Displacement

Displacement maps are grayscale textures applied to the mesh that push and pull the vertices according to the image's grayscale value. Displacement usually requires a high-resolution mesh for a finer level of detail because it deforms the mesh (unlike bump maps that only create the illusion of surface relief). An object with displacement can be at a low resolution in the viewport (for speed and real-time rendering issues) and at a ultra-high resolution at render time.

In Figure 10-31, the image at left shows how the procedural displacement map is applied on the plane. The image on the right shows how this information deforms the mesh.

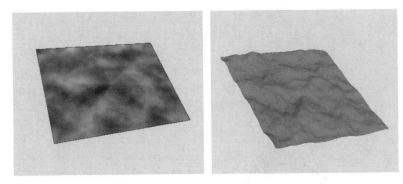

Figure 10-31

Figure 10-32 shows another displacement example. The checkerboard mapping, in pure black and white, produces very sharp results when the resolution of the mesh allows it.

Figure 10-32

The displacement resolution is pretty much related to the density of the mesh. The image on the left in Figure 10-33 has many more polygons than the image on the right. We can see the difference when comparing the displacement of both meshes.

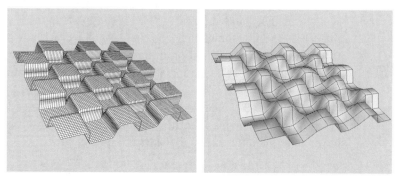

Figure 10-33

Figures 10-34 to 10-36 show the displacement map used at the left and the effect produced in the shape at the right. Notice that the white and gray areas push up the vertices and the black area pushes down.

Figure 10-34

Figure 10-37 shows a sharp 2D shape to be projected as a displacement map. Notice the hard edges and crisp polygons.

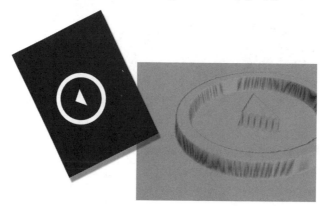

Figure 10-37

Now we add some smoothing using Gaussian blur on the above figure, which produces a much smoother result during displacement.

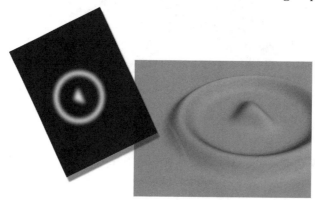

Figure 10-38

Note that displacement can be applied to any piece of geometry. However, to make it work properly it is recommended that the UV mapping be very accurate to ensure the correct mapping information will match the displacement.

Figure 10-39 shows a sphere with fractal noise displacement and a cylinder mapped with checkerboard displacement.

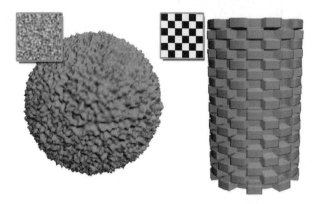

Figure 10-39

Displacement can be very useful for increasing the amount of detail in the geometry that otherwise would be difficult or impossible to create. But while displacement can be very handy, it's a nonintuitive way to achieve results because there isn't any real-time feedback. Because you can't see the mesh being deformed by the brush, it is almost impossible to achieve good results in organic forms. It's possible to paint the grayscale displacement maps with any 2D painting program, but the result may not be what the user was aiming for.

In the next chapter we discuss the benefits of using ZBrush, a software package that allows us to paint the displacement map and simultaneously see the results that the painting is actually producing on the piece of geometry we are working on. This lets us create the displacement map using one of the most artistic and intuitive ways possible today.

Chapter 11

Introduction to ZBrush

This chapter introduces the features of ZBrush that can be used for sculpting your mesh and discusses the advantages of using ZBrush in conjunction with your 3D package for mesh refinement sculpting using displacement. The tools and procedures presented here pertain to ZBrush 2; this chapter does not cover painting textures and 2D, 2.5D tools, or general workflow.

2D and 3D Differences in ZBrush

The first thing to point out about ZBrush 2 is that it is 2D, 2.5D, and 3D software, all in one package. ZBrush stores depth information when you paint on the canvas in what is called "pixols," that is, pixels with depth. Let's see how it works.

First, paint quickly with a noisy brush. Then use the standard brush slowly. When we hold the pressure while painting slowly, ZBrush adds depth to the stroke. In Figure 11-1, notice the noisy textured background underneath the horizontal clean stroke.

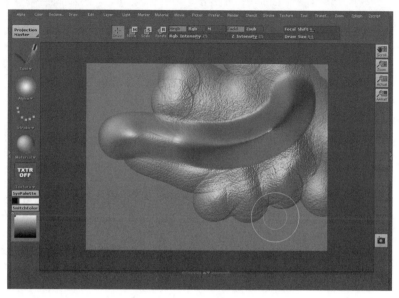

Figure 11-1

Working on the ZBrush Canvas

ZBrush is a unique software that has its own workflow, shortcuts, and user interface. As with most complex applications (especially 3D) that allow the user to configure shortcuts and customize the interface to better fit their own preferences, ZBrush allows you to completely customize your interface.

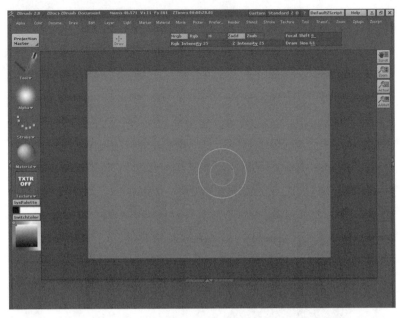

Figure 11-2: Default ZBrush interface.

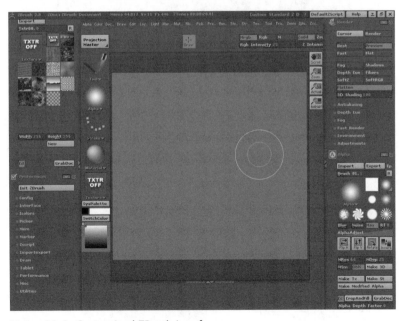

Figure 11-3: Customized ZBrush interface.

243

Importing

We start our modeling workflow in ZBrush by loading a mesh generated by a 3D application and exported to the Alias .obj object format. Click on the Tool menu to see the following options:

▶ **Load Tool**: Allows us to load a tool saved from ZBrush with all particular changes made by ZBrush, including those not supported by other applications.

▶ **Save As**: Allows us to save our tool to load later on (in ZBrush).

▶ **Import**: This option opens an import window to load our previously exported mesh .obj object.

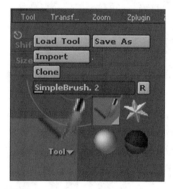

Figure 11-4

Select the ogre head modeled in Chapter 10.

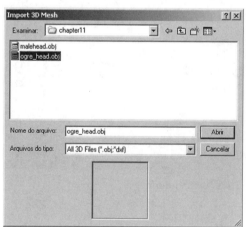

Figure 11-5

When we import the mesh, a thumbnail appears below the Projection Master, showing us that the head is our actual tool. When we click and drag inside the canvas, we create the head, then we hit T or click the Edit button to focus on our mesh. When the Edit mode is activated, it tells ZBrush that we want to modify the object we've just created. If we turn off Edit mode and draw another object (or paint on the canvas), the previous object will be dropped and is no longer editable.

Figure 11-6

If we hold the Shift key, ZBrush will place the shape in an orthogonal view.

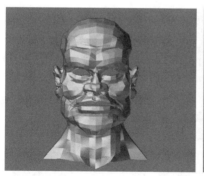

Figure 11-7

General Manipulation

There are a number of tools in ZBrush. This section discusses some of those used for general manipulation. Figure 11-8 shows the toolbar at the top of the ZBrush interface that contains the most basic ZBrush tools.

Figure 11-8: ZBrush toolbar.

From left to right, the tools are:

▶ **Quick**: Displays the faceted mesh (faster). When this button is turned off, ZBrush displays the smooth mesh (slower).

▶ **Edit**: Allows you to sculpt the 3D object. If you turn Edit off and create or import another object, the previous object becomes inaccessible for 3D editing.

▶ **Draw**: Enables you to create an object or draw, paint, or sculpt. You can't select the Draw button at the same time as the Move, Scale, or Rotate buttons.

▶ **Move**: Moves the entire shape if Edit mode is disabled. When Edit mode is enabled, it moves the selected portion of the mesh.

▶ **Scale**: Scales the entire shape if Edit mode is disabled. If Edit mode is enabled, it scales the selected portion of the mesh.

▶ **Rotate**: Rotates entire shape if Edit mode is disabled. If Edit mode is enabled, Rotate is disabled.

Figure 11-9 demonstrates the Frame option, which shows the wireframe mesh. The option is activated in the image at the left and deactivated in the image at right.

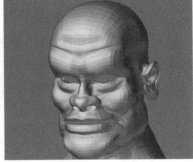

Figure 11-9

Move

The Move tool is commonly used to reshape the low-poly mesh before subdivision and to push a medium-resolution mesh that uses an attenuation falloff.

Figure 11-10 shows a vertex that has been moved without subdividing the mesh in the image at the left. The image at the right shows a vertex moving with focal shift attenuation. Notice that the Move tool acts perpendicularly to the user's camera view angle.

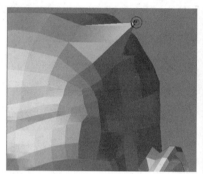 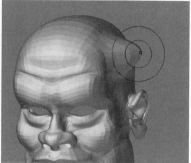

Figure 11-10

Scale

The Scale tool scales the vertices at the brush area using the brush's focal shift for sharpness attenuation during the operation.

Figure 11-11 shows scaling the brush size area, with different focal shift values.

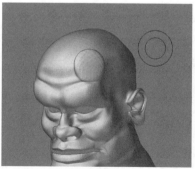 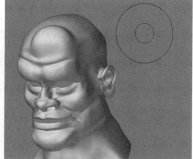

Figure 11-11

Zadd

Zadd stands for "Z (depth) add (addition)." This option bumps up the mesh, painting brighter values on the displacement map.

Notice the difference of the values and the increased height of the mesh in Figures 11-12 to 11-14.

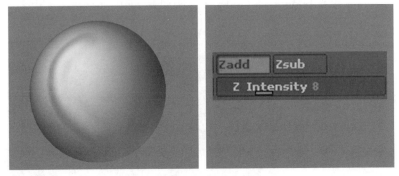

Figure 11-12: Zadd enabled, with Intensity of 8.

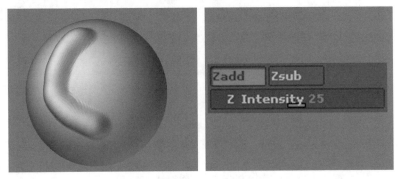

Figure 11-13: Zadd enabled, with Intensity of 25.

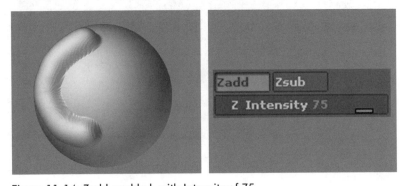

Figure 11-14: Zadd enabled, with Intensity of 75.

Zsub

Zsub stands for "Z (depth) sub (subtraction)." This option generates a depression on the mesh, painting darker values on the displacement map.

Figures 11-15 to 11-17 show different depressions based on the Intensity setting.

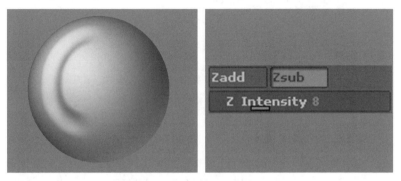

Figure 11-15: Zsub enabled, with Intensity of 8.

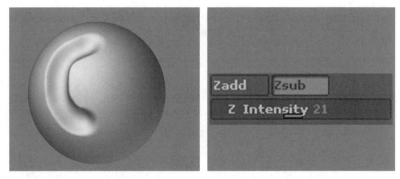

Figure 11-16: Zsub enabled, with Intensity of 21.

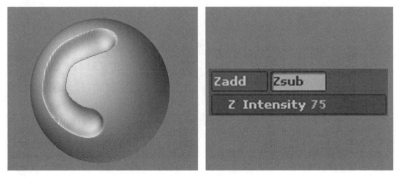

Figure 11-17: Zsub enabled, with Intensity of 75.

Right-clicking brings up a pop-up menu that allows us to change the main parameters of our brush.

Figure 11-18

Focal Shift

The Focal Shift setting determines the falloff of the brush and how sharp the effects of the brush will be. Figures 11-19 to 11-21 show various Focal Shift values and their effects.

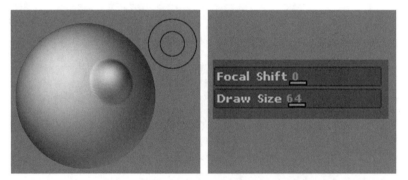

Figure 11-19: Neutral focal shift. The falloff causes a soft displacement.

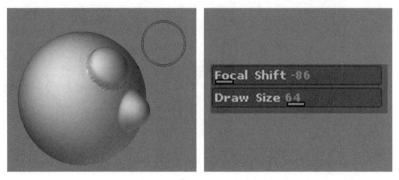

Figure 11-20: Focal Shift of –86. Notice the sharp displacement and the brush.

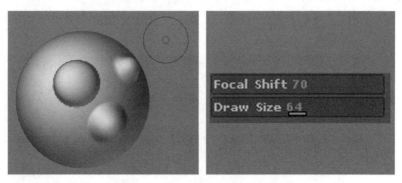

Figure 11-21: Focal Shift of 70. The displacement is sharp at the top.

Geometry Subdivision

ZBrush subdivides the mesh to increase the number of polygons for a smoother display of the displacement. ZBrush allows you to easily check out how many polygons your model has at each level of subdivision.

Under the Tool menu is the Geometry submenu. This allows us to subdivide the current mesh and easily change the slider to a higher or lower level of subdivision. The default shortcut for subdividing the mesh is Ctrl+D. Once subdivided, we can go down (Shift+D) or go up (D) on the subdivision level.

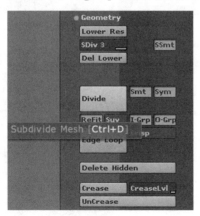

Figure 11-22

Figures 11-23 to 11-26 show the ogre head with varying subdivision levels.

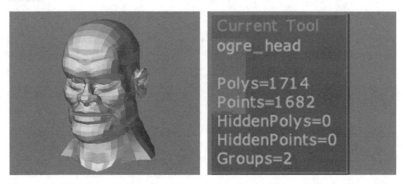

Figure 11-23: The ogre head with one level of subdivision (1,714 polygons).

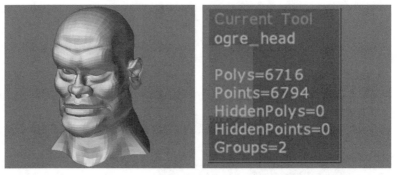

Figure 11-24: The ogre head with two levels of subdivision (6,716 polygons).

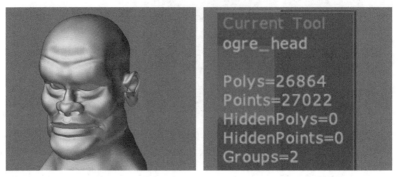

Figure 11-25: The ogre head with three levels of subdivision (26,864 polygons).

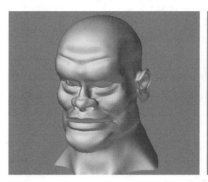

Figure 11-26: The ogre head with four levels of subdivision (107,456 polygons).

As stated earlier, the higher the level of subdivision, the more polygons the mesh will have and the denser the mesh will be. Having a high number of polygons can cause performance issues since the computer must show everything in real time, but in ZBrush you can always hide the part of your mesh you're not sculpting to improve the performance.

Hide/Unhide

Hiding polygons in ZBrush is pretty simple.

To hide everything outside the rectangle marquee, hold Ctrl, then press Shift (green selection).

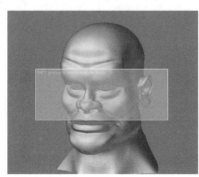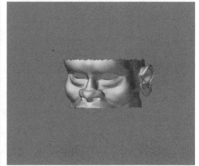

Figure 11-27

To hide everything inside the rectangle marquee, hold Ctrl, then press and release Shift (red selection).

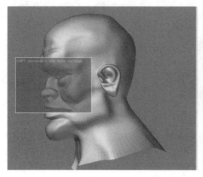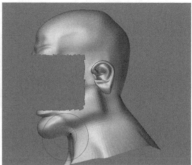

Figure 11-28

To unhide all, hold Ctrl+Shift, then click outside.

Figure 11-29

Mask

Masking in ZBrush is simple. This functionality lets you restrict the area in which you are working. The dark area is the protected area, which you can't edit. Only the white area is editable when some part of the object is masked.

Hold Ctrl, then click and drag to create the mask window.

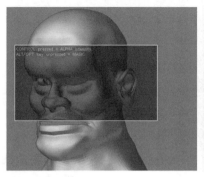 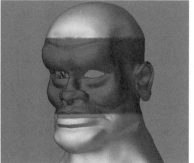

Figure 11-30

Hold Ctrl+Alt, then click and drag the mouse to create the unmask window.

 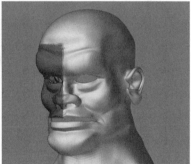

Figure 11-31

Hold Ctrl and click anywhere in the canvas to invert the mask selection.

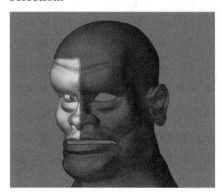

Figure 11-32

Figure 11-33 shows inflate sculpting on the unprotected (white) area.

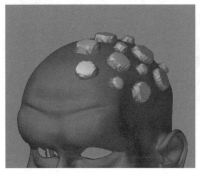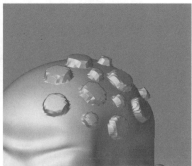

Figure 11-33

Basic Transform Tools

Transform tools can be found under the Transform menu. This section discusses some of the options available inside ZBrush 2.

Standard (Std)

The Standard option moves the vertices outward by polygon along the edit stroke. It can be adjusted with the Z intensity slider.

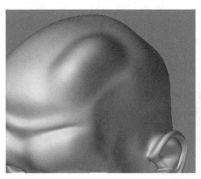

Figure 11-34

Standard Dot (StdDot)

The Standard Dot option is the same as the Standard option but works with one dot at a time.

Inflat

Inflat causes the vertices to move outward along their own surface normals. It can be adjusted with the depth of Z intensity slider.

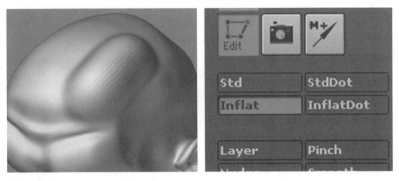

Figure 11-35

InflatDot

The InflatDot option is the same as Inflate but works with one dot at a time.

Nudge

The Nudge tool pushes the vertices in the direction you drag the cursor. Be careful when using this tool if you plan to export the displacement map since most 3D applications will have a hard time trying to reproduce the exact effect of this tool when reading the displacement map.

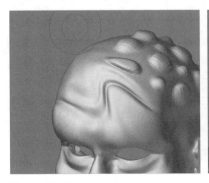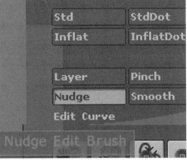

Figure 11-36

Morph

The Morph tool is enabled when you store a morph target. You use it as reference when you paint.

In this quick example we'll store the bare head by clicking the StoreMT button inside the Morph Target sub-menu of the Tool menu.

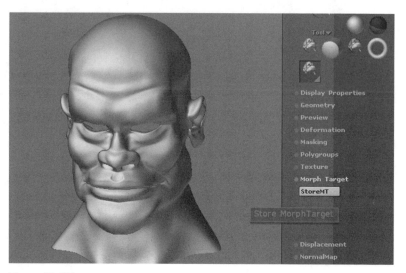

Figure 11-37

Then we can tweak our changes and use the Morph tool to get back to the original shape (stored by using the StoreMT button).

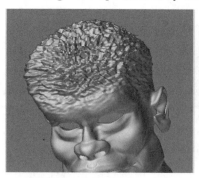 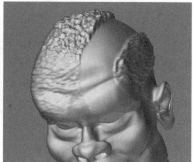

Figure 11-38

Layer

Layer sculpts the mesh to the predetermined value of the Z intensity slider. The value won't change until you release the mouse and click again.

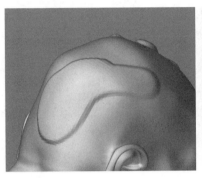 

Figure 11-39

Pinch

Pinch pushes the selected vertices toward their center, which is ideal for crisp edges. Again, be careful when using this tool if you are going to export your low-poly mesh with a displacement map to another 3D package because most 3D applications will have a hard time trying to correctly guess the Pinch value in the displacement map

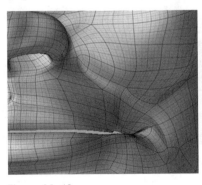 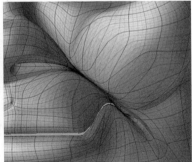

Figure 11-40

Smooth

The Smooth tool relaxes the mesh, blurs the displacement map, and smoothes rough and sharp areas of the mesh.

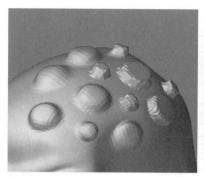 

Figure 11-41

Edit Curve

The Edit Curve option in the transform tools allows you to sculpt different shapes for the relief and even add noise. Figures 11-42 to 11-44 shows examples of using the Edit Curve option.

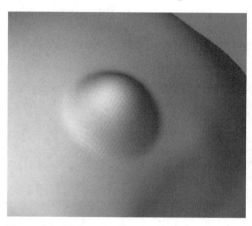 

Figure 11-42: Standard curve.

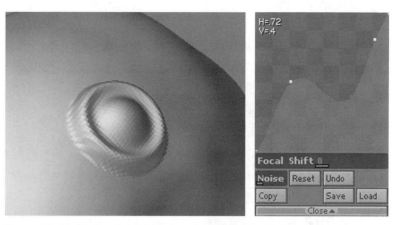

Figure 11-43: Notice the difference when the curve is changed.

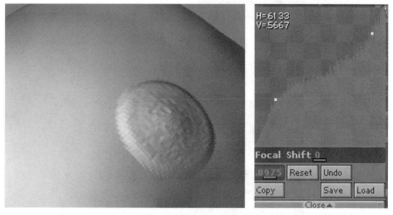

Figure 11-44: You can automatically add some random noise to the brush.

Symmetry

ZBrush allows you to sculpt and alter the geometry with three different symmetry axes.

Figure 11-45

Figure 11-46 shows three different symmetry orientations.

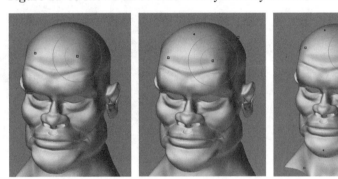

Figure 11-46: From left to right, X axis symmetry, X+Y axis symmetry, and X+Y+Z axis symmetry.

Projection Master

With Projection Master you can paint the displacement with a very fine level of detail. You can't rotate the mesh inside Projection Master, but you can use any of the 2D, 2.5D, and 3D tools to paint over the mesh.

Figure 11-47

Projection Master has the following options:

▶ **Colors**: Projection Master will pick up any color we add to the mesh.

▶ **Shaded** and **Material**: Projection Master will pick any shading and material setting added to the mesh.

▶ **Double Sided**: Projection Master will perform modifications on both the front and back of the polygons that are facing the camera.

▶ **Fade**: Projection Master will perform a fading of the brush as the polygon's normals are going away from the camera.

▶ **Deformation**: Projection Master will pick up any displacement information you add to the mesh.

▶ **Normalized**: This option performs the displacement along each polygon's normals. When this option is turned off, the displacement will be performed according to the Z axis canvas toward the viewer.

2D and 2.5D Tools to Use with Projection Master

With ZBrush you can directly paint displacement values into the mesh to save with the texture.

There are several alpha brushes inside the alpha palette that you can use alone or in combination. ZBrush also allows you to import your own alpha brushes.

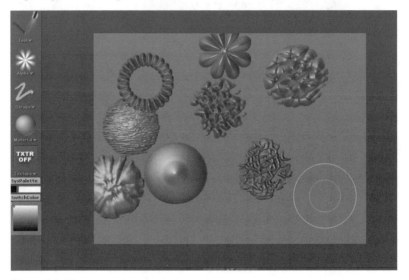

Figure 11-48

To take full advantage of the alpha brushes, we need to know the properties and the values we can change and their effects. The tool determines which kind of brush we'll use, and each has its own properties. The tools for 2D and 2.5D can be found mainly in the first row (see Figure 11-50), like simple brush, alpha brush, eraser, hook, and so on. Figure 11-49 shows a default brush.

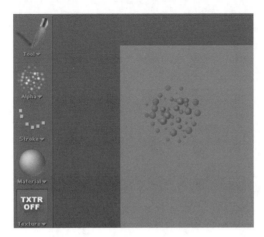

Figure 11-49

The stroke controls the instance and spacing during the painting process. Take a look at the following examples.

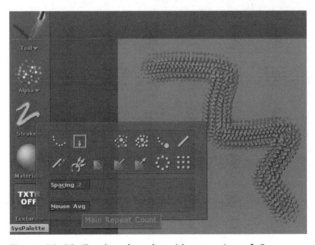

Figure 11-50: Freehand stroke with a spacing of .2.

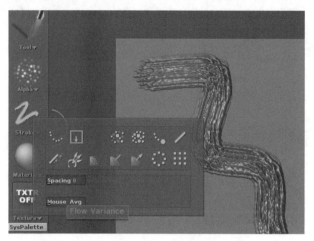

Figure 11-51: Freehand stroke with a spacing of 0.

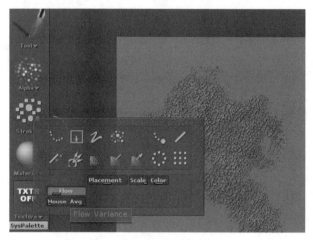

Figure 11-52: Spray stroke with flow of .25.

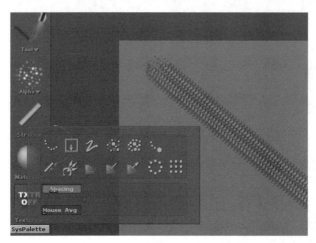

Figure 11-53: Line stroke. ZBrush traces a straight line using the selected spacing settings.

Once we've finished the painting process we can pick up the painting by pressing G or by opening the Projection Master again and pressing the Pick Up Now button.

UV and Displacement Map Settings

ZBrush also contains options for UV mapping. By default, if your imported mesh has UV coordinates, ZBrush will respect them and not modify the UV.

Figure 11-54

Figure 11-55 shows a UV exported from another 3D package with cylindrical mapping.

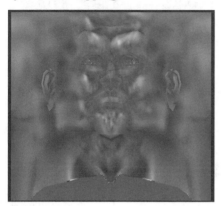

Figure 11-55

ZBrush offers two unique UV mapping methods: Group UV Tiles and Adaptive UV Tiles.

Adaptive UV Tiles will take the polygons that make up the mesh and paste them side by side, based on size. This results in as little distortion as possible but may be difficult to edit the texture in other 2D painting programs.

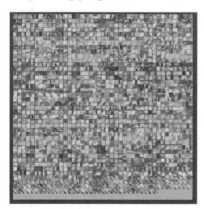

Figure 11-56: Adaptive UV Tiles.

Group UV Tiles will do nearly the same as Adaptive UV Tiles, except that it will keep the poly group as close as possible, which will make it a bit easier to read and understand when opening it from another 2D painting program.

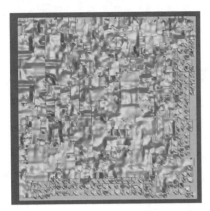

Figure 11-57: Group UV Tiles.

Grabbing and Exporting Displacement Maps

Once you have finished the process of sculpting, you must take the painted displacement map and export it to another package in order to read and render the map generated by ZBrush.

To create a displacement map, we must be at subdivision level 1 (Shift+D) in the Geometry submenu.

Figure 11-58

Then hit the Create DispMap button in the Displacement submenu of the Tool menu.

Figure 11-59

Notice that the displacement is generated and stored in the alpha palette.

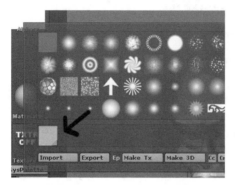

Figure 11-60

Now we can hit the Make Tx button and it will also be available in the Texture menu.

Before the export, be sure to take a look at the results. Fill the actual layer with the generated displacement map by hitting the FillLayer button.

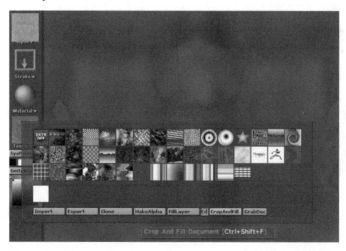

Figure 11-61

If everything is fine, export it using the Export button on the Texture menu.

Modeling with ZSpheres

With ZBrush you can also create a base mesh instead of importing one from a 3D package. ZSphere is a tool that allows you to create a multi-limbed exoskeleton that is pretty easy to adjust and manipulate. ZSphere is usually the last tool (red ball) at the right end of the palette (by default)

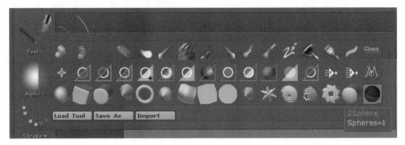

Figure 11-62

Click and drag to place a ZSphere on the canvas. Pressing T puts us in Edit mode, and the procedures for rotating, editing, and so forth are the same as for any other 3D tool (imported or not). As we move the cursor over the ZSphere in Edit mode, notice that a little circle is placed as we move and a line will be drawn to link it to the center circle. When the circle is green, it means it's in a perpendicular position, which is perfect for adding a new ZSphere; click and drag to insert a new ZSphere. Exit Draw mode so we can use the Move, Rotate, and Scale tools to perform modifications to the whole ZSphere structure.

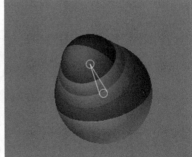

Figure 11-63

Press A to see a preview of how the mesh will look when converted to a polymesh. Press A again to turn it off. Notice that any

271

modification we make will be updated next time we activate the wireframe preview.

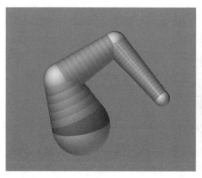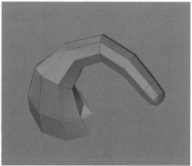

Figure 11-64

With ZSpheres you can perform three basic operations regarding the creation process:

▶ Add — To add a ZSphere to a limb, click on it with Draw mode activated.

▶ Remove — To remove a ZSphere, hold Alt and click the ZSphere with Draw mode activated.

▶ Add Magnet — To add a ZSphere magnet, choose a sphere and with Draw mode activated, Alt+Click the gray part of the limb.

Figure 11-65 shows four segments at the left. The right image shows the same object after two ZSpheres have been deleted.

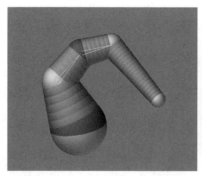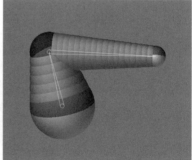

Figure 11-65

For this quick magnets example we create two symmetrical lateral horns for our character with ZSpheres.

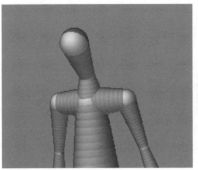

Figure 11-66

In Figure 11-67 the image on the left shows our preview mesh. When we Alt+Click in Draw mode and activate the gray part of the horn, the ZSphere becomes ZMagnets, and we can see the influence of the magnets when we activate the Preview mode (press the A key).

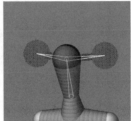

Figure 11-67

We can also carve the mesh using ZSpheres to apply a subtraction effect on the mesh, as shown in Figure 11-68.

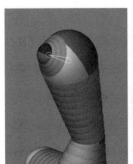

Figure 11-68: Left, the ZSphere is placed. Center, the ZSphere is pushed back until it enters the root ZSphere. Right, using Preview mode we can see that this process created a hole in our mesh that is topologically correct.

273

Once we've finished creating our ZSphere structure, we can press A again for a final preview and then hit Make Polymesh 3D under the Tool menu. A new copy of the polymesh will be created so you can clean the canvas (Ctrl+N), redraw the new copy, and start editing.

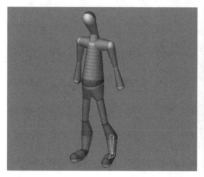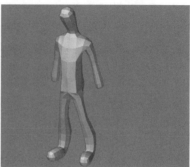

Figure 11-69

MultiMarkers

MultiMarkers are used to combine two or more pieces of geometry into one to be redrawn onto the canvas.

For this MultiMarkers exercise, first we import the ogre head we created in Chapter 10. Then we place it on the canvas and, before marking its position, adjust the options.

Figure 11-70 shows the Show, Tool, Draw, Position, and Normal options selected.

Figure 11-70

Press the Mark Object Position button in the right-click menu.

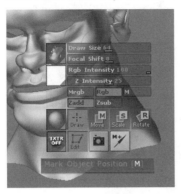

Figure 11-71

Or just press the M button.

Figure 11-72

The head position is marked and we can now add more objects. For this exercise we create a cone primitive and position it on the forehead. ZBrush asks if you want to switch or not; choose yes. Notice that ZBrush automatically adjusts the base of the object according to the surface's normal. We mark the cone position again and take a snapshot.

Figure 11-73

Move the cone to repeat the procedure. You can do this as many times as you want to and use another primitive or an imported mesh.

Once finished, we can convert it to polymesh 3D using the Make Polymesh button in the Modifiers submenu under the Tool menu.

Figure 11-74

With the tool done we can save it to use later or export to another application. We can use the tool inside ZBrush to add as many copies of the object as needed.

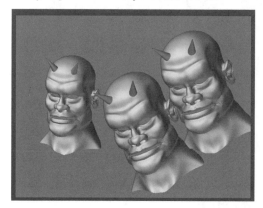

Figure 11-75

Unified Skin

The Unified Skin tool is found in the Tool menu. Unified Skin rebuilds the actual object and tries to correct the hard edges, especially the results of the MultiMarker tool. Figure 11-76 shows a polymesh object before and after applying Unified Skin.

Figure 11-76

Unified Skin has a few parameters that control the amount of smoothness and level of resolution. Be aware that a high resolution means a higher number of polygons.

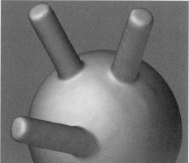

Figure 11-77

ZBrush Sculpting Workflow

In this chapter we introduced you to the basics of ZBrush sculpting. If you are in doubt about a certain button or function in ZBrush, hold Ctrl and move the cursor over the button; a brief explanation of the button's function will appear. To learn more about ZBrush techniques, you may want to look at the documentation and help files.

Figure 11-78 shows the basic workflow when using ZBrush.

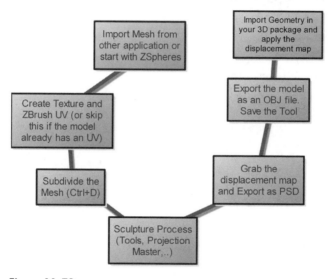

Figure 11-78

Useful Links for ZBrush

Here are some helpful sites for information about ZBrush:

www.pixologic.com — Official ZBrush developer's site.

http://www.zbrushcentral.com/ — Official forum/discussion group of ZBrush.

www.cgtalk.com — World's largest computer graphics discussion forum; they have a ZBrush forum, as well as a modeling forum and application-specific forums.

Shortcuts to Remember

Press **Alt** and **click** outside to frame an object.

Hold **Ctrl**, then press and release **Shift** (red selection) to hide everything inside the selection marquee.

Hold **Ctrl**, then **Shift** (green selection) to hide everything outside the rectangle marquee.

Hold **Ctrl+Shift**, then click outside to unhide all.

Hold **Ctrl+Alt** to unmask the selection.

Point select allows you to hide/unhide everything the selection touches.

Hold **Ctrl** to mask the selection.

Ctrl+click anywhere to invert the selection.

Chapter 12

Cartoon Modeling

Subdivision Applied to Cartoon Modeling

All the information presented in Chapter 3 about the behavior of the geometry during the subdivision process is crucial when modeling cartoon characters as long as we use a low-poly cage to model the object. In this quick exercise we discuss techniques to use when creating a rough model of a cartoon body.

Using the same technique applied to the human female body, we use half of a box and start shaping the arm from the top polygon.

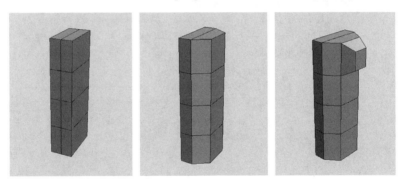

Figure 12-1

After a few extrusions and scaling, we have the arm ready and we can start extruding the leg using the same process.

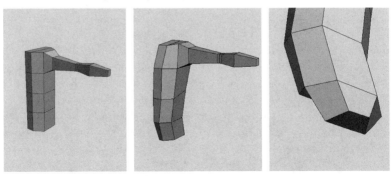

Figure 12-2

After a few extrusions and some tweaking, the torso, arm, and leg are finished.

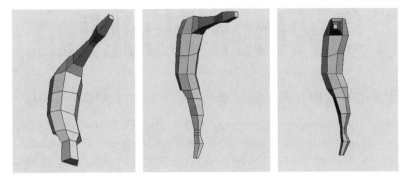

Figure 12-3

Then we start extruding down the polygon that will serve as the base for the foot.

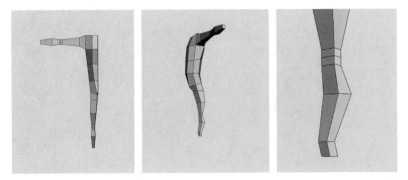

Figure 12-4

Notice that all the polygons for this character are quad and pretty simple.

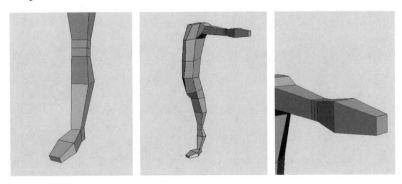

Figure 12-5

We start extruding the wrist a couple of times so we can have a nice deformation, and then extrude and cut to define the base for the fingers. This character will have only three fingers plus the thumb.

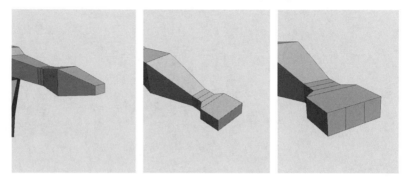

Figure 12-6

We extrude the fingers as shown below and use the same process to start creating the thumb.

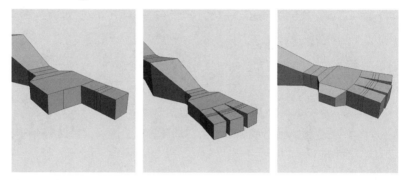

Figure 12-7

Be sure to avoid the big n-gon on the hand, as it will produce undesirable results.

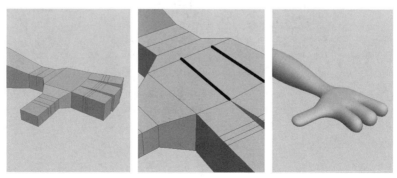

Figure 12-8

Extrude the neck polygon two times.

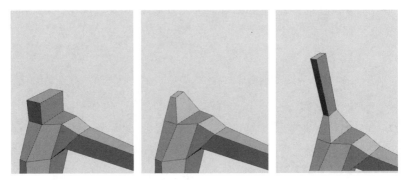

Figure 12-9

Cut the extruded polygon and reshape the vertices to conform to a head shape.

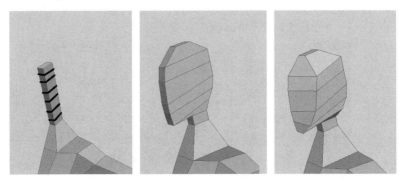

Figure 12-10

Delete the middle polygons so we can weld a mirrored side.

Figure 12-11

The result of this exercise is a simple poly cage for a basic cartoon character.

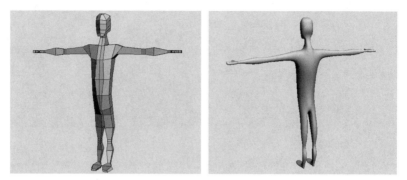

Figure 12-12

Exercise: Cartoon Head 1

Figure 12-13 shows the reference sketch we will use to create a cartoon head in this exercise.

Figure 12-13: Reference sketch for cartoon head.

For this lesson we start with a single polygon, just as we did when modeling the female head. After placing it correctly, we start extruding the edge to conform to the eye polygon ring.

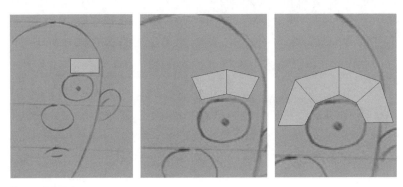

Figure 12-14

With the first ring completed, adjust the shape to fit the eye and expand the lateral polygon by extruding the edge.

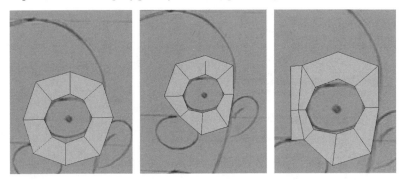

Figure 12-15

Extrude the polygons to create the forehead and the scalp.

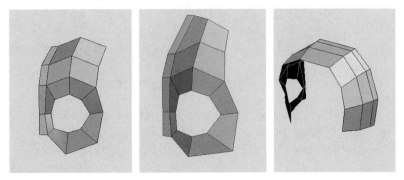

Figure 12-16

Then adjust the shape to match the reference sheet.

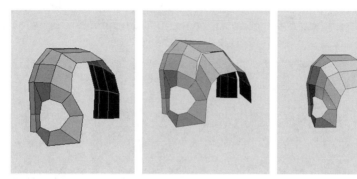

Figure 12-17

We close the upper part of the head by extruding the edge and welding the vertices as shown below.

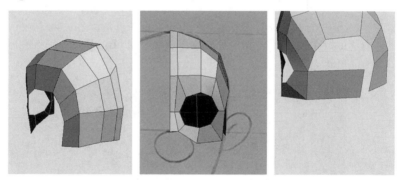

Figure 12-18

We now have a hole that we can easily repair by using the Cap tool and cutting the marked areas. Notice that everything is quad and we can now start extruding as shown at the right in Figure 12-19.

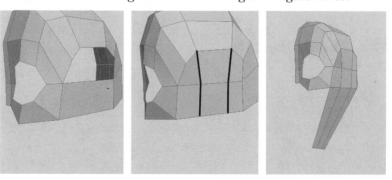

Figure 12-19

It's important to always check the proportions of the polygons extruded or created against the reference sheet as we extrude and stretch our polygons during the modeling process. Cut the marked areas and reshape according to the reference.

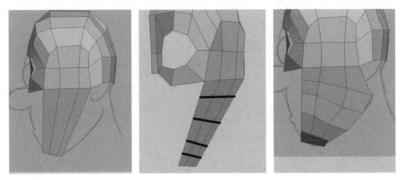

Figure 12-20

In Figure 12-21, notice the main line flow has already been established for the head and all we have to do is follow those established lines.

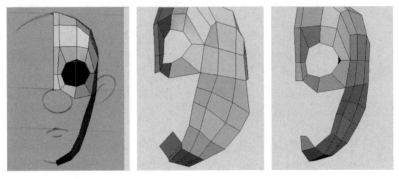

Figure 12-21

Notice that all the polygons fit perfectly as we extrude the edges and weld the vertices.

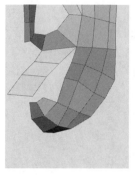
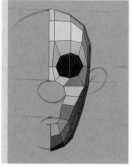
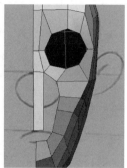

Figure 12-22

After finishing this step, the base of the head is done.

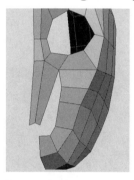

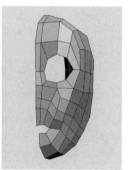

Figure 12-23

Complete the neck area by extruding the polygons and welding the vertices.

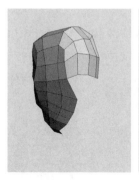
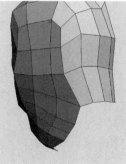
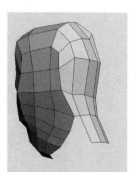

Figure 12-24

Now we have the base head and neck complete. From this step we can start increasing definition and refining our cartoon character.

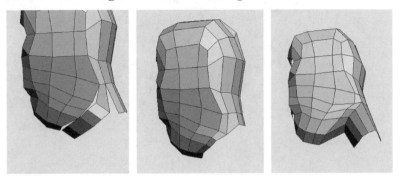

Figure 12-25

Be sure to check often how the wireframe is fitting the reference sheet.

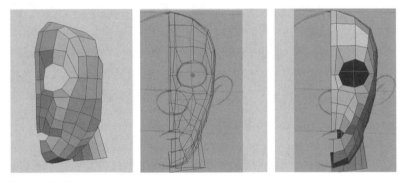

Figure 12-26

Extrude the upper edges of the eye socket border and start cutting the marked edges for finer control.

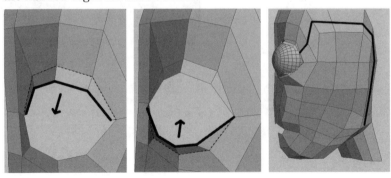

Figure 12-27

Cut the marked edges shown at left and center in Figure 12-28 and remove the dashed line shown at the right.

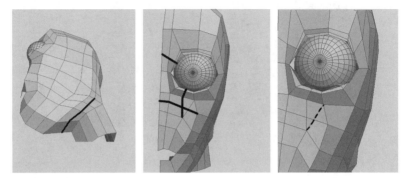

Figure 12-28

Keep the marked edge shown below at left and add the edges shown in the center. This is a continuous cut from the left figure that will avoid unfinished cuts.

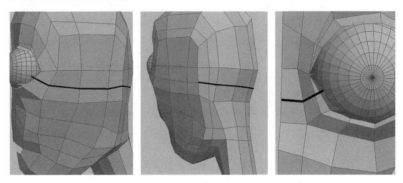

Figure 12-29

While you're tweaking, be sure to subdivide the mesh and turn back to level 0 of subdivision for a finer adjustment of the placement of the eyeball and its relationship with the skin.

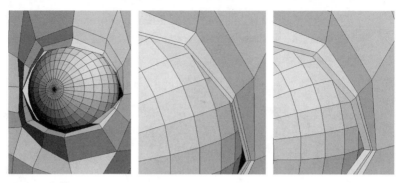

Figure 12-30

Notice that the closer edges are required to hold the tension on the skin around the eyeball.

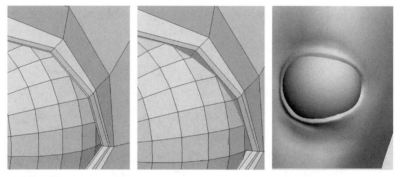

Figure 12-31

Figure 12-32 shows wire mesh and subdivided versions of the cartoon head with the eyes complete.

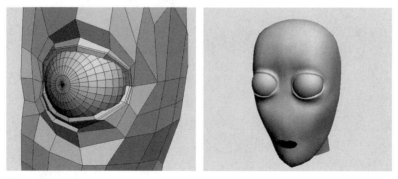

Figure 12-32

For the nose we select the marked polygons.

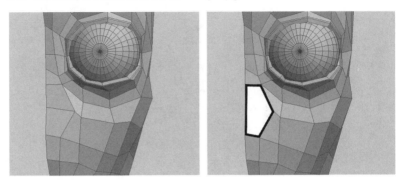

Figure 12-33

Extrude the polygons up and remove the polygons in the middle to avoid problems when we mirror this half of the head and weld the vertices.

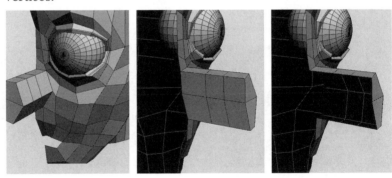

Figure 12-34

Figure 12-35 shows wire mesh and subdivided versions of the head with the nose complete.

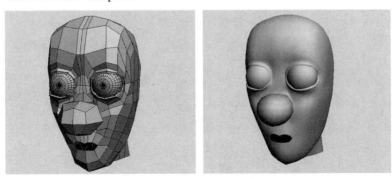

Figure 12-35

Add some edges below the mouth area to define the chin and jaw.

Figure 12-36

Now it's time to create edge loops around the mouth to hold the tension. In Figure 12-37, notice that the image in the center has a triangle at the corner of the mouth. This is a problem since the area is important for deformation. There's a quick way to solve this: Cut the marked area at the right of the figure.

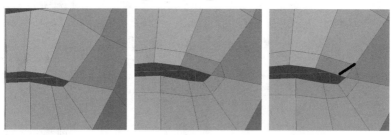

Figure 12-37

Then remove the old dashed line (shown below at left) and notice that everything is quad again. Cut a few more edges following the flow of the mouth.

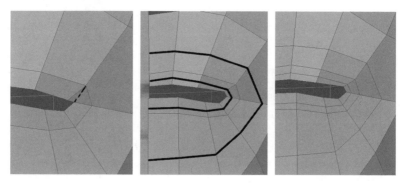

Figure 12-38

With the extra edges created, we can define the lips.

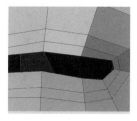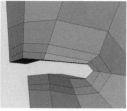

Figure 12-39

The subdivided version of the head is shown below at left. We now turn to the ear. Select the marked polygons.

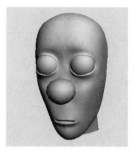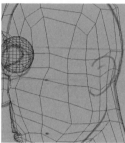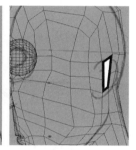

Figure 12-40

Extrude the polygons a little bit, then weld the marked vertices and extrude again as shown at the center and right in Figure 12-41.

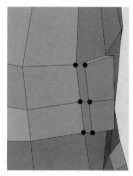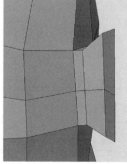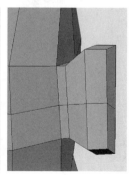

Figure 12-41

After finishing the extrusion, we need to reshape the ear to avoid having a flat ear.

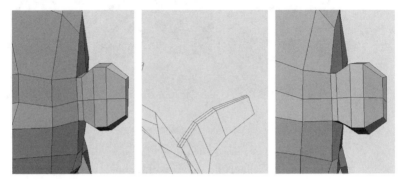

Figure 12-42

The base of the ear is done. Cut the marked edges and push back the marked vertices as shown at the right in Figure 12-43.

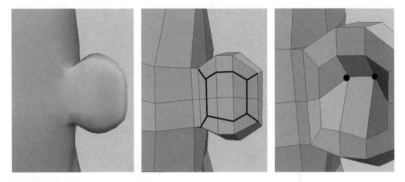

Figure 12-43

Cut the marked edges to produce the base of the polygons that will be the ear hole, then select them and extrude in.

Figure 12-44

Figure 12-45 shows the completed cartoon head.

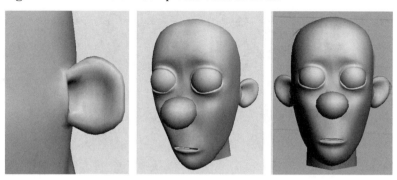

Figure 12-45

Exercise: Cartoon Body 1

In this lesson we are creating a cartoon body and adding detail to it. Figure 12-46 shows the reference sketch we will use in this exercise.

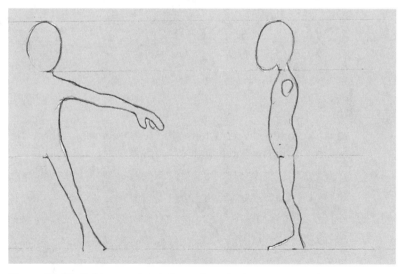

Figure 12-46: Reference sketch for cartoon body.

We start by placing a box and aligning it in the front and side views.

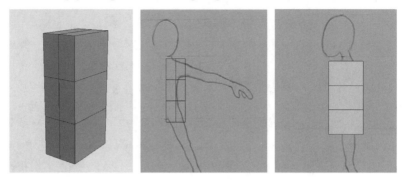

Figure 12-47

From the top view, we reshape the shoulder area accordingly.

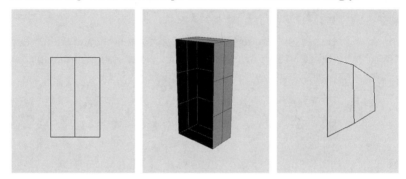

Figure 12-48

Make sure the shape matches the reference from all the views before cutting and adding more edges.

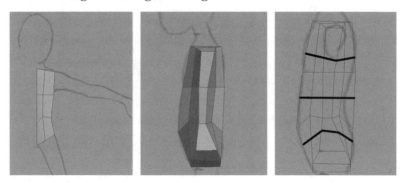

Figure 12-49

The torso is complete and it is time to work on the limbs.

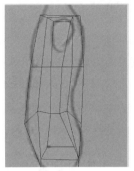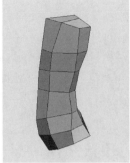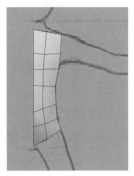

Figure 12-50

Select the marked polygon and extrude out to create the arm.

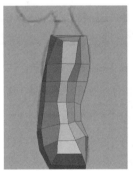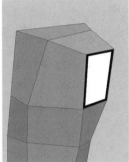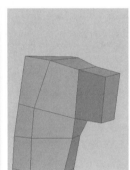

Figure 12-51

More cuts are needed to provide finer control for the arm. Continue extruding for the arm, but watch the reference sheet carefully.

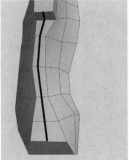

Figure 12-52

With the arm completely extruded, we can start adding more detail to create the leg. Notice the extra edges added in Figures 12-53 and 12-54 will allow for a perfect eight-sided n-gon for the leg.

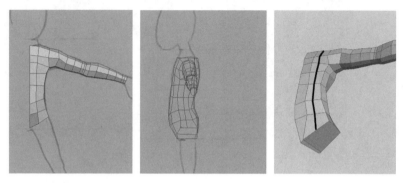

Figure 12-53

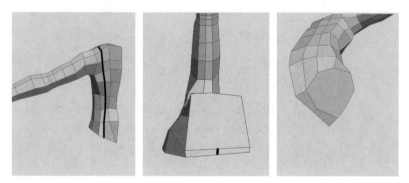

Figure 12-54

Select the marked polygon and start extruding down until you get the entire leg done and ready for the tweaking process.

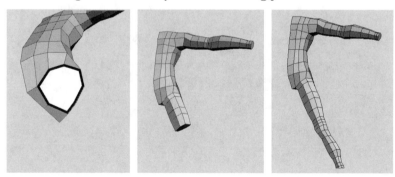

Figure 12-55

Continue extruding the polygons to follow the flow of the leg and create the foot.

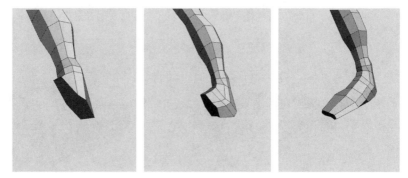

Figure 12-56

Figure 12-57 shows the complete cartoon body.

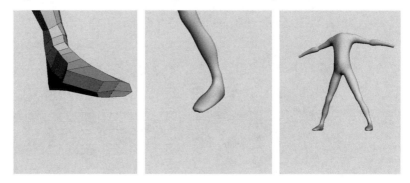

Figure 12-57

Exercise: Cartoon Hand 1

To start modeling the hand, we take a box and reshape the area near the wrist.

Figure 12-58

Then we extrude the polygons of the base of the thumb.

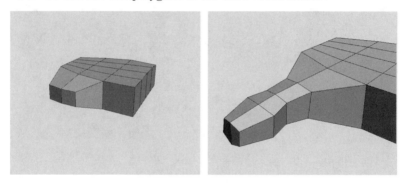

Figure 12-59

Figure 12-60 shows the extruded thumb and fingers from the perspective and top views.

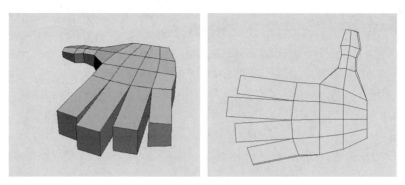

Figure 12-60

Cut the marked areas for animation deformation.

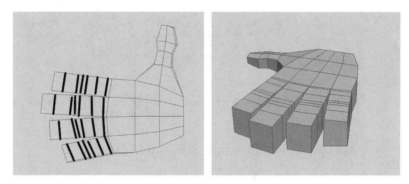

Figure 12-61

Figure 12-62 shows the subdivided and wire mesh hand.

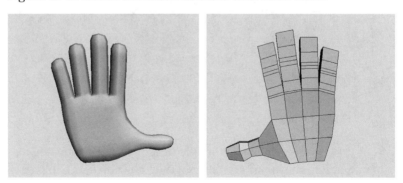

Figure 12-62

Exercise: Cartoon Head 2

This is a second example of a cartoon head. Figure 12-63 shows the reference sketch for this exercise.

Figure 12-63: Reference sketch for the cartoon head.

This time we begin with a sphere since the concept shape is pretty spherical. Start with a single sphere that has eight segments and delete one lateral half and the lower half. We end up with a mesh like that shown at the right in Figure 12-64.

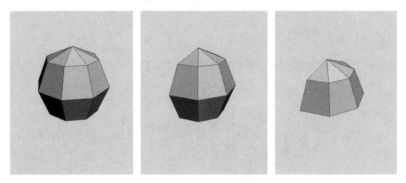

Figure 12-64

Place the polygon so it fits the reference and remove the dashed lines as shown in the center of the following figure to preserve the quad structure of the polygons.

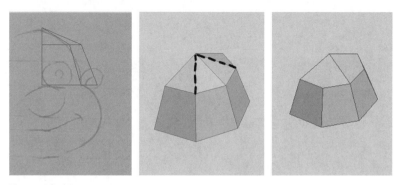

Figure 12-65

Next we place another sphere and delete half, as shown below, then remove the dashed lines.

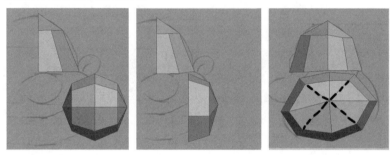

Figure 12-66

Merge the vertices as shown below.

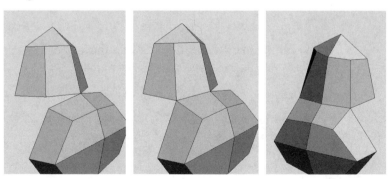

Figure 12-67

Now we extrude the edge, weld the vertices, and close the shape, both in the front and the back.

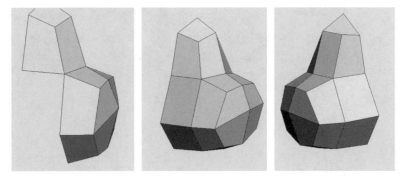

Figure 12-68

With the base form of the head finished, we can start cutting to add more detail and control.

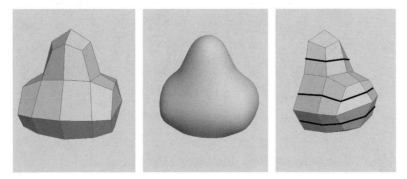

Figure 12-69

As you cut the marked areas, notice that the added edges provide more tension but the shape doesn't get rounder.

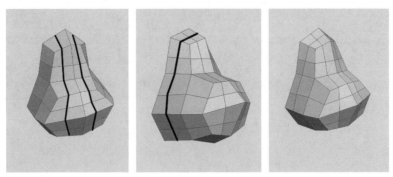

Figure 12-70

The shape is still a little too sharp, as shown at the left in Figure 12-71. To get a rounder shape we must move the vertices manually.

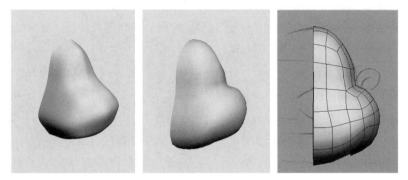

Figure 12-71

We create another low-poly sphere with eight segments, place it where the nose goes, and remove the dashed lines.

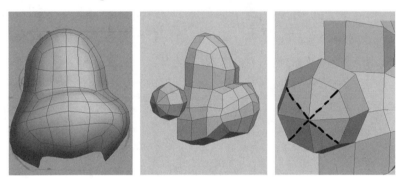

Figure 12-72

Make a hole on the back of the nose sphere and cut the marked area to improve the tension area near the hole's edges.

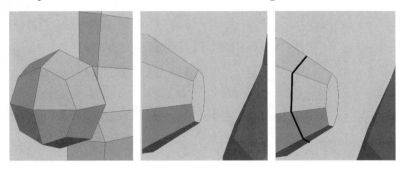

Figure 12-73

Cut the marked areas and delete the n-gon created by this process, then attach the sphere and start welding. Don't forget to delete half of the nose.

Figure 12-74

Now we start cutting the marked areas to form the base of the eye.

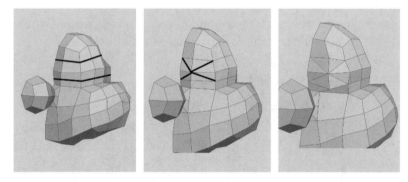

Figure 12-75

Cut the marked ring (below, left) and delete the internal polygons (below, right).

Figure 12-76

To define the geometry around the eye, place a sphere in the area for reference and to model around.

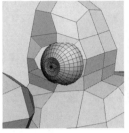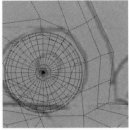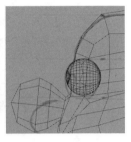

Figure 12-77

Continue cutting the geometry to increase the control around the sphere. Then select the border edges and chamfer.

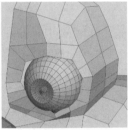

Figure 12-78

Select the border edges and extrude them again, then move forward and chamfer when getting closer to where the eyelid should be. Start extruding and scaling in.

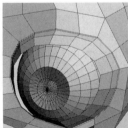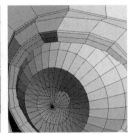

Figure 12-79

The image at the left of Figure 12-80 shows the subdivided version of the model at the current step. The image in the center shows the wireframe, and the image at the right shows the wireframe from the front view. Notice that the edges of the mouth already match the reference sheet.

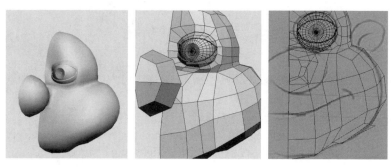

Figure 12-80

Next we can start modeling the mouth. Cut the marked areas shown at the left and center of Figure 12-81, then select the edges and chamfer them.

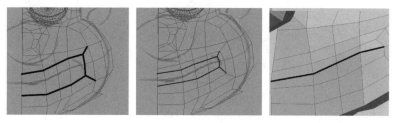

Figure 12-81

The polygon generated by the chamfer process will be deleted. Select the vertices at the corner of the mouth and push them back with a soft modifier until they match the reference.

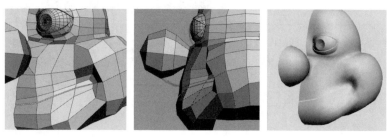

Figure 12-82

To model the ear we need to select the marked polygons and extrude, as shown in Figure 12-83.

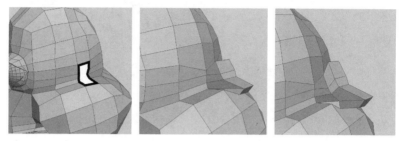

Figure 12-83

After a few extrusions and reshaping we are closer to the final shape.

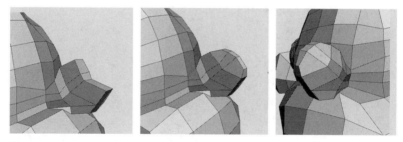

Figure 12-84

Figure 12-85 shows wire mesh and subdivided versions of the ear.

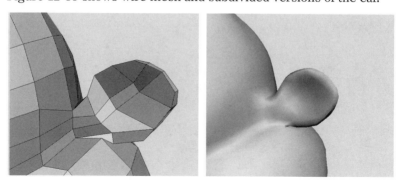

Figure 12-85

Cut the marked area shown below.

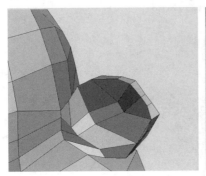 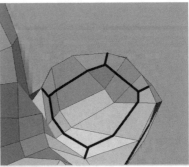

Figure 12-86

Moving the vertices in the center of the ear back a little bit gives us the final look of this cartoon ear.

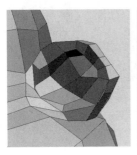 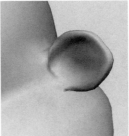 

Figure 12-87

Exercise: Cartoon Body 2

For this cartoon body exercise we move to a bigger body. By mastering the two generic forms — thin and fat — you will get a good understanding of the procedures to model any variation based on them.

Figure 12-88 shows the reference sketch used in this cartoon body modeling exercise.

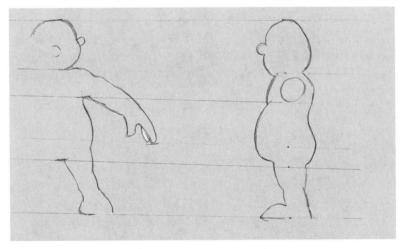

Figure 12-88: Reference sketch for the cartoon body.

Start with a box, delete half, and place it according to the reference.

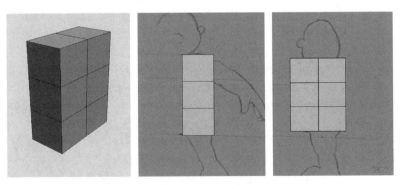

Figure 12-89

Then move the vertices in the top view. Although we don't have reference from the top view, we can still reshape the mesh to fit the rest of the reference as closely as possible.

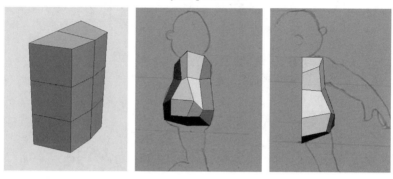

Figure 12-90

Cut the edges marked in Figure 12-91.

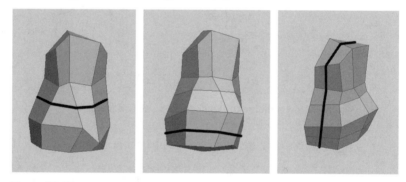

Figure 12-91

Make another cut so the hole for the arm is eight-sided, select the internal polygons, and extrude a little bit.

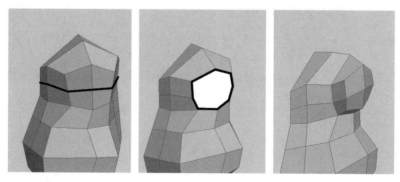

Figure 12-92

Extrude the arm until we reach the wrist position, as shown below. Then cut the areas marked at the right to produce the base edges for the leg extrusion.

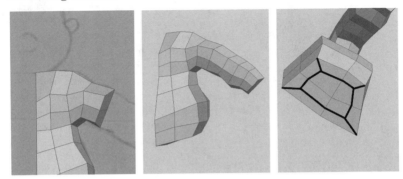

Figure 12-93

Select the marked polygons and extrude down a couple of times until you reach the spot where the foot will be attached.

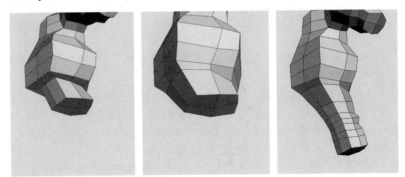

Figure 12-94

For the hand we start with a box, cut the middle edges of each finger, and reshape, as shown in the center image below. We start the finger with a cylinder and push the center vertex forward.

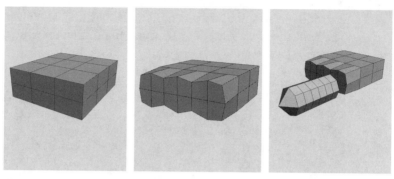

Figure 12-95

From the side view we can move the vertices to conform to the finger shape. Cut the marked edges, and the finger is done.

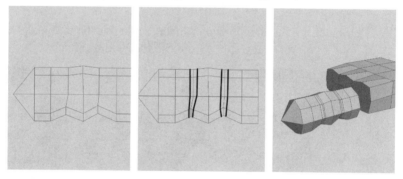

Figure 12-96

After two levels of subdivision we can see how the finger will look, as shown below on the left. Going back to level 0 of subdivision we can make two more copies of the finger and start joining them one at a time.

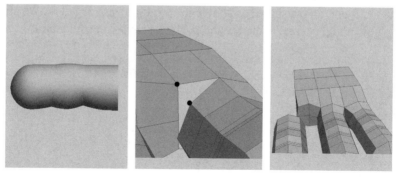

Figure 12-97

Figure 12-98 shows a subdivided version of the hand at the current step (left). Select the marked polygons, extrude forward, and scale down.

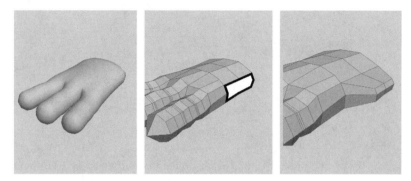

Figure 12-98

Before continue with the extrusion we need to make the thumb a little rounder and continue extruding until we get the whole thumb done. In looking at the thumb from the side, we can clearly see that we must rearrange the vertices a little bit.

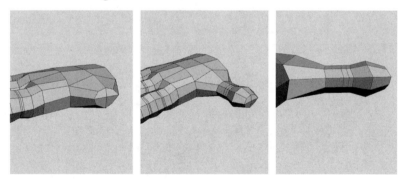

Figure 12-99

Notice the difference in the thumb after some tweaking (below, left). The images at the center and right of Figure 12-100 show the wire mesh and subdivided versions of the hand.

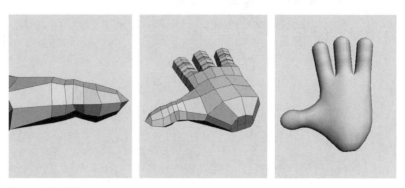

Figure 12-100

We need to continue the discontinued edges to avoid unnecessary tension in certain areas, so we cut the edges marked below.

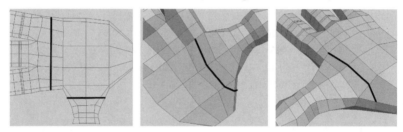

Figure 12-101

Make some more cuts.

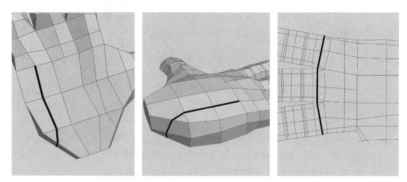

Figure 12-102

Cut the marked edges for a cartoon hand that has a bit more detail.

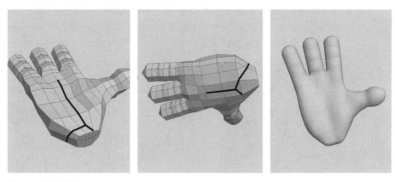

Figure 12-103

With the hand finished, we can move on to attach the hand to the arm and take care to remove all the triangulation in the wrist area.

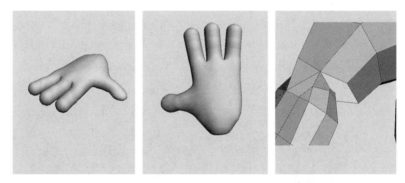

Figure 12-104

When we're finished with the welding process, we can continue cutting to avoid discontinued edges on the arm.

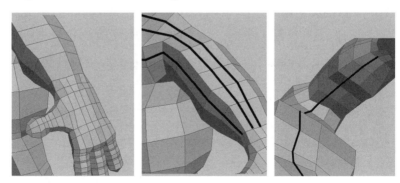

Figure 12-105

This process increases the number of edges, which require more attention to the tension as they often generate sharpness when you should have round limbs. So be careful and check out the subdivided version from time to time.

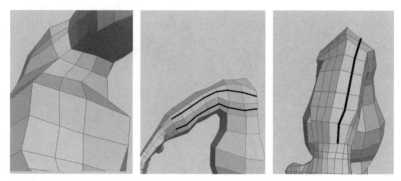

Figure 12-106

Figure 12-107 shows the body with hands attached. Now we can start modeling the foot. We start with an eight-segment sphere and squash it a little bit (below, right).

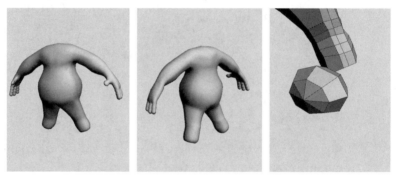

Figure 12-107

Remove the back polygons as shown at the left, select the border edges, and extrude forward until you reach the heel area (center). Then cap the hole.

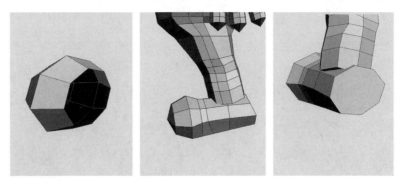

Figure 12-108

Cut the marked area to avoid the tension that the n-gon will generate.

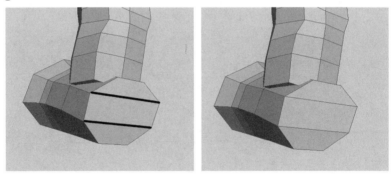

Figure 12-109

From the top view we start cutting based on the scheme discussed in Chapter 3.

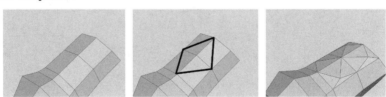

Figure 12-110

Select and delete the marked polygons.

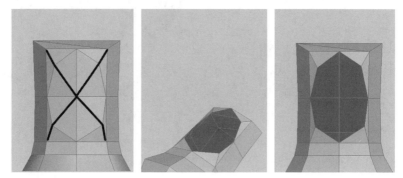

Figure 12-111

Then merge the foot and the leg using the same process we used to attach and weld the limbs previously, and make a few extra cuts.

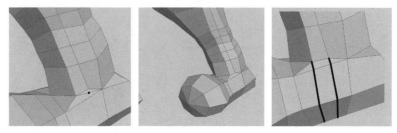

Figure 12-112

Now try to remove all the triangles and keep everything as much quad as possible, as this is an important deformation area.

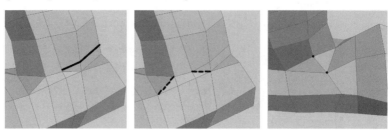

Figure 12-113

The foot is almost complete; it just needs a few tweaks.

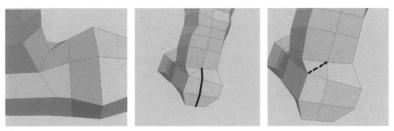

Figure 12-114

Remove the dashed lines, and the foot is done.

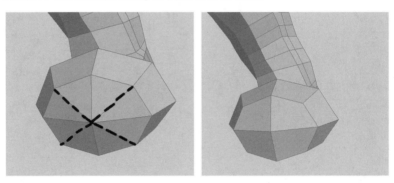

Figure 12-115

Figure 12-116 shows half of the body (with foot and hand) and the mirrored subdivided version.

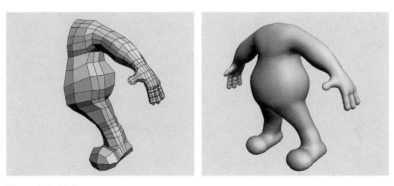

Figure 12-116

Cartoon modeling permits the modeling of a variety of shapes and forms. With polygonal modeling you can achieve finer results regarding mesh topology and deformation when animating, from stick-man-like characters to complex, fat, and multi-limbed characters. In this chapter we covered the basic topology for two generic characters that can be used to provide the base for any kind of cartoon character you may need to model in 3D.

Chapter 13

Modeling for Games

3D models for games are commonly referred to as low-poly objects since they have a limited polygonal count that varies according to the power of the 3D graphics card and the real-time 3D game engine. The continual increase in the graphics processing capacity of video game systems and computers directly affects the resolution of 3D models for games.

3D engines have a limited amount of processing power with which to display — in a minimum of 30 fps — all the textures, 3D animated models, scenery, sprites, and enemies, along with computing all the background events running in a game. That's why a 3D game modeler should be aware of the number of polygons used by the game's objects and characters. But with the power of game engines constantly increasing, why should you worry about the poly count? Even with the high processing capacity of game engines, the overall system must be optimized for maximum performance in a number of different PC systems (video game controllers have a standard system for computing and displaying graphics). The function of the game development team is to optimize the process and make the game run smoothly; this includes the 3D artist and the mesh resolution of the game models.

In this chapter we discuss the basics of real-time surfacing and structure regarding OpenGL display and processing.

Triangle Strips and Gouraud Shading

All the game geometry in OpenGL is decomposed into triangle strips. For example, a cube with six (quad) sides becomes triangulated with 12 sides.

Figure 13-1: Left, a simple cube primitive shown in Gouraud shading mode. Right, when the same light is decomposed into 16 colors on the surface of the cube, we can see how the light is processed and how the Gouraud shading calculates the light starting from the vertex corner.

The final quality of the object is directly related to the precision with which it is modeled and textured. The game engine is the interpreter of the 3D world, including the light, objects, textures, animation, effects, and the background programming that will run everything.

Here are some considerations for modeling using OpenGL:

▶ OpenGL will decompose the quad polygons into triangles before rasterization (rendering). It is recommended that you provide a triangulated model so you don't get unpredicted results.

▶ Avoid modeling where two triangles share an edge with another triangle, called a "T-intersection" or "T-vertex." This can cause unwanted cracks in the mesh, especially during animation.

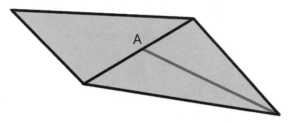

Figure 13-2: A T-intersection at point A.

▶ When viewed from outside, the orientation of the polygons of a surface should point in the same direction (clockwise or counterclockwise). This way, OpenGL will provide methods for face culling manipulation and display, which can be useful when dealing with convex surfaces and drawing the front faces and back faces of a polygonal surface.

The OpenGL documentation available at opengl.org indicates techniques about triangle-strip layouts that can speed up the OpenGL mode and save data storage space. Since most 3D applications use or allow the use of OpenGL resources with a 3D card, this information can be invaluable if you are going to model and fix triangulated geometry. If the polygonal mesh is directly generated from regular geometry such as NURBS surfaces, it is recommended that you connect the triangles into longer strips. One of the major rules about triangulation of the mesh refers to the clockwise or counterclockwise orientation of the triangle strips. The first triangle can start with either clockwise or counterclockwise winding, but the subsequent triangles must be alternated according to the orientation of the anterior triangle.

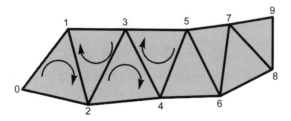

Figure 13-3: Alternated triangle strip.

A triangle-strip fan starts with the correct winding and all the subsequent triangles must point the same direction.

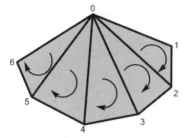

Figure 13-4: Triangle-strip fan.

When modeling regular geometry it's best to align the strips side by side as shown in Figure 13-5. Be sure to avoid the edges that can't be part of a longer strip (called "singleton strips").

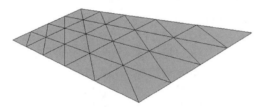

Figure 13-5: Continuous edges through a plane are ideal for regular geometry.

The Triangles Determine the Shading

Gouraud shading, which is the default in OpenGL real-time display mode and is available in most 3D game engines, is based on the vertices of the triangles as mentioned at the beginning of this chapter.

When we analyze the wireframe of the sphere and the Gouraud shading shown in Figure 13-6, we can see how the structure of the wireframe influences the final look of mesh shading.

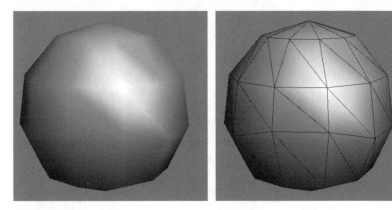

Figure 13-6

When we flip some of the edges of the triangles, we can see the result produced by the new render in the image at the left in Figure 13-7. The edge configuration has changed the final look of the shading.

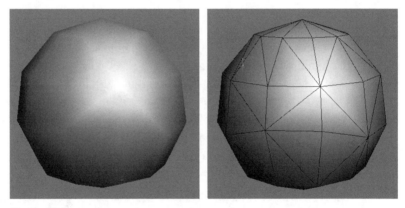

Figure 13-7

Pushing this theory further we can create complex topologies that are different for dealing with quad polygons and tri polygons. Game models are typically modeled in quad, where all the loops become clearer, and then refined in tri, if necessary. It is not recommended that you use a plug-in to do the triangulation since you'll have almost no control over the shading aspect determined by the triangulation. Be sure to keep an original file in quad so that you have a clean mesh ready if you need to go back and tweak a little more. Keep in mind that once you have triangulated your mesh it will be hard to find your edge loops and line flows.

When manipulating the triangles of the mesh, the orientation must be made according to the correct topology as much as possible. See the examples below.

When we see the mesh in faceted mode with quad polygons, it seems to be okay.

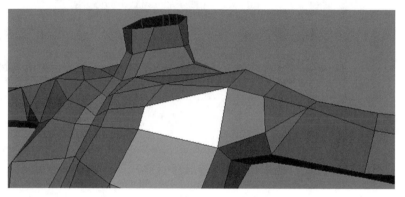

Figure 13-8

However, when we turn on the smooth Gouraud shading we can see that the shading determined by the triangle strips isn't correct for the line flow of the female body. In the deltoid area, a triangle-strip shade seems to be ripping off the deltoid and the sternocleidomastoid muscle. Remember that low-poly models cannot add too much mesh detail, so if we can tweak the triangle strips in a way that gives the impression of correct neck flow it will be well worth the effort.

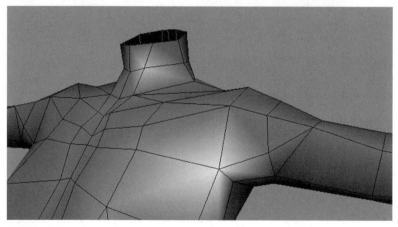

. Figure 13-9

The arrows in Figure 13-10 point out the flow of the light on the mesh surface. According to the correct anatomy and the flow of the musculature, these lines should be flipped to remove the visual impression that something is "broken" or incorrect.

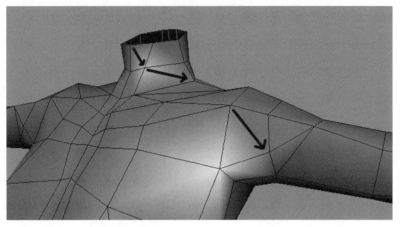

Figure 13-10

The actual musculature of the neck is opposite what is shown above.

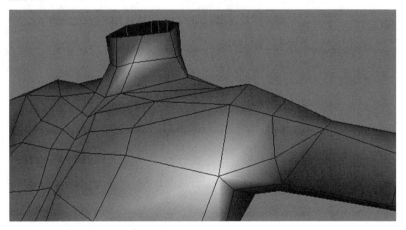

Figure 13-11

Now we've reversed some triangle edges to give the neck a more natural aspect since it now follows the correct flow of the neck musculature.

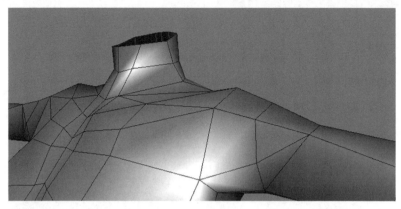

Figure 13-12

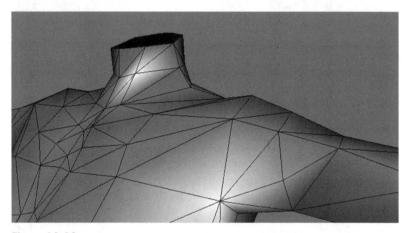

Figure 13-13

Continuity for Games

The mesh continuity for games is tied to the power of graphic processors that draw the polygons in real time. Early game systems such as Nintendo 64 used very rough quad shapes due to their low processing capacity. With Doom 3, shape edge continuity has been raised to a very acceptable quality. What is important to point out is that games use two types of meshes: high poly for cinematics, teasers, and so on, and low poly for real-time display inside the game. Continuity for high-poly models is achieved with a subdivision method, which is done automatically by the 3D application. Continuity for low-poly models is done manually, which means that you must be careful to keep the poly count below the acceptable limits of the 3D engine used.

Why Automatic Reduction Doesn't Work

Reducing the poly count with automatic tools will not work correctly because the computer cannot correctly analyze all the polygons and find the correct optimized topology for the joints and the mesh. This is extremely critical when dealing with 3D models for real-time applications and games.

Take a look at Figure 13-14. The image on the left shows a high-poly leg that is the best the computer can do with poly count optimization. As we can see, it wouldn't work for display in a game because it has too many triangles, many of which are placed incorrectly in the joints. The image at the right shows a better and cleaner scheme for a low-poly knee.

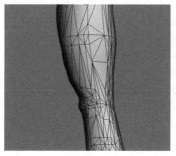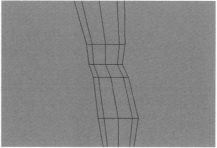

Figure 13-14

Mesh Resolution

One of the most critical aspects of low-poly character modeling is the character's joints. If the model is going to be animated, you need to remember that areas that will bend and undergo deformation must be well planned.

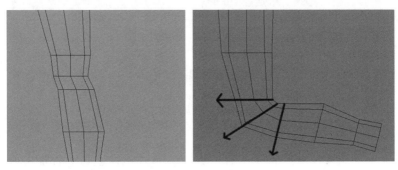

Figure 13-15: The three-span scheme for joints works in most cases and gives cleaner results.

Controlling the Poly Count

To control a character's poly count precisely you can split the complete body into parts and set limits for each part according to the needs of the character. For example, let's say you have a limit of 3,800 triangles for a character. Start by asking yourself a few questions: What are the needs of the character? How much of it will be displayed? What are the circumstances? How can mesh details be increased where necessary and simplified where they are not? What can the texture represent and what must be modeled?

Based on the answers to these questions you can set the desired proportions of the character. You have 3,800 triangles to be distributed among the head, body, hands, feet, and accessories. Focus on what is most important for representing the character as the player will actually see it inside the game.

General Tips

Limbs

If you start modeling a character's limbs from a primitive like a cylinder that closely matches the shape of a leg or an arm, be sure to tweak all the vertices in order to reduce the cylindrical regularity. Do the same for any primitive you use.

Folds

Depending on the polygonal count budget you can increase the modeling detail by adding folds that will be enhanced by the Gouraud shading.

Levels

Modeling game levels is a separate topic. A large number of engines have a level editor with its own system to build the levels, walls, doors, bridges, etc. If the engine does not provide a level editor, it likely accepts entire levels made by another 3D application. If that's the case, you may want to set up the grids and snaps for your 3D application and check the scale between those two programs. Without snapping tools, modeling a simple room can become a nightmare during alignment.

Final Tips

▶ Try to keep the poly count as low as possible for each object/character.

▶ Models for games should be clean blocked models. The objective of the modeler is to provide a good mesh for the texture artist to detail.

▶ You can manipulate the final look of the shading to some degree by flipping triangle strips.

▶ Never use polygonal reduction tools for games.

▶ Models for games should be made with polygons, not NURBS.

▶ Keep the models as clean as possible and save a copy of the object in quads before triangulating.

Conclusion

The use of polygonal modeling for multiple purposes — from organic to inorganic and from characters to objects — shown through the theoretical and practical lessons in this book is an efficient way to create digital sculptures and 3D models. The topology presented in the practical lessons using the Catmull-Clark subdivision scheme can be planned and applied to any type of object or creature you may need to model, as the structure of the actual subdivision scheme allows the software to rearrange the control points, which preserves the intended structure of the surface during the subdivision process.

In this book we also discussed the importance of good reference before starting the modeling process and the need to plan the anatomy of the model or object. We also saw that when the technical side of polygonal modeling starts to affect the balance of level of detail versus the weight of the mesh, you can use displacement at rendering time using a large number of polygons in the subdivision step to achieve details that otherwise would be difficult or impossible to make by hand.

With these foundations of polygonal modeling with a multi-resolution displacement mesh, today it is possible to make extremely complex organic characters as well as inorganic objects and complex scenes through the use of polygons.

Here are some final tips for polygonal modeling:

▶ Rotate the camera and view your object from as many angles as necessary to achieve the true volume of the mesh you are modeling.

▶ Focus on studying the basic knowledge and structure of how polygonal modeling works rather than a specific software tool, since there may be times when you may be required to use other 3D packages.

▶ Last and probably the most important advice: Computer graphics are constantly changing at a fast pace. Keep up with the major computer graphics news portals for announcements in this field.

Appendix A

3ds Max Polygonal Modeling Quick Start Guide

3ds Max allows the user to customize the user interface completely, changing shortcuts, panels, toolbars, colors, and many other functions to improve the workflow. In this appendix, we discuss how you can customize 3ds Max.

The letters in Figure A-1 correspond to the list below the figure.

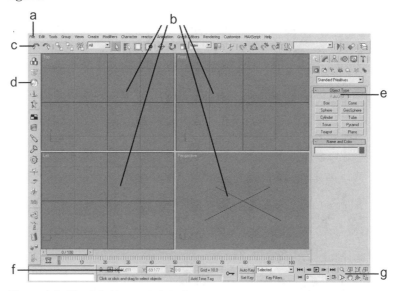

Figure A-1: The 3ds Max user interface.

a - Menus: 3ds Max main menus contain options for loading, saving, importing, and many other functions found in the Command Panel.

339

b - Viewports: 3ds Max work area.

c - Toolbar: The main area where you can find basic tools for object manipulation.

d - Docked toolbar: Toolbar that can be attached to the main window or used as a floating toolbar. By default 3ds Max has a Reactor docked toolbar.

e - Command Panel: Probably the most used panel in 3ds Max. This is where most of the options related to modeling in 3ds Max will appear.

f - Lower interface bar: Contains controls for animation.

g - Navigation and playback controls: Controls that are used to move around in 3ds Max and play the animation.

Customization

To customize your interface in 3ds Max, choose Customize from the main menu and select Customize User Interface. This will open a new window filled with options that allow you to change shortcuts and preferences, such as navigation hotkeys, tools, and menus.

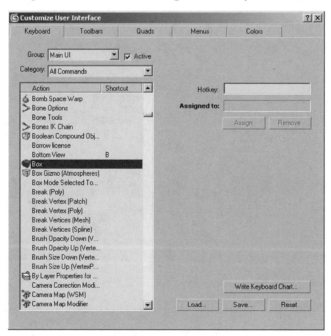

Figure A-2: Customize User Interface window.

Assigning Hotkeys

The Keyboard tab in the Customize User Interface window refers to the keyboard shortcuts. To assign a shortcut, make a selection in the Group list box, then choose from the Category list box. Place the desired shortcut in the Hotkey box and press Assign.

Creating a New Toolbar

In 3ds Max it is possible to create a new toolbar (or "shelf" as it's called in Maya) on which you can place an icon for quickly accessing tools you use often.

To create a new toolbar, go to Customize | Customize User Interface and select the Toolbars tab. When you press the New button, a new toolbar will be created. For this demonstration, name it "Modeling1," as shown in Figure A-3, and click OK. A small window will appear; click on an action in the list and drag it inside the toolbar.

Figure A-3: New Toolbar window.

Now our new toolbar has three tools: Cap Border, Bevel, and Break.

Figure A-4: Modeling1 toolbar.

If the action you selected does not have a proper icon, it will appear as text. The text will be gray when it is not available and black when it is available. If you prefer, you can create your own icons for your toolbar.

Creating Icons

Icons to be used inside 3ds Max must be in one of two resolution formats: 24x24 pixels and 16x16 pixels, plus versions in 24x24 and 16x24 pixels for a black and white mask. This means that 3ds Max will read the image file once for the color that will appear and then read the black and white image file to set the transparency of the icon.

It is recommended that you save the icons as bitmap (.bmp) files.

Be sure to correctly name your icon file. As an example, let's use "IconName" for our new icons:

IconName_24i.bmp — for the 24x24-pixel color icon
IconName_16i.bmp — for the 16x16-pixel color icon
IconName_24a.bmp — for the 24x24-pixel mask icon
IconName_16a.bmp — for the 16x16-pixel mask icon

Notice that color icons have an "i" after the number of pixels and the mask, or alpha, has an "a" to indicate it's the transparency orientation reference. The black represents what will be invisible and the white indicates what will be visible. Grayscale tones indicate semi-transparency.

Figure A-5: Icons for the color mode example.

Figure A-6: Icons for the mask/alpha example.

You can also make new icons and place them side by side to create a set of four 24x24 icons that is 96x24 pixels.

When you're done with the new icons, place them inside the discreet and Icon folders inside the UI folder on the root 3ds Max installation folder.

If you have questions about the general aspects of 3ds Max icons, be sure to check the UI\Icons folder and take a closer look at the examples there.

Now we can place the icons inside our toolbar. Right-click on the text you want to change to an icon and choose Edit Button Appearance. Select the Image Button radio button, and in the Group list box select the set of icons you've created and then choose the icon.

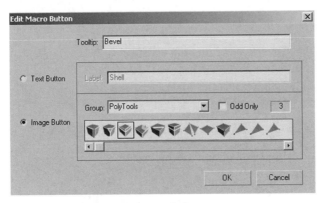

Figure A-7: Edit Macro Button window.

Be sure to take a look at the icons that discreet provides; there are a lot of icons for modeling that aren't used.

General Performance

To change viewport parameters such as the vertex dot size or backface culling at primitive creation, and to set the OpenGL or Direct3D properties of your graphic 3D card, go to Customize | Preferences in the Viewport tab.

To manage other viewport properties, right-click the viewport's label and select the Rendering Method tab. The main properties that can be changed for modeling purposes in the Rendering Method tab are Rendering Level and Rendering Options. Rendering Level changes the aspect of surface display like smooth highlights, facets, etc. Rendering Options lets you select and unselect the Force Two Sided option, which relates directly to the display of faces with flipped normals.

If you mess up the UI at any time, go to the menu item Customize | Load Custom UI Scheme and select DefaultUI.ui file. If you are satisfied with the UI scheme and want to preserve it, go to Customize | Save Custom UI Scheme and then select Customize | Lock UI Layout to prevent any accidental changes to the UI.

Navigation

The navigation tools in 3ds Max are located at the bottom right of the user interface. These tools can be accessed by pressing the buttons, but it's highly recommended that you customize shortcuts to speed up your workflow.

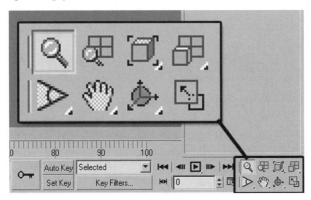

Figure A-8: The navigation tools.

Perspective and Axonometric (orthographic and isometric) views are available in 3ds Max. Perspective is most often used because it simulates the way our eyes see the world, with the correct perspective of vanishing points. Axonometric orthographic view is constrained to 90 degrees in one of the planes (top, left, right, or bottom), and Axonometric isometric is similar to CAD programs, where parallel lines remain parallel to infinity instead of converging to a vanishing point as in Perspective view.

From left to right and top to bottom, the navigation options are:

Zoom: This tool moves the view closer or farther from the objects in the active viewport.

Zoom All: Zoom closer or farther from objects in all viewports simultaneously.

Zoom Extents All: Zoom in on all objects of the screen.

Zoom Extents Selected: Zoom in on all selected objects.

Field-of-View (only in Perspective view): Control the view's width (FOV).

Pan View: Move the view by clicking and dragging.

Arc Rotate: Rotate the perspective around. The arc rotate with a white center rotates around the selection. The arc rotate with a yellow center rotates around a selected subobject.

Maximize Viewport Toggle: Resizes the active viewport to fill the space of all four viewports. Pressing the toggle again causes the viewport to go back to the previous layout scheme.

Layouts

To change the viewport layout in 3ds Max, right-click the viewport's label and choose Configure, as shown in Figure A-9. The Viewport Configuration window is displayed. Then choose the Layout tab, as shown in Figure A-10.

Figure A-9

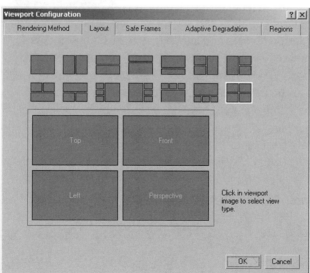

Figure A-10

In the Layout tab you can choose the layout scheme from predefined layouts and then right-click the viewport panel to select which view will be displayed. You can also change the viewport by right-clicking the viewport's label after choosing the layout.

Gizmos and Basic Manipulation

The gizmos in 3ds Max are similar to those in Maya and Softimage XSI.

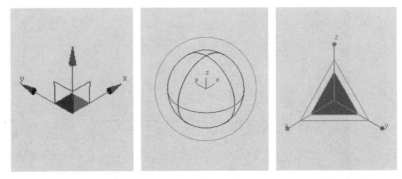

Figure A-11: From left to right, Move gizmo, Rotate gizmo, and Scale gizmo.

3ds Max introduced better gizmos in version 5, which clearly has had a positive influence in the quality and precision of selection and manipulation objects and subobjects in basic operations.

The Move tool ✛ now has the 90-degree right angle relative to the axis in three dimensions. If you select an angle, it will move locked in the two axes relative to the angle you selected.

The Gimbal Rotate tool ↻ has an intuitive way of manipulating the object and also displays precise angle rotation information while performing the operation.

The Scale tool ◼ acts like the Move tool. When selecting the middle triangle, 3ds Max will perform uniform scaling operation. When selecting an exterior transparent strip, 3ds Max will lock the scale in the two corresponding axes.

Axis

The Reference coordinate system in 3ds Max has seven options available:

Figure A-12

The local and world axis related to the object can be selected from the drop-down list in the main toolbar.

Snap

The snaps are most useful for precise modeling, architectural wall placement, or other modeling that requires perfect placement of objects along a grid system.

In 3ds Max you can choose from four types of snapping mode.

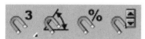

Figure A-13: Snap options.

The options are:

Snap toggle: Snaps the cursor to the grid's unit.

Angle Snap toggle: Snaps the angle at every 5 degree rotation.

Percent Snap toggle: Snaps the scale to a specific percentage.

Spinner Snap toggle: Determines the spinner value at each click.

The snap settings can be changed with the Customize | Grid and Snap Settings menu option.

Mirror/Duplicate

To duplicate objects, hold Shift and apply a transformation tool (like move, rotate, scale). The Clone Options window will appear with parameters to choose from like copy, instance, or reference and the number of copies and name for the new object.

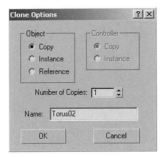

Figure A-14: Clone Options window.

To mirror an object, press the Mirror button 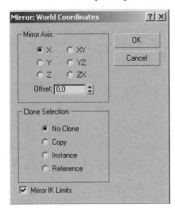.

Figure A-15: Mirror window.

The Mirror window has two main choices. The Mirror Axis area allows you to choose from one or more axes on which to perform the mirroring operation. In the Clone Selection area, you can choose whether the mirrored object will be No Clone, Copy, Instance, or Reference.

Layers

Since version 5, 3ds Max has had a nice layer system that allows the user to easily manage the objects in a scene. It is accessed with the Layer button 🖹.

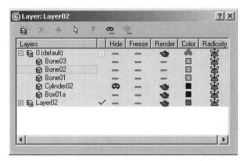

Figure A-16: The Layer window.

There are a number of buttons at the top of the Layer window.

Figure A-17

From left to right these buttons are:

Create a New Layer: Creates a new layer. To rename the new layers, double-click on the layer's name.

Delete Highlighted Empty Layers: Delete empty selected layer.

Add Selected Objects to Highlighted Layers: Add the selected object to the selected layer. When you add new objects to an empty layer, there will be a plus sign preceding the layer label. This indicates that the layer has objects inside and can be expanded.

Select Highlighted Objects and Layers: Select everything inside the selected layer.

Select Highlighted Object's Layers: Select the layer to which the selected object belongs.

Hide/Unhide All Layers: Hide and Unhide Layers toggle.

Freeze/Unfreeze All Layers: Freeze and Unfreeze layers toggle.

Pivot

Pivot can be found in the Hierarchy Panel tab. Pivots are treated like subobjects. To edit the pivot position and rotation you must access one of the options available under the Adjust Pivot rollout.

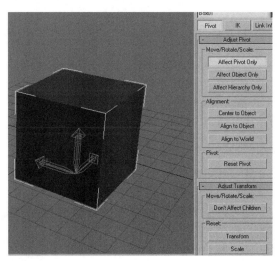

Figure A-18

Affect Pivot Only will allow you to manually adjust the pivot point. It also offers a few other options to automatically align the pivot point to the object, center the pivot point to the object's center, or world alignment.

Display Panel

In the Display Panel you will find options for hiding, unhiding, and making the selection of specific objects unavailable (freezing), as well as other display properties.

Subelements Structure

3ds Max has two ways to deal with meshes: Edit Mesh and Edit Poly. The main differences are that Edit Mesh splits the polygons into triangular faces and has a subobject foundation that is a bit different.

In Edit Mesh we have Vertex, Edge, Face, Polygon, and Element options. In Edit Poly we can work with Vertex, Edge, Border, Polygon, and Element options. Additionally, some tools are available only in Edit Mesh mode or only in Edit Poly mode. Most of the improvements in the modeling part of 3ds Max were made to Edit Poly and provide many benefits for polygonal modeling. To simplify the process of understanding polygonal modeling in 3ds Max, this quick start guide only presents the Edit Poly functions.

The subelements structure in Edit Poly mode is shown in Figure A-19.

Figure A-19: The Vertex, Edge, Border, Polygon, and Element options.

The vertex subelement can be accessed through the quad menu (by right-clicking) or by pressing the 1 key.

The edge subelement can be accessed through the quad menu (by right-clicking) or by pressing the 2 key.

The border subelement can be accessed through the quad menu (by right-clicking) or by pressing the 3 key.

The polygon subelement can be accessed through the quad menu (by right-clicking) or by pressing the 4 key.

The whole mesh element can be through the quad menu (by right-clicking) or by pressing the 5 key.

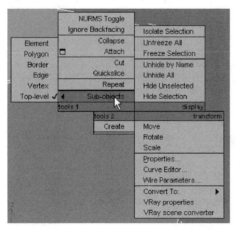

Figure A-20

Editing Polygons

The tools for editing polygons in 3ds Max are located in the Modifier Panel. There are more buttons than your resolution can probably display at one time, so if you feel that something is missing, click and hold in an empty area of the Modifier Panel, and scroll down to find the other buttons.

Cut

You can cut polygons in 3ds Max in several different ways. When you point the cursor over a vertex, the cursor changes to ▨ to indicate you are over a vertex and the cut will start precisely over the vertex.

When you position the cursor over an edge, the cursor will be changed to ▨ to indicate the cut will start from the edge the cursor is over.

When you position the cursor over a polygonal face, the cursor changes to ▨ to indicate that the cut will start from the point of the face the cursor is over.

3ds Max indicates the path of the cut in a real-time display.

Bevel

Bevel functions in 3ds Max have three main parameters to define, as shown in Figure A-21.

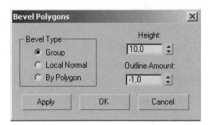

Figure A-21: Bevel Polygons window.

The Bevel Type sets how the bevel will work: by group, local normal, or polygon. This works like extrude, which was discussed in Chapter 2. Height determines how much the polygon will be extruded before the beveling action. Outline Amount specifies how much the face will be scaled down after the extrusion.

Chamfer

Chamfer in 3ds Max has one option, which determines the size of the edge chamfer. Note that chamfer commands exist for both edges and vertices, and they perform differently.

Figure A-22: Chamfer Edges window.

Extrude

Extrude has two main parameters: Extrusion Type (as discussed in Chapter 2) and Extrusion Height, which determines the height to which the polygon will be extruded.

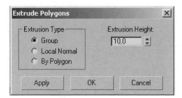

Figure A-23: Extrude Polygons window.

Weld

The Weld Threshold option in the Weld Vertices window determines the range of vertices that will be picked and merged together.

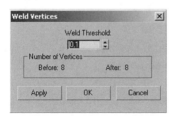

Figure A-24: Weld Vertices window.

353

Soft Selection

Soft Selection is one of the greatest features inside 3ds Max.

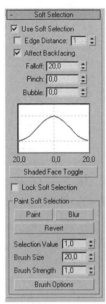

Figure A-25: Soft Selection window.

The Use Soft Selection check box activates the tool.

The Edge Distance check box will affect only the vertices/edges related to the edge distance you selected to affect. If there is a hole near the selected portion, the edge distance will not allow the selection to influence the vertices on the other side. If this option is turned off, all the vertices inside the attenuation falloff will be affected.

Falloff determines the attenuation area of the Soft Selection tool related to the portion of the subelement you picked.

The Shaded Face Toggle will display in the mesh surface the colors corresponding to attenuation falloff. The colors can be customized by selecting Customize | Customize UI Interface in the Colors tab.

Attributes

The basic attributes related to the 3ds Max objects can be found in the Modifier Panel. After you create an object, click the Modifier Panel tab icon and scroll down the menu to find all the control parameters.

Understanding the Command Panel

The Command Panel is shown in Figure A-26 and each item is discussed below.

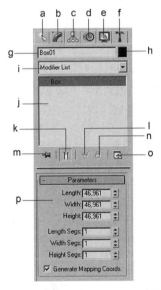

Figure A-26: The Command Panel.

a - Create tab: The Create tab provides access to the full menu for creating polygonal primitive objects and other objects such as particles, NURBS, patches, etc.

b - Modify tab: The Modify tab lets you access the main properties and parameters to be changed. If you've already created your object, switch to the Modify tab so the parameters and options related to any modifier you applied can be changed here.

c - Hierarchy tab: The Hierarchy tab offers options related to pivots and hierarchy object controls.

d - Motion tab: The Motion tab includes specific options related to animation controls.

e - Display tab: The Display tab contain options and parameters for the geometry display in the viewport as well as some management tools for freezing (making unselectable) and hiding objects in the viewports.

f - Utilities tab: This contains a set of vertical buttons that can be configured to suit your needs.

g - Name: The name of a selected object can easily be seen and changed in the modifier panel. After creating the object, when you select the modifier panel, the name of the primitive you created appears at the top of the object's properties. In Figure A-26 we can see "Box01" is the standard name for the box primitive that was just created. To change the name of an object, click in the edit box and type in an appropriate name for your object.

h - Color: If your object doesn't have any material applied to it, the color you choose will be applied to the whole object. If your object has a material applied, the selected color will change only the wireframe color.

i - Modifier List: The modifier list lets you choose a modifier to apply to the mesh.

j - Modifier Stack: The modifier stack contains all the historical information about the object. All the modifiers applied to the object will be displayed in the modifier stack hierarchy from bottom to top. The light bulb in the modifier stack indicates whether the modifier is active. If the light bulb is white, it is active. If the light bulb is dark, it is inactive. To toggle the modifier stack, just click on it. The "+" sign means the modifier has subobjects to be accessed.

Figure A-27: The modifier stack with MeshSmooth applied. The Editable Poly at the base does not have a light bulb icon, meaning it can't be disabled. For the MeshSmooth modifier, the light bulb is white, which means it's active. Notice that both have a black square with the plus sign to indicate they can be expanded.

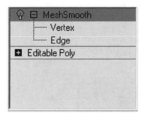

Figure A-28: Now we can see a minus (–) sign in the MeshSmooth modifier, indicating it is already expanded. It will retract if we click on it. Also, notice the lamp is dark, which means the MeshSmooth modifier is not active.

k - Show End Result on/off Toggle: This button shows the result of the last modifier applied when it's disabled. When enabled, it shows the results of all modifiers.

l - Make Unique: When you duplicate objects with the instance option and then apply a modification (like MeshSmooth), that modification will affect all of the objects. Selecting Make Unique will make this object unique, and a modification made to the other instance will not affect the unique object.

m - Pin Stack: Pin Stack allows you to lock the modifier for editing even if you select another object. For example, let's say you applied MeshSmooth to a cube, selected Pin Stack, and selected a sphere. The MeshSmooth parameter change will affect the cube, even if the sphere is selected.

n - Remove Modifier from Stack: Deletes the modifier from the stack.

o - Configure Modifier Sets: This button enables you to set buttons above the modifier stack and set the available command. This is useful if you use 3ds Max with high resolution and use specific modifiers a lot.

p - Rollout options: The rollout options for modifications appear here when available.

Figure A-29: Set of standard mesh editing tools.

357

Display Modes

3ds Max has six display modes for real-time geometry viewing and manipulation:

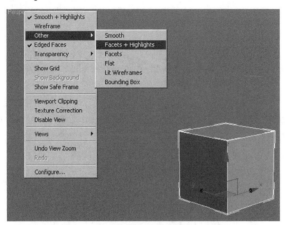

Figure A-30: Display mode options.

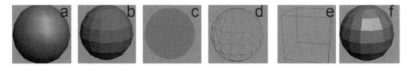

Figure A-31: Examples of display mode options. The letters in the figure correspond to the options listed below.

a - Smooth: Displays the geometry with Gouraud shading.

b - Facets: Displays constant shading without highlights.

c - Flat: Displays a complete flat shade. This option disabled any highlighting or shading at the object's surface.

d - Lit Wireframes: Shows shaded wireframes.

e - Bounding Box: Displays the entire shape as a box.

f - Facets+Highlights: Displays constant shading with highlights.

Selecting

There are several tools used for selecting objects.

Select tool: The Select tool activates the selection mode and de-selects the Move, Rotate, or Scale tool if any of them are selected.

Select By Name: The Selection By Name tools allows you to view an alphabetical list of all the objects in your scene so you can easily select them. By default in the Windows OS, you can press and hold Shift and select an entire list, or you can pick specific items by pressing and holding Ctrl and clicking the name in the list.

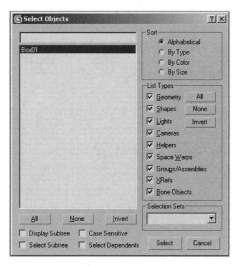

Figure A-32: Select Objects window.

Selection Sets: Selection sets allow you to save specific selected objects that would take time to select again. For example, if you are modeling a complex machine and want to quickly se-lect all the bolts and pipes, you can save a selection set that will recall and reselect all the objects in the selection set.

Selecting From Layers: With the layer system it is possible to pick all the objects inside a layer or hide or freeze the objects.

Selection Marquee

In 3ds Max you can select from four different methods of creating the selection marquee.

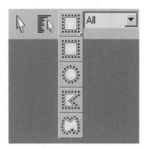

Figure A-33: Selection marquee options.

Rectangular selection region: The standard selection method.

Circular selection region: Creates a symmetrical circular selection marquee.

Fence selection region: Creates a faceted marquee selection similar to the polygonal lasso in Photoshop.

Lasso selection region: Creates a freehand selection marquee

The toolbar has an icon that represents the behavior of the edge of the selection marquee: ▣▣. The icon on the left selects everything the selection marquee touches, and the icon on the right selects everything inside the selection marquee.

Grouping and Linking

In 3ds Max we can link objects to one another and group them together.

To group objects, select them, go to the menu item Group | Group, enter the group's name, and press Enter or click on the OK button. When you select any of the objects, the entire group will be selected. Go to the menu item Group | Open to make an open group so you can select the objects individually. Notice that the selection bracket will be visible even if the group is unselected. The brackets will enable you to select the group.

Link and Unlink can be accessed by the Select and Link button ▣ and the Unlink Selection button ▣.

To link two objects, click on the geometry that you want to be the "child" object, hold the Select and Link button, and release when the cursor is over the object that will be the "parent" object. Notice the link line being drawn in the viewport to indicate the link.

To break the link to the child object, select the child object and click the Unlink Selection button.

Colors and Shading

The colors and shading of an object can be easily changed by applying a simple Blinn standard material.

To change the color of the wireframe, select the color box in the Name and Color tab in the modifier panel, then make changes in the Object Color window.

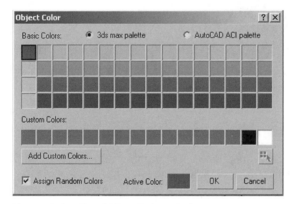

Figure A-34: The Object Color window.

You can increase or decrease the specular value before starting to model, as shown in Figure A-35.

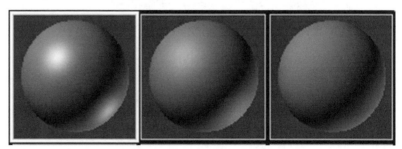

Figure A-35

Normals

Normals can be accessed with either the Edit Normals or Normals modifier.

The Normals modifier is a bit older and has only two options: Unify and Flip.

The Edit Normals modifier offers more options for manipulating and controlling normals. If you check the Show Handles option, you'll be able to manipulate the normals freehand.

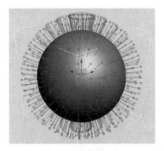

Figure A-36: 3ds Max's normal handles using the Edit Normals modifier.

Polygon Creation

3ds Max probably has the largest number of primitives available in any 3D package on the market. The standard primitives you can choose from are shown in Figure A-37, and the extended primitives are shown in Figure A-38.

Figure A-37:
Standard primitives.

Figure A-38:
Extended primitives.

The standard primitives are Box, Cone, Sphere, Geosphere, Cylinder, Tube, Torus, Pyramid, Teapot, and Plane. The extended primitives are Hedra, Torus Knot, ChamferBox, ChamferCyl, OilTank, Capsule, Spindle, L-Ext, Gengon, C-Ext, RingWave, Hose, and Prism. To create primitives in 3ds Max, you must click and drag to create instead of the primitive just popping into the center of the viewport as it does in Maya and SoftImage XSI.

Operational Tools

3ds Max offers a variety of spline tools to be used for creating a mesh with the Extrude, Loft, and Lathe tools. The splines are available in the Create menu's Shapes submenu.

Figure A-39

In 3ds Max the splines have the same control options as in most vector drawing programs. If you select the vertices of the splines and right-click, the quad menu will appear and show the options to convert that vertex to a bezier vertex.

Operational tools in 3ds Max are available under the Create panel with the Geometry button selected. The first option in the list is Standard Primitives. Click on the list and more options will appear. The operational tools mentioned are located under the Compound Object option.

Boolean: 3ds Max allows you to perform union, subtraction, and intersection operations.

363

Scatter: Scatter is located in the same panel as Boolean. It will pick an object and distribute it along another object's surface according its surface.

Loft: To use the loft operation you must have at least two splines: one (or more) for the shape and one for the path. 3ds Max will pick the shape and run along the path to generate a lofted mesh.

Lathe: Lathe is located in the modifier list. It will pick the spline and rotate it around an axis.

Pass Through

In 3ds Max the Pass Through function can be found in the Properties options in the quad menu under the See-Through option. You can toggle the enabling and disabling of the pass-through options. You can also press the hotkey Alt+X.

General Deformation

In 3ds Max, most of the general deformation described in this book can be found in the modifier list. Here we describe some of those most commonly used for 3ds Max polygonal modeling:

Bend: Creates a lattice cage that bends the mesh globally.

Edit Poly: Modifier for editing the polygons without having to collapse the modifier stack

Edit Normals: Modifier to edit the normals with several options.

FFD 2x2x2: Creates a box lattice cage with 2x2x2 segments.

FFD 3x3x3: Creates a box lattice cage with 3x3x3 segments.

FFD 4x4x4: Creates a box lattice cage with 4x4x4 segments.

FFDbox: Creates a box lattice cage with the option to change the number of control points.

FFDCyl: Creates a cylindrical lattice cage with option to change the number of control points.

MeshSmooth: Applies subdivision to the mesh.

Mirror: An interactive way to place the mirror.

MultiRes: Tool for polygonal reduction, with more options than Optimize.

Noise: Generates fractal bumps in the geometry.

Optimize: Polygonal reduction tool.

Twist: Creates a cage that globally twists the mesh.

Shell: Creates thickness in the mesh.

Symmetry: Variation of Mirror, which allows the user to interactively place the flipped half with real-time vertex merging.

Poly Count

A tool for monitoring polygon statistics can be found under the Utilities panel. By default, 3ds Max does not provide the poly count function in the standard set of buttons. You can configure the buttons and place the poly count with the Configure Buttons Sets option.

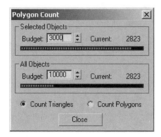

Figure A-40: Polygon Count window.

The Polygon Count window contains a visual bar indicating your polygon limit and how many polygons you have used. It also provides options for seeing the triangles and the polygons.

Problem Solving

How do I subdivide my mesh in 3ds Max?

Select MeshSmooth in the modifier list.

I've just created my primitive. How do I edit the vertices, edges, etc.?

You must collapse the modifier stack or add the Edit Poly modifier. You can also use the Edit Mesh modifier.

I've just subdivided my mesh. How do I go back to an earlier step without removing the modifier?

Play with the Iterations parameter inside Subdivision Amount.

When I rotate my viewport, all my scene objects become boxes. Why?

You may have accidentally tapped the O key, which by default activates the Adaptive Degradation toggle that turns the objects into bounding boxes to increase the performance of the system while you rotate the viewport.

Appendix B

Maya Polygonal Modeling Quick Start Guide

Maya allows the user to customize the user interface completely, changing shortcuts, panels, toolbar, colors, and many other functions to improve the workflow. In this appendix, we discuss how you can customize Maya, along with basic functions discussed elsewhere in this book.

The letters in Figure B-1 correspond to the list below the figure.

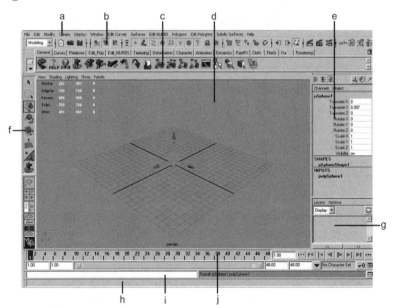

Figure B-1: The Maya user interface.

a - Menu bar: The menu bar contains a number of standard menus (File, Edit, Modify, Create, Display, Window, and Help), plus other menus depending on the module you choose. In the modeling module are these menus: Edit Curves, Surfaces, Edit NURBS, Polygons, Edit Polygons, and Subdiv Surfaces.

b - Status line: The status line contains buttons that are mostly used for modeling and working with objects.

c - Shelf: The shelf is where you can quickly access most of the tools and items related to creation and modification of geometry, dynamics, texturing, and so on. Maya allows you to completely customize your own shelf with the commands you use most often and separate them with a custom label.

d - Workspace: The Maya workspace is where you perform the transformations and object manipulations. The workspace has a Panel menu, which you can use to change functions related to the object's display in the view, lightning, camera, etc.

e - Channel box: The channel box shows basic information about the object such as position coordinates, rotations, and scaling, as well as general modification inputs.

f - Toolbox: The toolbox provides quick access to basic operations like select, move, rotation scaling, etc.

g - Layer editor: Maya's layer system.

h - Help line: Line of context-sensitive tips and hints.

i - Command line: Place to enter MEL Script commands.

j - Time and Range slider: Animation related section of timeline and slider to view specific areas of the timeline.

Customization

Customization in Maya starts with the menu selection Window | Settings/Preferences | Preferences, as shown in Figure B-2. To change the preferences related to polygons, for example, select the Polygons category from the list in the Preferences window (see Figure B-3). You'll see important options about polygons display in the viewport such as backface culling, faces display, normal size, and so on. You can set many other options in the Preferences window for user interface optimization for modeling.

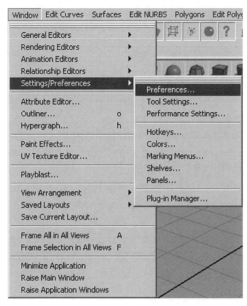

Figure B-2: Window | Settings/Preferences | Preferences menu choice.

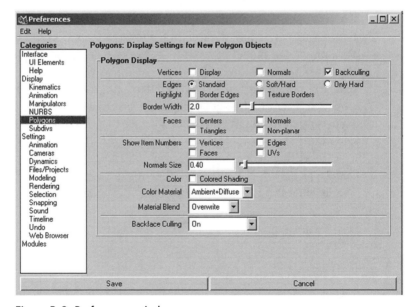

Figure B-3: Preferences window.

Navigation

There are a number of ways to navigate in Maya, including using the following tools.

The Tumble tool rotates the camera around the center of interest. You can access it by selecting the button on the shelf 🎱 or by pressing Alt+left mouse button.

The Track tool tracks the camera in the opposite direction you drag the mouse. You can access it by selecting the button on the shelf 🎱 or by pressing Alt+middle mouse button.

The Dolly tool moves the camera in and out. You can access it by selecting the button on the shelf 🎱 or by pressing Alt+right mouse button.

The Zoom tool zooms the camera in and out. You can access it by selecting the button on the shelf 🎱. The main difference between the Dolly and Zoom tools is that the Zoom tool distorts the perspective if pushed too far.

Layouts

The viewport layout can be customized to fit the needs of modelers, texture artists, technical directors, and anyone else who is working with Maya. For modeling we can set the basic four viewports, tap the Spacebar to maximize the view we are working in, and then go back to the four-view layout. When managing a complex scene we can set a layout that is half perspective and half Outliner or Hypergraph. It's up to you to set a layout that is most comfortable and intuitive for you.

To set the layout, select Window | Settings/Preferences | Panels, as shown in Figure B-4, then make your selection in the Panels window.

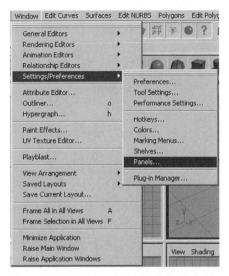

Figure B-4: Window | Settings/Preferences | Panels menu choice.

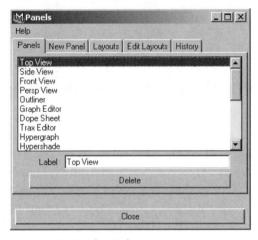

Figure B-5: Panels window.

By default, Maya has predefined five viewport layouts:

Single Perspective View

Four Views: Top, Side, Front, and Perspective (Persp)

Outliner/Perspective, for scene management

Perspective/Curve Editor, for animators

Hypergraph and Perspective, for node management of complex objects

Gizmos and Manipulation

The Move, Rotate, and Scale gizmos in Maya are similar to those in many other packages.

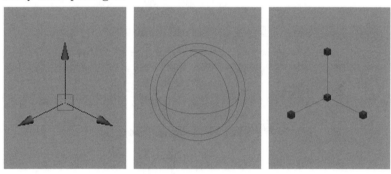

Figure B-6: Move, Rotate, and Scale gizmos.

The Move tool translates the object in the selected axis. The center square moves in all three axes perpendicular to the camera's view. Ctrl+click in the gizmo's axis to lock the gizmo in two axes.

The Rotate tool rotates the object in the selected axis.

The Scale tool scales the object in the selected axis. The middle square scales in all three axes.

Axis

To change the axis referencing system (the way the axis behaves related to the object), press the Tool Settings button. This will bring up a window that shows the options available for the tool you are using to manipulate the object (Translate or Move, Rotate, or Scale).

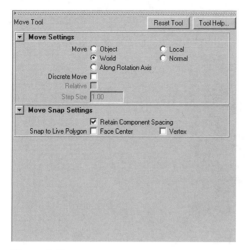

Figure B-7

Mirror/Duplicate

To mirror a polygonal mesh in Maya, select the object and go to the Polygons | Mirror Geometry menu option. The option box enables you to choose from a variety of axes to mirror.

To duplicate the polygon mesh in Maya, select the geometry and press Ctrl+D. This simply duplicates the object at the same position as the original object. It is possible to duplicate the geometry scaling, translating, and rotating along any axis by using the Duplicate Options window.

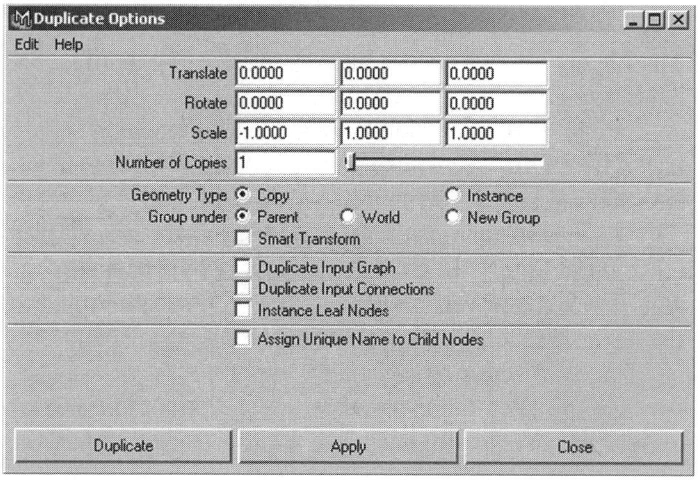

Figure B-8: Duplicate Options window.

The –1.0000 value will mirror the geometry and scale it in negative direction. This is an alternative to the Mirror Geometry option.

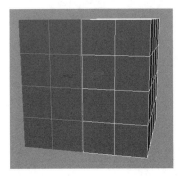

Figure B-9

Layers

The layers in Maya are quite simple to manage by using the Layers and Options menus.

Figure B-10: Layers and Options menus.

The Layers menu provides options for creating, editing, and deleting the selected layer. In each layer you'll notice three columns.

The first column is for visibility. You can turn on or off the "V" letter. When the "V" is displayed, the layer is visible. If the square is blank, the layer is invisible.

The second column enables the options for template and reference. If the letter "T" is displayed, all the objects inside the layer will be visible but you can't select them or snap anything to them. If the letter "R" is displayed, you can see the objects and snap to them but cannot select or modify them.

The third column is for colors. Setting colors for the layers make it easier to distinguish layers if there are a number of them.

To the right of the color box is the name of the layer. It is recommended that you give the layers appropriate names so you can quickly recognize what kind of objects are in that layer.

Pivot

To view and manipulate the pivot, select the Transform mode and press the Insert key.

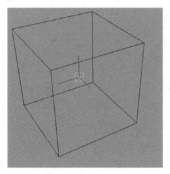

Figure B-11

You can move and change the pivot point. To center the pivot, select Modify | Center Pivot. This will automatically place the pivot at the center of the object.

Subelements Structure

Maya's subelements, called components, can only be accessed in component mode, which is accessed through the marking menus by right-clicking inside the object or assigning a specific hotkey for component mode. Also notice that Maya treats the UV as a component. Choosing object mode exits the component mode.

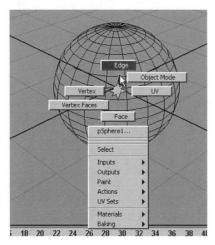

Figure B-12: Subelements in Maya can be easily accessed from the marking menus.

Attributes

The Attribute Editor can be accessed by pressing ▦ or by pressing Ctrl+A. The Attribute Editor contains tabs with parameters created with the object and parameters of tools applied later. When you create a polygonal primitive in Maya, the internal Maya architecture creates some nodes that will compose that object. In Figure B-13, we can see that Maya creates five nodes when we create a single sphere: pSphere1, pSphereShape1, polySphere1, initialShading-Group, and lambert1. These tabs can be confusing at first, but in time you'll notice that they allow you to have greater control of the object that will be reflected in it's final shape.

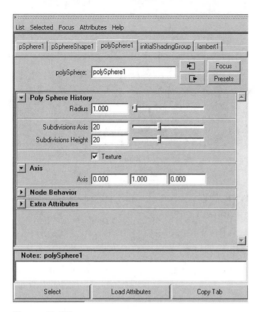

Figure B-13

There are also several other buttons near the Attribute Editor:

Show/Hide Tool Settings — Toggles the tool settings.

Show/Hide Channel Box/Layer Editor — Toggles the Channel box and the Layer Editor.

The History button is located in the status line. Maya history stores information about the changes you make to your mesh. If the button is set to off , the information will not be stored. For optimization issues, it is recommended that you turn the history off. To remove the history of a specific object, select it and choose Edit | Delete All by Type | History.

Display Modes

Maya offers several options for polygonal mesh display.

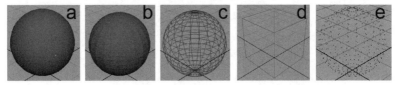

Figure B-14

Examples of display mode options. The letters in the figure correspond to the options listed below.

a - Smooth Shade All: Smooths the surface and displays the volume of the mesh.

b - Flat Shade All: Displays the faces of the mesh with constant shading.

c - Wireframe: Displays the wires without shading properties.

d - Bounding Box: Displays the whole object as a box. This is a good option for speed optimization in the viewport.

e - Points: Displays only the vertex points of the geometry.

Name

In the Channel box you can click on the object's name, such as pSphere1 in the following figure, and rename it whatever you wish. The nodes of the archive can be renamed as well but is not necessary.

Figure B-15

Selecting

Maya provides various ways to select objects and components, including ways to precisely select an object or group of objects in a complex scene. You can select objects with the Select tool (shortcut Q) or with a Lasso Selection tool. The Select tool individually selects the objects by clicking on them. The Lasso Selection tool creates a freehand marquee selection and selects everything inside the marquee.

There are a number of selection options available in the Edit menu:

Select All: Selects everything.

Select Hierarchy: Selects lower nodes of the current selected node in the scene hierarchy.

Invert Selection: Inverts the selection. This will unselect the objects that are selected and select everything that was unselected.

Select All by Type: Selects all objects of specific types such as polygons, NURBS, joints, etc.

Quick Select Type: Shows the options to quick select the sets you've created.

Paint Selection Tools: Activates the paint selection for components.

Selection Sets: As in 3ds Max, you can create selection sets when working with complex scenes or objects that require you to select a large number of specific objects instead of selecting them one by one. To create a selection set, select Create | Sets | Create Selection Sets and type in the name you want. To recall that set, select Edit | Quick Select Sets | <created sets>.

The following sections discuss other methods Maya provides for selecting and managing objects.

The Outliner

The Outliner is similar to the Select by Name option in 3ds Max. It's a list where you can view and manage the scene files with ease. The object's name is preceded by an icon that shows you the type of object.

Figure B-16: Outliner window.

In Figure B-16, we can see a curve, a NURBS cone, a subdivision cube, and a polygonal sphere that are parented together, as indicated by the light gray line. Notice that the icons for each object differ. The plus and minus signs indicate that the object has attributes or other objects connected to it. In the Display and Show menus you can set the level of nodes and the type of objects you want displayed. If you are working exclusively with polygons, for example, you may want to disable all the other items from being displayed in the Outliner.

The Hypergraph

The Hypergraph provides a clear understanding of Maya's internal architecture for managing objects and their nodes. Maya has a DAG (Directed Acrylic Graphic), which is a graphical representation of the arrangement of objects and their connection nodes. In Hypergraph it is possible to select the objects and/or manipulate the nodes of a specific object. The navigation commands inside Hypergraph are the same as for viewport navigation (except for 3D navigation since Hypergraph is a 2D window). With the Buttons menu you can frame the nodes, show and hide input connections between them, and bookmark specific regions where nodes are connected to recall later without losing time trying to find them in complex scenes.

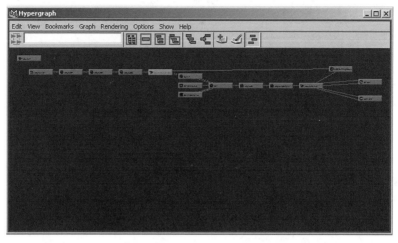

Figure B-17: Hypergraph window.

For modeling, it is important to notice that every change we make to the object like cuts, extrusion, and so forth will be referenced in the Hypergraph, but if we delete the history these nodes will also be deleted because they represent changes we made.

Grouping and Parenting

Grouping is a very powerful way to make a set of objects unified by a node. In Maya you can group objects and select them individually or select the group node to select all at once. Parenting is the same as "linking" in 3ds Max. Parenting objects creates a hierarchy relationship.

Grouping and parenting options can be found in the Edit menu.

Colors and Shading

The colors and shading in Maya can be changed by applying a specific material created via hypershade or by accessing the lambert1 tab in the Attribute Editor. The Lambert shader is applied by default to every primitive you create.

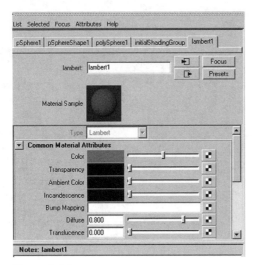

List   Selected   Focus   Attributes   Help

pSphere1 | pSphereShape1 | polySphere1 | initialShadingGroup | lambert1

Figure B-18

In the Shader tab you can set the color and many other surfacing aspects of your object.

If you want to change the color of the wireframe, select Display | Wireframe Color. You can choose from eight default colors.

Normals

In Maya the normals can be viewed by selecting the Display | Polygon Components | Normals menu option and choosing from long, medium, and short normals. You can show or hide the normals by selecting Display | Custom Polygon Display option box.

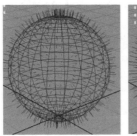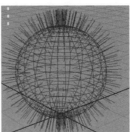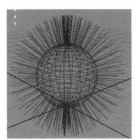

Figure B-19: Normals options.

You can also change the length of the normals by using the menu option Display | Custom Polygon Display.

Polygon Creation

The polygonal primitives available in Maya can be created from the predefined shelf or by using the Create | Polygonal Primitives menu option.

The default polygonal objects available are sphere, cube, cylinder, cone, plane, and torus.

Figure B-20

We can also create a single polygon and extrude the edges. More polygonal shapes can be created by using NURBS and then converting the shape to polygons by selecting Modify | Convert | NURBS to Polygons.

Operational Tools

Most of the operational tools described in this book can be found in the Polygons or Edit Polygons menus, or in Maya's default shelf. Don't forget that you can customize your own shelf as well.

In the Polygons menu you will find tools that generally affect the object as a whole, like Smooth (subdivision), Combine (attach), Triangulate, Quadrangulate, etc.

In the Edit Polygons menu you will find tools that affect the components of a polygonal mesh such as Split (cut) Polygon, Extrude Face, Extrude Edge, Bevel, Merge, etc.

Notice the small cube at the right side of the following figure. This indicates that Maya opens a dialog box that offers options for this tool that can be selected before you actually apply the tool.

Figure B-21

Pass Through

In Maya you can activate X-Ray mode by selecting Shading | X-Ray from the viewport menu.

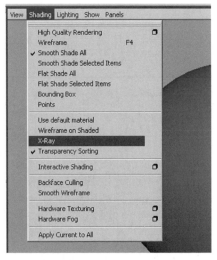

Figure B-22: Shading menu options.

General Deformation

Tools that globally affect objects in Maya can be found in the Deform menu in the Animation module. Those most useful for modeling are Cluster, Lattice, and Sculpt Deformer.

Cluster

Cluster is accessed through Deform | Create Cluster. This is a deformer that allows you to control a set of points (vertices, CV, etc.) based on a variety of weight attributes.

To effectively create and manipulate a cluster, select a section of vertices. Notice in the following figure that the axis is placed according to the section we've chosen.

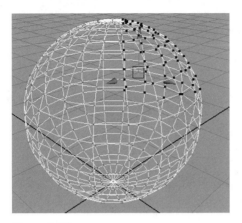

Figure B-23

A small "c" will be created in the center of the axis. This is the cluster handle. Manipulating this cluster will affect the section of vertices according to the weight.

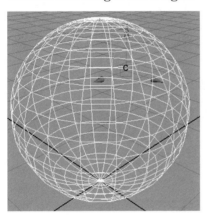

Figure B-24

When in the paint weight mode, the object will be converted into black and white tones. The black areas indicate no influence at all, and white indicates 100 percent influence. The gray areas along the surface indicate moderate influence. As we can see in the following figure, the weight has considerable influence over the mesh deformation.

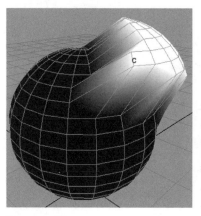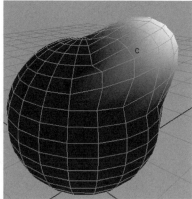

Figure B-25

Lattice

Lattice is accessed by selecting Deform | Create Lattice.

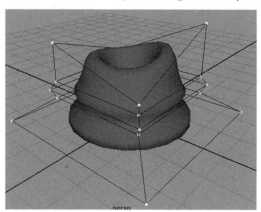

Figure B-26

The Lattice can be customized before it is applied so that you can set up the number of points you want to deform in the mesh.

Sculpt Deformer

Sculpt Deformer is accessed by selecting Deform | Create Sculpt Deform. The Sculpt Deformer will displace the mesh based on a spherical wireframe called the "sculptor."

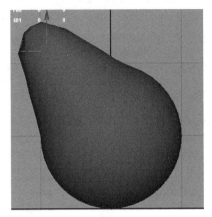

Figure B-27

In wireframe mode we can clearly see the sculptor inside the sphere and the deformed wireframe. Sculpt deformer is mostly used for animation purposes, but it can also be useful in polygonal modeling. The advantage is that you can easily place the deformer where you want and see the results in real time.

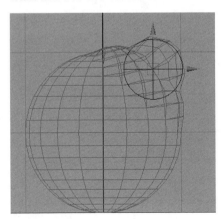

Figure B-28

Marking Menus

Maya has a quick way of displaying all the menus available by pressing and holding the Spacebar. With the marking menus you can quickly access all of the menus for polygons or change the viewports. The menus can be easily configured in the preferences.

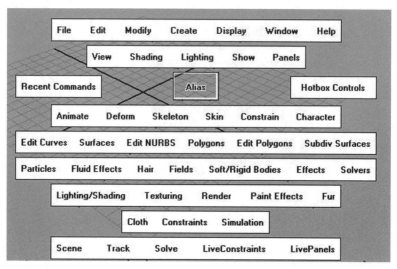

Figure B-29

If you click outside the menu — at the left, right, bottom, or top — you get different sets of menus.

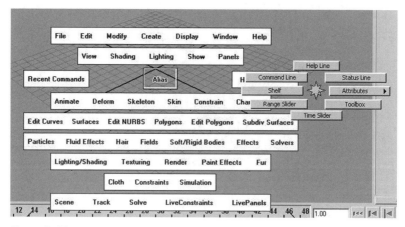

Figure B-30

At the right of Figure B-30 is a menu accessed by clicking at the right side of another menu. These menu options allow you to show or hide different portions of the UI, such as Shelf, Command Line, Time Slider, and so on.

Poly Count

To display information about the poly count in Maya, select Display | Heads up display | Polycount. The heads-up display allows you to select other functions like frame rate and object properties.

Maya's polycount system also allows you to see the number of vertices, edges, and UVs of the object.

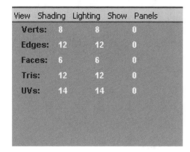

Figure B-31

Glossary

algorithm — In computer graphics programming, defined as an expression or a set of ordered steps for solving complex mathematical problems.

aliasing — Undesired artifacts in straight lines generally produced by limitations of pixel resolution display.

antialiasing — Set of mathematical oversampling techniques for removing aliasing problems related to limitations of pixel display resolution.

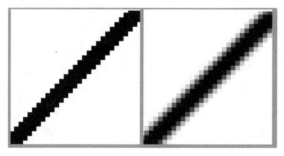

Left, edge with aliasing; right, edge with antialiasing.

Attach — In 3ds Max, means to join two distinct meshes and combine into one. This is called Combine in Maya.

axis — In 3D, one of the three space coordinates — X, Y or Z.

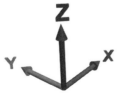

3D axis.

B-spline — A basis spline; smooth spline curve controlled by at least three control vertices.

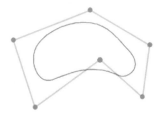

B-spline closed curve.

backface culling — In 3D modeling, a technique to hide the wireframe (vertices, edges, and faces) of the surface that faces the camera.

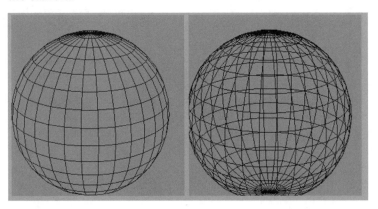

Left, sphere with backface culling. Right, sphere without backface culling.

bevel — In 3D, bevel is related to an expansion of the edges and vertices into a new polygonal face.

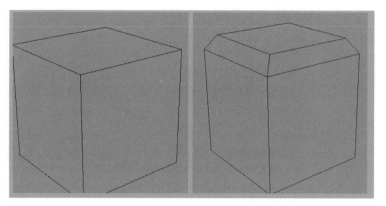

Left, box; right, box with top polygon after bevel operation.

Bézier curve — Curves defined by four points: initial and final positions (also called anchor points) and the middle control points. Manipulating these points causes the shape of the curve to change. Created by Pierre Bézier.

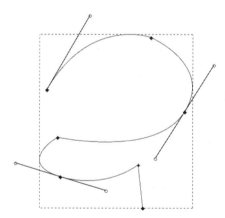

Bézier curve.

blocking — A technique to simplify a complex shape, form, or object by starting work on the parts separately.

blueprint — References from an orthographic point of view of mechanical devices, vehicles, etc.

Boolean — Logical mathematical operations developed by George Boole. In 3D, Boolean operations consist of picking two objects and joining them together, subtracting them, or having them intersect each other.

Boolean operations.

border subelement — In 3ds Max, defined edges at the limit of the mesh and the hole.

bump — A technique for simulating bumps, wrinkles, and irregularities on objects by using a grayscale texture. The 3D application interprets the darker values as depressions and lighter values as bumps.

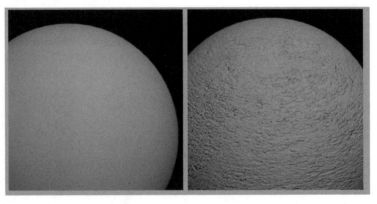

Butterfly — A subdivision technique proposed by Nira Dyn, David Levine, and John Gregory.

CAD — Abbreviation for computer-assisted design.

Cartesian system — Coordinate space system devised by René Descartes that designates the height, length, and deepness of the 3D space represented by three axes — X, Y, and Z.

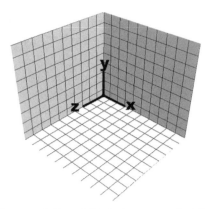

Representation of Cartesian system in 3D space.

Catmull-Clark — A subdivision technique proposed by Edward Catmull and Jim Clark in 1978.

Chaikin — A curve cut-corner refinement algorithm proposed by George Chaikin in 1974.

chamfer — In 3D modeling, the removal of a vertex to create non-90-degree corners.

Combine — See Attach.

continuity — Relates to a mathematical measure about the smoothness of two curves or 3D surface. Good or bad continuity has direct effects on the final look of a 3D surface.

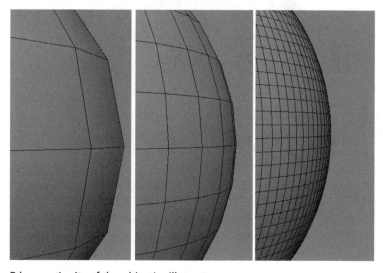

Edge continuity of the object's silhouette.

customization — Changes made by the user to change the software user interface to fit the user's needs related to ergonomic workflow.

Detach — In 3ds Max, the Detach command separates the selected meshes or vertices. Known as Separate in Maya.

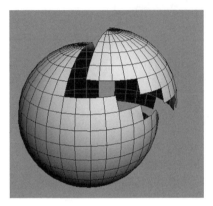

Detached sphere.

displacement — A technique to push and pull vertices of a geometry using a grayscale map as the reference base on its dark or light value.

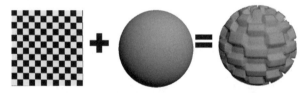

Display — In 3ds Max, Display determines the aspect of the shading of the 3D model inside the viewport for real-time manipulation.

Doo-Sabin — A subdivision technique for bi-quadratic B-splines proposed by Daniel Doo and Malcolm Sabin.

edge loop — Polygonal edges that loop around an object or specific area and return to the origin. See also line flow.

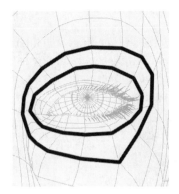

Edge loop.

extraordinary vertex — A vertex with a valence less than or greater than 4.

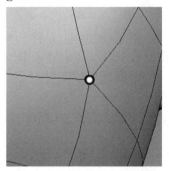

Extraordinary vertex with a valence of 5.

extrude — In 3D, the process of creating a 3D surface by sweeping a line shape along a curve. Known as Loft in 3ds Max.

face — In 3D, a face is defined as a renderable 2D triangle plane.

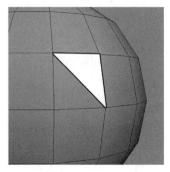

Face.

facets — See flat shading

flat shading — Also called constant shading. A rendering method that does not apply any smoothing technique over the mesh's surface, resulting in a faceted appearance.

Gouraud shading — A technique developed by Henri Gouraud to compute and display a shaded surface based on the color and illumination at the corner of polygonal planes.

high poly — Term for models with a high number of polygons.

hole — The absence of one or more faces on a mesh structure.

inorganic modeling — The modeling of inorganic objects or objects that are very complex.

interpolation — A method of constructing new data points from known data points. In 3D, some subdivision techniques use interpolating methods of mesh refinement.

iterations — A repetition of a piece of code. In 3D mesh subdivision, the iterations determine how much the mesh will be subdivided.

Kobbelt — Subdivision scheme proposed by Leif Kobbelt.

Lathe — Operation in 3ds Max that picks a profile spline curve and revolves it using an axis, generating a 3D object. Known as Revolve in Maya.

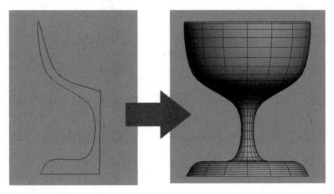

lattice — In 3D, a structure of points around a mesh that deform its surface by manipulating the lattice's points.

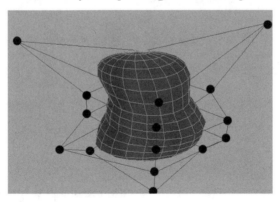

layout — The arrangement of the viewports inside the user interface of a 3D application.

line flow — The edge structure of an anatomy of a specific model, character, or object. See also edge loops.

Loft — Method of surfacing using a cross section of splines.

Loop — Subdivision technique proposed by Charles Loop.

low poly — Term for models with a low number of polygons to be rendered in real time in a game engine.

masks — Refers to the mathematical procedures that rule the process of subdivision. In other words, the "mask" defines the visual scheme for mathematical procedures of how the software will pick the unrefined mesh, subdivide the actual mesh cage, and try to make it as smooth as possible.

mesh — A 3D object composed of triangular faces. A mesh's smoothness is relative to the number of mesh refinement (subdivision iterations).

MeshSmooth — In 3ds Max, the command to apply subdivision to a mesh. See also subdivision.

mirror — In 3D, a procedure to duplicate a mesh by inverting it along one or two axes.

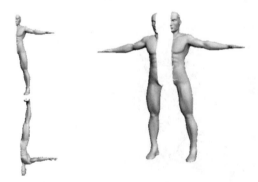

mirror line — Edges at the center of the object that will be mirrored.

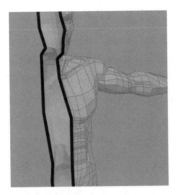

Mirror line.

n-gon — Polygon with n sides. For example, a 5-gon is a pentagon (polygon with five sides).

normal — A non-rendering vector line that points perpendicular (in or out depending on the configuration of the polygon's normal) to a polygonal face.

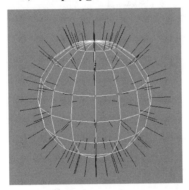

ordinary vertex — Vertex with a valence of 4.

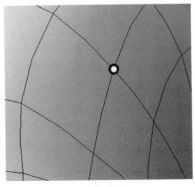

Ordinary vertex with a valence of 4.

organic modeling — The modeling of a character, creature, or organic object.

orthographic view — View of a scene projected onto a drawing surface or screen in which the lines of projection are perpendicular to the screen. In 3D graphics, orthographic views are always aligned with the axes of the global Cartesian coordinate system.

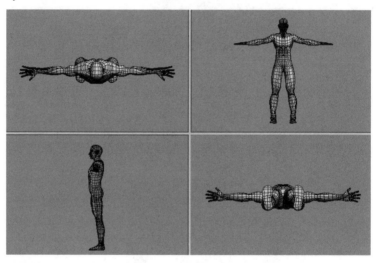

Object seen from four orthogonal views.

pivot — In 3D, the pivot controls the exact position of objects in 3D space and also has influence over the basic transformation of the mesh (move, rotate, scale).

pixel — Short for pixel element. A computer image is composed of small dots called pixels.

pixol — Term from Pixologic that means "pixels with depth."

poly — Abbreviation for polygon. See also polygon.

polygon — A plane defined by at least three vertices. A tri polygon is made up of three vertices, a quad polygon is made of two triangular polygons, a pentagon is made of three triangles, and so on.

poly cage — See mesh.

poly count — Refers to the number of polygons.

primitive — A simple object generated mathematically by default in most 3D applications. These include cubes, spheres, cones, cylinders, torii, and planes.

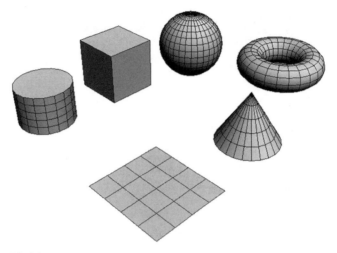

Primitives.

quads — Polygons with four sides.

real time — A one-to-one relationship between display time and real-life time.

refinement — In 3D subdivision, the procedure of picking a rough poly cage and using a specific algorithm to subdivide it and make it smoother.

shading — In 3D, shading determines the look and the physical aspects of a surface shadow, highlights, and diffuse colors.

smoothing — See subdivision.

SoftModificator — See Soft Selection.

Soft Selection — In 3D, a tool that allows you to pick a selected portion of vertices, edges, or faces and push or pull with an attenuation falloff degree.

spline — A curved line made of segments controlled by vertices/control points. The term is generally used to refer to any curved line. See Bezier curve and B-spline.

subdivision — In 3D, the process of picking a polygonal mesh and applying a mesh refining algorithm technique to increase the smoothness and the continuity of the mesh.

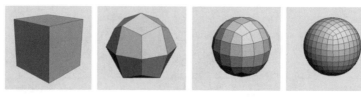

A cube subdivided into a sphere.

triangles (tris) — Three-sided polygons. See also face.

UV — Abbreviation for UWV. UVW are the coordinates for texture mapping. These are different from XYZ, which are the coordinates for geometry in the 3D space.

valence — The number of edge boundaries connected to a vertex.

vertex — A point in the mesh cage without length or volume that is responsible for controlling the shape of the polygonal 3D surface.

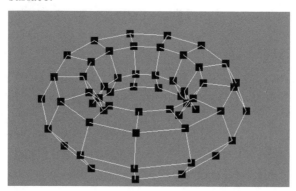

Vertex points.

weld — In 3D, an operation related to picking two or more vertices inside a tolerance range and merging them togther.

wireframe — 3D surface display method that shows the mesh cage without any surface shading technique.

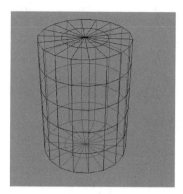

Wireframe display of a cylinder.

X,Y,Z — Space coordinates. Generally, X represents the length, Y the height, and Z the depth.

ZBrush — 3D application developed by Pixologic (www.pixologic.com).

Bibliography

Biermann, Henning, Adi Levin, and Denis Zorin. "Piecewise Smooth Subdivision Surfaces with Normal Control." Proceedings of ACM SIGGRAPH 2000, pp. 113-120.

Catmull, E., and J. Clark. "Recursively Generated B-Spline Surfaces on Arbitrary Topological Meshes." *Computer-Aided Design*, vol. 10, no. 6 (November 1978): 350-355.

Chaikin, G. "An Algorithm for High-Speed Curve Generation." *Computer Graphics and Image Processing*, 3 (1974): pp. 346-349.

DeRose, Tony, Michael Kass, and Tien Truong. "Subdivision Surfaces in Character Animation." Proceedings of ACM SIGGRAPH 1998, pp. 85-94.

Dyn, Nira, David Leven, and John Gregory. "A Butterfly Subdivision Scheme for Surface Interpolation with Tension Control." *ACM Transactions on Graphics*, vol. 9, no. 2 (April 1990): pp. 160-169.

Halstead, Mark, Michael Kass, and Tony DeRose. "Efficient, Fair Interpolation Using Catmull-Clark Surfaces." Proceedings of ACM SIGGRAPH 1993, pp. 35-44.

Hoppe, H., T. DeRose, T. Duchamp, M. Halstead, H. Jin, J. McDonald, J. Schweitzer, and W. Stuetzle. "Piecewise Smooth Surface Reconstruction." Proceedings of ACM SIGGRAPH 1994, pp. 295-302.

Kobbelt, Leif. "A Subdivision Scheme for Smooth Interpolation of Quad-Mesh Data." Eurographics '98 tutorial.

_____. "Interpolatory Subdivision on Open Quadrilateral Nets with Arbitrary Topology." Proceedings of Eurographics '96, pp. 409-420.

Loop, Charles T. "Smooth Subdivision Surfaces Based on Triangles." Master's thesis, Department of Mathematics, University of Utah, 1987.

Maierhofer, Stefan. "Rule-Based Mesh Growing and Generalized Subdivision Meshes." Ph.D. diss., Vienna University of Technology, 2002.

Netter, Frank H., and John T. Hansen. *Atlas of Human Anatomy.* 3rd edition. Icon Learning Systems, 2002.

Peters, Jörg. "Patching Catmull-Clark Meshes." Proceedings of ACM SIGGRAPH 2000, pp. 255-258.

Reif, Ulrich. "A Unified Approach to Subdivision Algorithms." Mathematisches Institute A 92-16, University of Stuttgart, 1992.

Simblet, Sarah, and John Davis. *Anatomy for the Artist.*, DK Adult: 2001.

Stam, Jos. "Evaluation of Loop Subdivision Surfaces." SIGGRAPH '99 Course Notes.

Terzopoulos, Demetri, John Platt, Alan Barr, and Kurt Fleischer. "Elastically Deformable Models." *Computer Graphics* (SIGGRAPH '87 Proceedings), vol. 21 (July 1987), pp. 205-214.

Zorin, Denis. "Stationary Subdivision and Multiresolution Surface Representations." Ph.D. diss., Caltech, 1997.

Zorin, Denis, and Daniel Kristjansson. "Evaluation of Piecewise Smooth Subdivision Surfaces." *The Visual Computer,* vol. 18, no. 5-6 (August 2002): pp. 299-315.

Zorin, Denis, Peter Schröder, and Wim Sweldens. "Interpolating Subdivision for Meshes with Arbitrary Topology." Proceedings of ACM SIGGRAPH 1996, pp. 189-192.

Zorin, Denis, Peter Schröder, Tony DeRose, Jos Stam, Leif Kobbelt, and Joe Warren. "Subdivision for Modeling and Animation." SIGGRAPH '99 Course Notes.

Index